Handbook of $uccessful Ecological Lawn Care

by
Paul D. Sachs

Newbury, Vermont

Handbook of $uccessful Ecological Lawn Care
by Paul D. Sachs

THE EDAPHIC PRESS
P.O. Box 107
Newbury, Vermont 05051

Library of Congress Catalog Card Number: 95-61669

ISBN 0-9636053-1-3

DEDICATED TO SANFORD
for teaching me the value
of ethics, morality, and trust.

ACKNOWLEDGMENTS

Special thanks to Jack Kittredge and Robin Barone for their careful and diligent proofreading and to Laurie Broccolo, Michelle Chamberlain, Paul Chu, Tony Grizzaffi, Cliff Maske, Michael Merner, Erik Morgan, Eric Nelson, Eric Smassanow, Michael Talbot, and Michael Warren Thomas for sharing their knowledge and experience with me.

Extra special thanks to Ruth, Dave and Jeff for their love and support and for putting up with my alarm clock going off every morning at 5:00 am for over two years.

Cover photo: Saint Gaudens National Historic Site, National Park Service, U.S. Department of the Interior; photographed by William Noble.

ABOUT THE AUTHOR

In 1983, when Sachs founded North Country Organics*, he decided it was important to learn something about the soil if he was going to sell natural fertilizers. However, as time went on, the objective changed from an obligatory curiosity to a quest of passion. As the information accumulated, Sachs began to see metaphoric similarities between the soil system and all other terrestrial dynamics, including the social and economic structures established by human civilization. He decided that many analogies from the soil such as competition, growth, adaptation and symbiosis could be applied to all of life's relationships. He also applied these analogies to running a successful business.

After only two years of study, Sachs became known as a source of good information for people involved in organic crop production or land care. Requests for articles and seminar appearances began to increase. In 1993, Sachs completed his first book, **EDAPHOS: Dynamics of a Natural Soil System**, to help disseminate the tremendous amount of valuable information to the people who need it the most. This work represented almost ten years of research on the subject of soil system dynamics. His work on this handbook began soon after the completion of **Edaphos**, and took over two years to complete.

* North Country Organics is a Bradford, VT based supplier of natural fertilizers and soil amendments for commercial use.

CONTENTS

Introduction

A warm sun, a slight breeze, birds singing, and a freshly mowed lawn together develop an intoxicating picture of the quintessential summer day. What is it that is so appealing about tens of thousands of nearly identical plants cut at exactly the same height?

This attraction goes back thousands of years. It is thought that the first lawn was created by an animal tethered to a rock or a stake. The uniformly grazed surface it created was extremely attractive, not only for sedentary activity, but also to the active youth who quickly changed the purpose of the pasture into what we now call recreational turf.

Ancient farmers found grazed areas to be useful protection against the predators of the forest. The buffer zones of pasture around the huts and cabins of yesteryear did not have the cover needed by many carnivorous pests, who required the elements of stealth and surprise to secure their prey. These areas inadvertently became the first residential lawns.

The genetic ancestors of the grass plant actually date back some seventy million years. The earliest known use of grass as an ornamental plant is estimated to have been over 2000 years ago. The Chinese Emperor Wu-Ti (157 - 87 B.C.) supposedly kept 30,000 slaves to maintain his extensive turf and pleasure gardens.

Although it is probably the most enduring of sports played on turf, golf actually evolved from bowling. According to history books, the crowned heads of Europe bowled on grass back in the fourteenth century. Regardless of the sport, the lawns back then had to be mowed by sheep which, in retrospect, were very efficient, multitasking turf tools. They mowed very close, compacted the ground into a hard playing surface, and fertilized at the same time. Too often, however, the fertilizer was a nuisance to the players and needed to be swept away.

Back then varieties of grass plants had to be edible if the four legged, gang-type lawn mowers were to work effectively. Although not documented, it is easy to imagine our ancestors gathering seeds from the more palatable varieties of grasses. Looks and performance were probably secondary considerations. Varieties today no longer have that same criterion of palatability. In fact, many grasses are bred with endophytes (natural fungi) that render them bitter and distasteful to grazing animals and insects.

The most significant change in turf over the centuries has been the explosive expansion of the areas where it is used. Airports, athletic fields, campuses, churches, cemeteries, public gardens, golf courses, highways, hospitals, parks, military bases, racetracks, resorts, and residences all use turf to adorn the landscape. The installation and maintenance of turf has become a multi-billion dollar industry that employs millions of workers, from landscapers and lawn care professionals to turfgrass scientists, with sales, support, and management technicians in between.

Unfortunately, the evolution of turf management has become an attempt to cultivate living plants into as uniform a picture as possible. If the genetic engineers could combine the atoms of a broad loom carpet with the cells of Kentucky Bluegrass, they would. However, nature doesn't like this very much. Producing two living organisms that are identical is not part of nature's strategy. Man's struggle to produce this freak of nature is not without its challenges because natural diversity has an ecological purpose. As the functioning components of a naturally diverse ecosystem are slowly eradicated or changed, imbalances are created that need constant attention. The greater the change, the more attention needed to keep the lawn from reverting back to a naturally diverse pasture, meadow, or forest. This attention is commonly referred to as *maintenance*.

The unnatural environment that we create is not restricted to plants. Our soils are mixed, moved in, moved out, neutralized, fertilized, sterilized, limed, desalinated, aerated, dethatched, topdressed, compressed, decompressed, de-stoned, denuded, tilled, turned and raked. Ironically, this is all done in the interest of creating a better soil environment. Unfortunately, these activities will more often than not accomplish the opposite.

As we apply artificial inputs to suppress nature's reaction to the environmental imbalances we cause, we often stimulate other natural reactions that require more artificial inputs. By trying futilely to debug this chain reaction, some professionals have come to the realization that many of nature's original ideas are difficult to improve upon.

The turf managers of a half century ago didn't have a fraction of the mechanical or chemical tools we have today. They also lacked much of the information gathered from modern turfgrass research. Yet they were able to create and maintain magnificent turfgrass environments. Their techniques required cooperation from nature or, more accurately, their cooperation with nature.

The purpose of this book is to expose the natural system to the reader and help him or her understand ways to use the powers of nature instead of fighting against them. Each time we disturb a natural environment we create imbalances. The less we disturb it, the more easy it is to maintain that environment.

The *freedom lawn* *, for example, is a man-made ecosystem where anything that grows beneath the height of the mower blade is a vital component of the system. This natural system requires no fertilizer, seed, or pesticides. What does not survive is naturally replaced by a plant that does. Eventually a self-sustaining ecosystem evolves in the freedom lawn that keeps it perpetually green and healthy. At the other extreme is an *industrial lawn* * where only one variety of grass exists and weeds, insects, pathogens, moles, voles and sometimes even earthworms are not tolerated. This lawn requires constant maintenance with fertilizers, pesticides, and energy. From a distance the difference between the freedom lawn and the industrial one is difficult to discern. Close-up, most notable differences are the amounts of time, energy and money spent on one as compared to the other. Customers making a cost-based analysis of a freedom

---

*Freedom lawn and industrial lawn are phrases from a new book called Redesigning the American Lawn (Bormann 1993). This book describes alternatives to conventional lawns and their maintenance.

lawn versus an industrial one can easily see the advantage of natural choices.

To some, the lawn has joined ranks with expensive cars, clothes, and other symbols of wealth, power, or status. To others, the lawn may just be an icon of membership: participation in a community tradition of conventional appearance.

Once in a while, an item in the newspaper may appear describing a conspiracy by a community to stop a neighbor from inappropriate or negligent lawn maintenance. Some of these disputes have even ended up in court. Many municipalities have passed ordinances that mandate a maximum height to which a lawn can be grown. The lawn's psychological significance to some is a state of mind that may not be logical but cannot be changed easily.

This is okay. If customers are willing to dedicate a significant amount of resources toward their image of a beautiful lawn, that is their choice. There is no reason, however, why that end cannot be accomplished without the use of products that disrupt the soil and plant ecosystem.

This book examines the many facets of lawn installation and maintenance and attempts to analyze the effect many of our conventional activities have on the soil ecosystem. The alternative methods discussed are, in many cases, less labor intensive, less expensive and potentially more profitable.

Like the natural lawn, humans must also survive and thrive. If we, as practitioners of ecological turf care, cannot sustain ourselves in a comfortable manner, then we cannot become the altruistic stewards of the soil we would like to be. There is nothing ignoble about doing something worthwhile and earning a decent living from it. It is the same symbiosis that is ubiquitous in the natural world. The section on *Business* discusses different approaches to conducting a natural lawn care business in a profitable manner.

Time and energy must be viewed as assets that need to be managed like any others. Topics such as labor, customer relations, job costing, marketing, contractual arrangements and double entry accounting will be discussed in an effort to help the natural lawn care business endure the economic stresses of modern civilization. In a natural system finding the appropriate niche is vital for every living thing to survive and sustain its species. The small business is no different.

The **Handbook of Successful Ecological Lawn Care** is designed for those professionals who want to survive and thrive in this business. The knowledge it proposes to introduce, however, should only be a beginning in the never-ending quest for new information.

Sources:

Bormann, F.H., D. Balmori, and G.T. Geballe, 1993, **Redesigning the American Lawn: A Search for Environmental Harmony**. Yale University Press. New Haven, CT.

Craul P.J. 1992, **Urban Soil in Landscape Design**. John Wiley and Sons, Inc. New York, NY.

Leslie, A.R. (editor) 1994, **Handbook of Integrated Pest Management for Turf and Ornamentals**. Lewis Publishers. Boca Raton, FL.

Part I
IN THE FIELD

Chapter 1
Turfgrass Dynamics

The relationship that a plant has with the soil, the atmosphere, the climate and itself is nothing short of fascinating. Plants are organisms that can produce the wealth of the world almost from thin air by using carbon dioxide from the atmosphere and energy from the sun. Plants not only produce food, fiber and fuel for almost all species of consumer organisms on earth, but also make oxygen available for air breathers. Their residues renew the soil with life-giving humus.

The plant functions like two distinctly different organisms living together symbiotically. The root system of the plant requires oxygen from the soil and nutrients manufactured by the plant's leaves to live while producing carbon dioxide as a waste product. The above-ground portion of the plant uses carbon dioxide from the atmosphere, energy from the sun, minerals from the soil and water from various sources while giving off oxygen as a waste product. The root system acts as a consumer, using nutrients produced by the plant tops while providing a crucial connection to the earth that sustains the whole organism.

Turfgrasses are particularly persistent species of plants that function both agriculturally and horticulturally. Their existence dates back more than 70 million years. Before the midwestern United States was developed for agriculture, natural stands of grasses dominated an area of close to one million square miles.

At the same time that turfgrasses provide esthetic pleasure, they also provide other benefits, such as improved water infiltration, erosion protection, groundwater protection, reduced soil surface temperature (from shade and a 7-14° F reduction from the cooling effect of evapotranspiration), improved air quality, noise reduction, absorption of pollutants (such as sulfur dioxide, carbon monoxide, and ozone), utilization of carbon dioxide, and production of oxygen. Compared to other outdoor utility surfaces, turfgrasses reduce sports injuries and provide habitat to certain wildlife.

To many people involved in horticulture, grasses are the quintessential landscape plant; to farmers growing row crops, they are pests with enormous potential to do harm. Grasses have the ability to compete effectively with other plants so much that they can become the scourge of farmers who grow clean crops. In an unnatural environment, where we stress the grasses with inappropriate care, they can lose their competitive edge.

Grasses do well in a rich, fertile soil which they replenish by creating significant contributions of organic matter. Turf root systems are generally annuals that regenerate every year. The old roots can add anywhere from one half to four tons of organic matter to an acre of soil, depending on the plant varieties, growing conditions, and the way in which the turf is managed. If clippings are returned to the soil when the plants are mowed, even more organic matter is contributed. Additionally, twenty percent of the energy manufactured by photosynthesis in the plant leaves is exuded through the roots into the soil. There, teeming masses of bacteria and other soil organisms use these nutrients to implement necessary biological functions that create a rich and fertile soil environment and protect the plant from pathogens and other harmful organisms.

PHOTOSYNTHESIS

Photosynthesis is a critical function in all plants. It combines the energy from the sun with carbon dioxide from the atmosphere, hydrogen and oxygen from water, and all the necessary mineral nutrients it extracts from the soil to create sugars, starches, proteins, fats, waxes, lignin, cellulose, hormones, enzymes, and other organic compounds that enable the plant and the soil to function. The production of these compounds is crucial not only for plants but for all of the other organisms on the planet that depend on plants for food. Photosynthesis occurs in the leaves of the plants, where energy from the sun sets off a complicated chemical chain reaction. The end result is the production of carbon compounds, many of which contain energy (derived originally from the sun) that can be used by the plant or passed on to other organisms that rely on plants for sustenance.

Unfortunately, mowing—the cultural practice that gives a lawn most of its esthetic value—removes the part of the plant where photosynthesis takes place. This activity is analogous to shutting down a manufacturing facility and funding the entire operation from the sales of inventory. Eventually, the production line must start up again or the business will fail. If too much of the turf shoots is cut off at once, the production of energy and protein from photosynthesis is shut down and the plant must use nutrients stored in the root system to regenerate new leaves. When this occurs, the roots stop growing and the plant can take almost a month to rebuild itself and its energy reserves back to the point where the roots begin to grow again. Researchers often advise us of the *one third rule* which states simply that no more than one third of the turf's current height should be mowed off at once. There are times, however, when it is impractical to follow this rule and significantly more than one third is removed. The result is, of course, a month's delay in new root growth.

ROOTS

Although the root system is dependent on functioning plant leaves to grow, it is also influenced by several other factors in the soil environment. Levels of organic matter, available moisture, soil porosity and available nutrients will have both direct and indirect effects on root production. Organic matter governs the levels of moisture reserves in the soil as well as soil porosity and the biological activity that makes many essential nutrients available. As organic matter is depleted by natural causes or cultural practices (or both), there is a relative decrease in the production of roots.

Available moisture in the soil depends entirely on the amount of pore space between soil particles. As the space gets smaller there is less ability to hold available water. There is also less space for oxygen, which is essential for roots to survive. The water trapped in the very small capillaries in the soil is often unavailable to plants. Plants will wilt and die in a heavy clay soil containing significantly more water than a sandy soil could hold under the best of conditions (see figure 1-1). The reason is that the pore space in clay is so small that, although there is plenty of water, it is trapped between the clay particles and held too tightly for plants to gain access to it. Another

SOIL MOISTURE RELATIONSHIPS

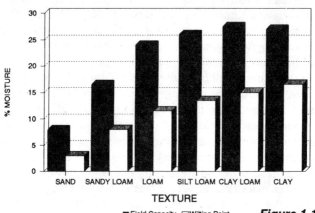

Figure 1-1

problem associated with inadequate porosity is the exchange of oxygen from the atmosphere into the soil. Roots cannot survive without oxygen. As levels of oxygen are depleted, the entire plant is stressed and cannot compete.

The availability of mineral nutrients is also affected by the size and abundance of pore space in the soil. Obviously, the movement of nutrients dissolved in the soil solution is greatly inhibited in a compacted or heavy soil. Biological activity, which is actively involved in making nutrients available to plants from mineral particles and organic matter, is also influenced by the availability of water. Like roots, many microbes in the soil require oxygen - which can be limited in a heavy soil. Low soil temperatures can also limit biological activity.

Soil health is inextricably linked to the development and welfare of plant roots, and roots are a vital link to the health of the entire plant. Beginning new plants in poor soil is, most often, an exercise in frustration and futility. The more energy spent on improving the sub-surface portion of the growing system, the less needed to care for the tops.

ORGANIC MATTER

All of these factors can be improved with organic matter, but increasing the level of organic matter in the soil is easier said than done. Soil amendments such as aged composts or other organic materials will help improve soils over time, but applications of large quantities designed specifically to raise the level of organic matter in the soil are not practical on turf. In situations where the soil is being prepared for a new seeding, more material can be initially applied but must be worked into the soil to avoid layering (see the section entitled WATER in this chapter).

Another fact to consider is that less than one percent of a compost application may actually become stable soil humus, depending on soil conditions, climate, and the way in which the soil is managed. Increasing soil organic matter levels significantly can be a monumental task. If an acre of topsoil (6 to 7 inches deep) weighs two million pounds, then increasing organic matter content by one percent would require 20,000 pounds of *stable humus*. Although compost contributes significantly to the creation of stable humus, it is not yet in that condition.

Creation of organic matter occurs naturally in turf. The roots of the plants contribute significant amounts to the soil every year. The way in which the turf is maintained, however, affects the level of those contributions. Mowing height and frequency have a great influence on turf root production. Obviously, if the roots stop growing from cutting too much of the plant at once, there will be less production of organic matter. The average height at which a turf is maintained also plays a major role in root production (see chapter 3).

As old roots decay, canals are left in the soil where air and water can pass. The increase in movement of both moisture and atmosphere will inevitably increase the production of roots. Soils that endure excessive traffic, whether by foot or vehicle, become compacted and inhibit the movement of water and air and the growth of roots. Soil compaction can be alleviated by the occurrence of organic matter but it takes time. If the traffic is continuous, mechanical methods may have to be employed.

COMPACTION

Soils need to breath a little like we do. The gases in the soil developed from biological activity need to exchange with the above-ground atmosphere or toxic levels can accumulate in the soil and plant roots can suffocate from a lack of oxygen. Soils that become compacted suffer from a loss of pore space between soil particles, resulting in a reduction of water and air movement through the soil. Compaction usually results from excessive traffic, especially during times of the year when the soil is excessively moist. Soils that are naturally wet or have very low levels of organic matter are more susceptible to compaction. Nature will often decompress the soils in the early spring with recurring frost. The repeated freezing and thawing of water between soil particles expands the pore spaces throughout the soil's surface and some of the subsurface. Heavily compacted soils do not hold very much water and, therefore, cannot benefit as much from frost activity.

Core aeration is an effective treatment for this condition, but should be done during the spring or fall when turf growth is most vigorous. Hollow tines will remove cores of soil whereas solid tines will only fracture the soil in the immediate area where they penetrate. Topdressing with well aged compost after aeration is a step toward permanently mitigating compaction. Increasing levels of soil organic matter by whatever means possible can eventually solve chronic compaction problems. Like anything else, core aeration can be over applied. Introducing too much oxygen into the soil can accelerate the decomposition of soil organic matter and eventually make the soil more susceptible to compaction.

SOIL AGGREGATION

Many soil-dwelling organisms produce mucilage and other sticky substances that bind soil particles together into aggregates. The aggregation of soil particles is extremely important for implementing good soil structure and porosity. Without it, water infiltration, root penetration, and the exchange of vital gases—such as oxygen and carbon dioxide—with the atmosphere would be immeasurably inhibited. All of this can translate into stress for turf plants. Cultural practices that do not stimulate or actually inhibit the growth and welfare of soil organisms ultimately sacrifice the ability of these organisms to aggregate soil particles. Pesticides or other materials that mitigate biological activity in the soil reduce its potential to maintain structural integrity. Fertilizers that ignore the nutritional needs of soil organisms will help the plant in one respect but may hinder it in several others. Soils with poor aggregation are prone to compaction and have a smaller capacity for moisture, oxygen, and nutrients.

The biological activities that enhance soil aggregation can be stimulated by several different practices. Leaving clippings where they are mowed is a practice that is very beneficial to earthworms and other organisms that contribute to aggregation. Using natural organic fertilizers or composts that require biological processing before they actually become plant nutrients is another beneficial procedure. Mowing higher can not only produce greater root systems which harbor much greater populations of soil organisms, but can also shade the soil, preserving moisture that is vital to the organism's existence. Excessive mechanical disruption of the soil such as tillage or unnecessary core aeration can fracture aggregates and introduce too much oxygen, hastening the decomposition of valuable soil organic matter. Pesticides that affect non-target organisms can also inhibit aggregating activities. The long and the short of it is that the cultural practices we engage in for short term esthetic reward can lead to long term problems that are difficult to solve.

SOIL TEMPERATURE

Temperature can have a profound effect on turf and the soil. At a soil temperature of 88 degrees F, with adequate air and moisture, organic matter is destroyed faster than it can be produced. This is a common condition in tropical soils where high temperature, moisture from tropical rains, and an abundance of air from extremely sandy (porous) soils are all at an optimum level for bacterial decay. The loss of this valuable soil component can have severe consequences on the viability of turf. Moisture reserves are diminished along with populations of beneficial organisms and available levels of many turf nutrients, all of which can create significant stress for plants. During these times, pest organisms such as weeds or insects can gain a competitive edge.

Figure 1-2 shows that as we move closer to the equator, lower levels of soil organic matter naturally occur. Rich loamy soil with ample amounts of organic matter is a natural phenomenon of the

INFLUENCE OF TEMPERATURE
ON SOIL ORGANIC MATTER
CONTENT

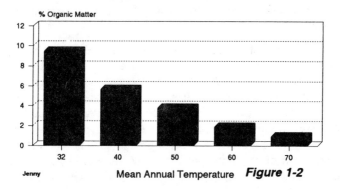

Mean Annual Temperature   *Figure 1-2*

temperate zones where climate moderation inhibits the activities of decay bacteria. This is not to say that soils cannot be improved anywhere else. The maintenance and preservation of soil organic matter must be an integral part of every turf manager's program, no matter where on the globe that turf is situated.

Shading the soil can reduce soil surface temperatures and slow down the decomposition of organic matter. Turf stands that are mowed at maximum height during the hottest part of the year can shade the soil and reduce soil surface temperature by as much as 20 degrees. Increasing mowing height not only increases the production of roots, which add organic matter to the soil, but also provides more shade, which lowers the soil temperature and preserves more of the existing organic matter. This is not always possible because of use restrictions (e.g. on golf greens and tees). In many instances, however, a tall green stand of turf is much preferred over a short brown one. It is true that taller turf uses slightly more water because of evaporation from a greater leaf surface area, but the increase in availability of water from deeper and more invasive roots more than compensates for the extra need. Leaving the clippings where they are cut can also provide some relief during drought periods. Small contributions of clippings can act as a short term mulch that slows the evaporation of moisture from the soil's surface (see chapter 3).

CARBON CYCLE

The production and the decomposition of organic matter are part of a phenomenon called the carbon cycle which is the basis for all life on the planet Earth (see figure 1-3). Carbon dioxide in the

CARBON CYCLE

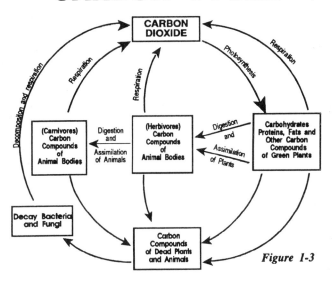

Figure 1-3

atmosphere is used by plants in the process of photosynthesis to create carbon compounds such as proteins and carbohydrates. These compounds contain energy and nutrients that organisms, ranging from microbes to mammals, can use for sustenance. A by-product of this energy consumption is carbon dioxide, which escapes back into the atmosphere where it can begin the cycle again. Each time energy is used by any organism, carbon dioxide is given back to the atmosphere. When carbon compounds (from plant and animal residues) are added to the soil, 60-70% of the carbon is released back into the atmosphere within the first year by microbial decay. Much of the carbon that was once carbon dioxide in the earth's prehistoric atmosphere is now located in all the living organisms on the planet

RELATIVE PROPORTIONS OF TOTAL SOIL ORGANIC MATTER

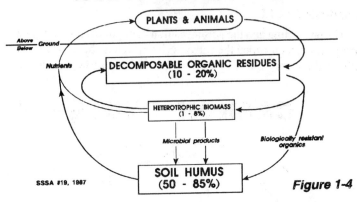

Figure 1-4

and in the fraction of organic matter (see figure 1-4) in the soil.

Figure 1-5 illustrates that the progression of energy consumption through the food chain leaves very little for soil saprophytes (decay organisms). Not all energy products, however, will travel through the entire food chain before they reach the soil. Plants give twenty percent of the photosynthesized compounds directly to soil organ-

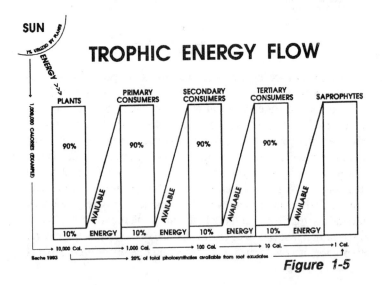

Figure 1-5

isms through the root system. This fuels a very biologically active zone around each root where plant nutrients can be mineralized from both organic and inorganic sources, beneficial competition, antagonism, or parasitism can take place, and many other advantageous functions can occur.

NITROGEN CYCLE

Like carbon, nitrogen originates in the atmosphere, but it does not have to re-enter the atmosphere to complete the cycle. Nitrogen is a component of protein. Whether it is derived from plants or animals it must undergo a biological process before it can be used by plants. Figure 1-6 illustrates how nitrogen from the atmosphere is first converted into protein by nitrogen fixing bacteria. When these bacteria die the protein is biologically converted into a mineral that is taken up into plants and changed back into protein. Whether the plants enter the food chain or are returned to the soil,

NITROGEN CYCLE

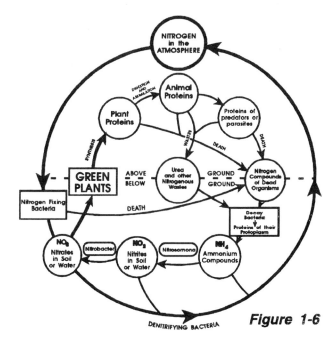

Figure 1-6

the residues of both plants or animals are broken down and assimilated by bacteria and other soil organisms. When this happens, a complex process begins that eventually makes mineral nitrogen available to plants again. Certain conditions (such as water saturation) that deplete the soil of oxygen can cause denitrification, where nitrogen is returned to the atmosphere. Nitrogen in the soil can accumulate to a certain level where, depending on climatic conditions and cultural practices, it achieves an equilibrium with the forces that use or destroy it.

NUTRITION, FERTILITY

The soil acts as the plant's digestive system. Without it, the plant could not survive. It is somewhat ironic that almost all the organic compounds produced by plants cannot be used as plant nutrients unless they are first decomposed by microorganisms and transformed back into inorganic forms. Nitrogen, for example, is a component of protein but must undergo a complex process of simplification, mineralization and nitrification before it can be used by the plant again. Once used as a mineral nutrient, it is immediately transformed back into protein where it can begin the cycle again (see figure 1-6).

Ninety-five percent of the plant's diet is comprised of three elements that cannot be purchased from any supplier. They are car-

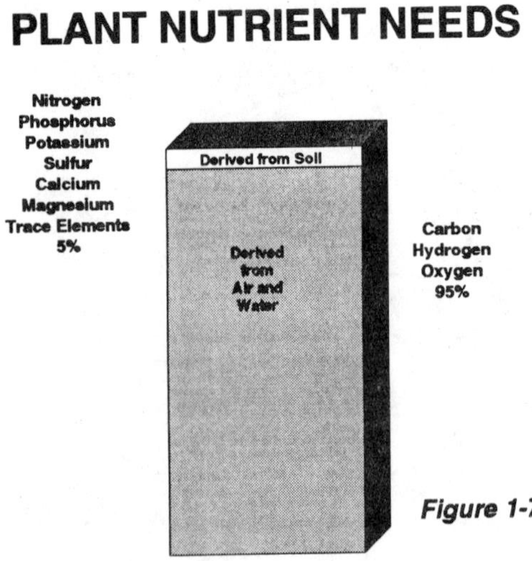

PLANT NUTRIENT NEEDS

Nitrogen
Phosphorus
Potassium
Sulfur
Calcium
Magnesium
Trace Elements
5%

Derived from Soil

Derived from Air and Water

Carbon
Hydrogen
Oxygen
95%

Figure 1-7

bon, oxygen, and hydrogen (see figure 1-7). These elements come from the atmosphere and from water. The remaining five percent is essential nutrients which come from the organic and the mineral components of the soil. The five percent is the only portion we can truly influence (with the exception of water from irrigation). Infusions of nutrients into the soil obviously can have significant effects on most plants. Like anything else, however, exceeding or falling short of the optimum balance can cause problems. Trace elements are a glaring example of this rule. The introduction of certain elements in quantities even slightly above optimum can kill the plant. The old axiom stating that *if a little is good, more is better* could not be farther from the truth in horticulture and agriculture. Quantities of nutrients beyond optimum can have an adverse affect on the chemistry and biology of plants and the soil.

Too much nitrogen can lead to insect and disease problems as well as to changes in the physical structure of the soil. Excess phosphorus can fix with other nutrients making both the phosphorus and the other nutrients unavailable to plants. Heavy applications of potash can affect plant turgidity and influence the availability of calcium and magnesium in the soil. The side effects of over-use can be documented for almost all elements essential to plants and for other elements that are needed by soil organisms. In almost all cases, applications beyond optimum can lead to some degree of environmental pollution.

Changes in an area's ecology because of excessive applications of nutrients can influence many different factors of plant growth, including: beneficial predator and parasite activity, plant defense mechanisms, the potential of the soil to mineralize nutrients from organic and inorganic sources, the ability of soil organisms to recycle plant and animal residues, and the chemical and biological changes necessary for the soil system to function. Input levels of nutrients need to be relative to the production of a given soil and often exceed those levels offered by nature. A balance should be maintained, however, and it is important to understand that there is a limit to what every soil can produce. Forcing more nutrients into an organism (or system of organisms) than it can use does not always help increase production; indeed, poor health can result.

PRESERVING ORGANIC MATTER

If one agrees that organic matter is a valuable asset to both the owner and the steward of a lawn, steps should be taken to preserve the existing level in the soil and, if possible or practical, add to it. Chapter 3 looks at different cultural practices and how they affect the existence of soil organic matter. Learning how to make compost is an excellent way to familiarize oneself with the factors that destroy organic matter. If conditions are right, the compost pile decomposes so quickly that it becomes hot from the biological energy that is expended. In the soil, the steward must take care not to expose the soil organic matter to those same conditions. Compost needs plenty of air and water, a balanced pH, higher temperatures and the correct ratio of carbon to nitrogen. Soil requires the same factors for plants to grow, but in different ratios. The introduction of too much air into the soil is probably the most significant cultural mistake we can make. Improper irrigation and excessive liming, however, can also contribute to significant loses of soil organic matter. Mowing too short can reduce the amount of shade provided by turf and increase soil surface temperatures, providing more favorable conditions for decay bacteria.

Organic matter should be a primary concern for everyone who makes a living from, or with, the soil. The benefits it provides are analogous to having three shifts of full time employees who work for free.

DYNAMICS OF THATCH

Thatch, in small amounts, can be beneficial to turf. Its ability to absorb water, exchange gases with the atmosphere, and to shade the soil can mitigate some stress associated with heat and drought. Excessive amounts of thatch is generally a sign that the biological activity in a given area is suppressed for some reason. Healthy soils rarely have a excessive thatch problem. There are several reasons why microbial activity may be inhibited, but the most common is from the use of certain pesticides. The existence of earthworms and other decay organisms is temporarily curtailed by many different pesticides, and thatch production soon exceeds the rate at which it is decomposed back into useful organic matter. Excessive applications of nitrogen only serve to exacerbate the situation by increasing the production of plant parts that contribute to the thatch layer (see chapter 4).

WATER

Water is as essential to turf as it is to any other living organism. The properties and dynamics of water play a critical role in the plant/soil system. Water is chemically known as H_2O, which identifies its molecule as having two atoms of hydrogen and one atom of oxygen. Figure 1-8 shows that the way in which this molecule is constructed gives it a polarity that is responsible for both adhesion and cohesion. Adhesion is water's ability to cling to surfaces. The way in which a water droplet will cling to a car's windshield even at high speeds is evidence of the strength of adhesion. Cohesion is water's

WATER POLARITY

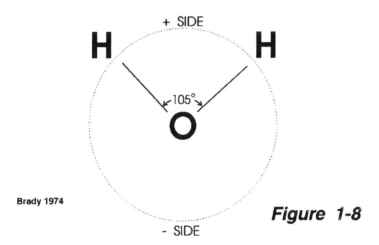

Brady 1974

Figure 1-8

ability to cling to itself. An example of cohesion is when two droplets of water merge after making contact. The combined strength of both adhesion and cohesion is exemplified when two panes of glass are held together by a thin film of water. Attempts to separate the panes without sliding them apart will often result in a broken pane.

Water also has energy referred to as *free energy*. The concept of energy in water may be confusing but there are many familiar examples that make it easier to understand. A good example of free energy in water is an experiment with a small spill and a dry paper towel. When the paper towel comes in contact with the water it is instantly absorbed. The movement of the water into the paper towel illustrates the energy difference between the spill and the towel, and the tendency for an energy equilibrium to be established. It is important to understand that the movement of any substance on earth requires energy in one form or another. Ice cubes melting in a glass of water show thermal energy flowing from the water to the ice (i.e., the warmer to the colder material). This example, which involves heat as the energy that is causing movement, illustrates the natural tendency for an energy equilibrium to be found.

The energy in water fluctuates in intensity as it reacts to variables in the soil, such as uptake by plants, dissolution of nutrients, or surface evaporation. Where there is more water in the soil, there is more energy. Physical law dictates that energy flows from levels of high to levels of low energy. So, just as heat flows to cold, the moisture from a wet area in the soil will flow to dryer areas, as long as the soil texture remains relatively consistent.

As water moves from high to low energy areas its cohesive attachment to itself drags more water with it and a flow is created. On a hot sunny day when high rates of evaporation are occurring at the surface of the soil, an area of low energy is created which attracts water from beneath the surface through capillaries--passages in between soil particles. This movement of water is similar to how liquids are drawn up a wick. During a rain storm, when the surface contains more moisture than the soil beneath it, the direction of the water movement is reversed. As root hairs absorb water the moisture level in the immediate area surrounding the root is reduced, creating a low energy area which attracts new water into the root zone.

The negative energy force that moves water is called suction (so that soil scientists can refer to it in positive terms). As the soil dries out, the suction in the desiccated area is increased and water from surrounding areas is drawn to it.

Heavy rains may saturate soils to the point where all the pores and capillaries in the soil are filled with water. In this condition suction is reduced to zero and gravity becomes the dominant force controlling water movement. Water that is drawn out of the soil by gravity eventually finds its way to rivers, lakes and oceans, where it evaporates and is recycled to the soil in the form of precipitation.

After a short period of time (depending on soil texture), gravity will draw off enough water to create an energy equilibrium between gravity and the force of suction. This equilibrium also forms a balance of air and moisture in the soil. The moisture level of the soil in this condition is said to be at *field capacity*.

As plants and surface evaporation draw more water from the soil, suction is increased and water is drawn from reserves beneath the surface. If moisture removal continues but little reserve water is available, the soil will eventually reach a moisture level known as the *wilting point*—when plant tops can become permanently wilted. The free energy of the soil at this point is very low, which creates very high suction.

As the soil dries further, the remaining moisture is held tightly to soil particles by adhesion and is unavailable to plants or other organisms.

All of this information is enlightening and useful for soils that remain consistent to depths of a few feet or more. Unfortunately, there are very few places (especially in New England) where that occurs. Water movement is significantly disrupted when it meets with a soil horizon that has a different texture. An example of this phenomenon is shown by an experiment that was done many years ago. Several inches of loam were placed on top of a thick layer of sand in a glass case (see figure 1-9). As water was slowly added to the surface of the loam, it was evident through the glass that the water preferred to move horizontally through the loam rather than down into the sand. The loam reached near saturation before gravity could pull any water down into the sand. This was because the force of suction is greater than gravity until the saturation level is reached. This reaction would occur with a number of different textured materials beneath the loam.

The research suggests that abrupt changes in soil consistencies from one horizon to another can affect both the movement of water and the soil's ability to store it. Thus thin applications of topsoil to a well drained base may do more harm than good in terms of water dynamics (see chapter 2).

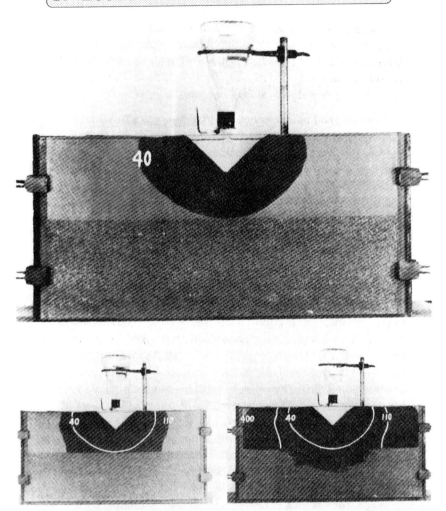

Brady 1974 *Courtesy W.H. Gardner* **Figure 1-9**

The movement of water in plants is governed by the same physical laws that govern movement through the soil. Water that is evaporated from the leaves of plants to the atmosphere reduces the energy level in the leaves which creates suction in the stems and/or branches. When moisture is drawn up into the leaves, there is a reduction of energy in the stems. This energy reduction draws water from the roots which, in turn, draws it from the soil. In all cases there is more energy in the source than the location to which the moisture is moving. As energy levels equalize in the different locations, suction diminishes.

The last link in the moisture cycle is the atmosphere, which is also regulated by moisture energy relationships. If moisture levels in the atmosphere are low, such as on a warm, dry and windy day, the movement of water through the cycle is accelerated. Conversely, on still days with high humidity, water evaporates from the soil and plant leaves more slowly. The difference between the moisture level in the soil and that in the atmosphere is called the *vapor pressure gradient;* it controls the rate of water movement through the cycle. On a cool, foggy morning, the energy levels in the soil, plant and atmosphere may be close to equal, which slows, and perhaps even stops, the movement of water through the cycle. One of the new technologies in moisture control systems for greenhouses is a fog generator, which creates an atmosphere with 100% relative humidity. In this environment the transpiration of water through the plant is slowed and often stopped. Because of the high energy levels in the atmosphere, water moves from the air to the soil instead of in the direction normally caused by evaporation.

The leaves of plants provide further regulation of the cycle. Leaves contain small pores, called stomata, that can open and close, regulating the amount of water and gases that flows through them. On hot, dry days, when evapotranspiration is highest, the stomata can contract, slowing down the flow of moisture through the plant.

Nutrients that dissolve in soil water use some of its free energy, which can inhibit the water's flow through the moisture cycle. This phenomenon is referred to as *osmotic suction* and is demonstrated by water's migration to soluble salts. For example, rural municipalities will often apply calcium chloride (a soluble salt) as a dust control on gravel roads. Moisture is drawn from the humidity in the air to the dry salt which dissolves and seeps into the surface of the road. The osmotic suction created by the concentrated solution continues to attract moisture from the air because its energy level is lower than the water vapor in the atmosphere. The reversed flow of moisture from the air to the road continues until the salt is diluted enough to reduce the force of osmotic suction.

In the soil, water that is rich in dissolved nutrients has less energy and moves more slowly into plant roots. The membranes on the surface of roots will filter much of the dissolved salts, which can further impede water's progress into the plant.

WINTER DYNAMICS OF TURF

When the temperatures turn cold the basic functions of the soil and plant slow to almost a complete stop. Water movement through the plant ceases because the frozen ground moisture can no longer migrate through its cycle. Desiccation can often occur when cold, dry winds draw moisture from exposed leaves that can not be replaced from the frozen ground. Chlorophyll slowly degenerates from the cold, removing most of the color from the shoots. Carbohydrates from most of the plant are moved into its perennial parts, such as the crowns, stolons, rhizomes, and leaf sheaths.

Even though the plants are dormant, they are still alive and functioning. Evidence of respiration is apparent when ice forms over the top of a lawn, cutting off its supply of oxygen. Many species can suffocate from prolonged exposure to thick ice in the winter.

Deep freezes, especially in the early spring when plants begin to break dormancy, can cause significant damage to turf. Ice crystals form inside the plant tissues and can rupture cell membranes and imperil the plant's survival.

Snow protects grass from desiccating winds and from extreme cold. Heavy snows, especially in the fall before the ground freezes, can keep grasses healthy through the winter. Unfortunately, snow can also provide habitat for snow molds which are potentially very damaging to turf. Plants grown in rich, biologically active soils are less susceptible to snow molds. Topdressing with well aged compost in the fall seems to be very effective at preventing snow molds from getting established.

Traffic during the winter can cause a surprising amount of damage to stands of grass. The crushing and bruising of frozen leaves severely limits their ability to survive. Snow provides some protection against traffic but sledding, snowmobiling, and other winter sports can pack snow into ice that may cause damage to turf.

SUMMARY

It is important to understand that the turf plant is only one component of a system that functions as a whole. Focusing only on the needs of the plant can lead to a loss of benefits offered by the other components of the system. Feeding plants and ignoring the balance of the plant/soil system is analogous to feeding yourself intravenously. The necessary nutrients may be available to you, but, in a short period of time, your unused digestive system will shut down and imperil the survival of your entire being. The soil has more resilience than the human body to unbalanced or improper forms of nutrition, but, eventually, problems can and probably will appear from sustained programs that ignore the needs of the entire system. In any cultivated environment there is a correlation between the level of human intervention and the amount of necessary maintenance. As the level of intervention increases, so does the amount of care needed to maintain the system.

Sources:

Adams, W.A. and R.J. Gibbs, 1994. **Natural Turf for Sport and Amenity: Science and Practice**. CAB International. Wallingford, United Kingdom.

Albrecht, W.A. 1938, **Loss of Organic Matter and its Restoration**. U.S. Dept. of Agriculture Yearbook 1938, pp347-376.

Arshad, M.A. and G.M. Coen, 1992, **Characterization of Soil Quality: Physical and Chemical Criteria**. American Journal of Alternative Agriculture v7 #1 and #2, 1992 pp 25-31. Institute for Alternative Agriculture, Greenbelt, MD.

ASA# 47. 1979, **Microbial - Plant Interactions**. American Society of Agronomy. Madison, WI.

Bear, F.E. 1924, **Soils and Fertilizers**. John Wiley and Sons, Inc. New York, NY.

Beard, J.B. 1995, **Mowing Practices for Conserving Water**. Grounds Maintenance, January 1995. Intertec Publishing. Overland Park, KS.

Bhowmik, P.C., R.J.Cooper, M.C. Owen, G. Schumann, P. Vittum, and R. Wick, 1994, **Professional Turfgrass Management Guide**. University of Massachusetts Cooperative Extension System. Amherst, MA.

Bormann, F.H., D. Balmori, and G.T. Geballe, 1993, **Redesigning the American Lawn: A Search for Environmental Harmony**. Yale University Press. New Haven, CT.

Brady, N.C. 1974, **The Nature and Properties of Soils**. MacMillan Publishing Co. Inc. New York, NY.

Bunce, R.G.H., L. Ryszkowski, and M.G. Paoletti, 1993, **Landscape Ecology and Agroecosystems**. Lewis Publishers. Boca Raton, FL.

Carrow, R.N. 1994, **Understanding and Using Canopy Temperatures**. Grounds Maintenance, May 1994. Intertec Publishing. Overland Park, KS.

Craul P.J. 1992, **Urban Soil in Landscape Design**. John Wiley and Sons, Inc. New York, NY.

Deal, E.E. 1967, **Mowing Heights for Kentucky Bluegrass Turf**. Agronomy Abstracts Vol. 59 Nov. 1967 pp. 150. American Society of Agronomy, Madison, WI.

Dernoeden, P.H., M.J. Carroll, and J.M. Krouse, 1993, **Weed Management and Tall Fescue Quality as Influenced by Mowing, Nitrogen, and Herbicides**. Crop Science 33:1055-1061. Crop Science Society of America. Madison, WI.

Dest, W.M., S.C. Albin, and K. Guillard, 1992, **Turfgrass Clipping Management**. Rutgers Turfgrass Proceedings 1992. Rutgers University. New Brunswick, NJ.

Elam, P. 1994, **Earthworms: We Need an Attitude Adjustment**. Landscape Management July, 1994. Advanstar Communications. Cleveland, OH.

Franklin, S. 1988, **Building a Healthy Lawn: A Safe and Natural Approach**. Storey Communications, Inc. Pownal, VT.

Greulach, V. A. 1968, **Botany Made Simple**. Doubleday & Company, Inc. Garden City, NY.

Huang, P.M. and M. Schnitzer, 1986, **Interactions of Soil Minerals with Natural Organics and Microbes**. Soil Science Society of America, Inc. Madison, WI.

Jackson, N. 1994, **Winter Turf Problems**. Turf Notes, November/

December 1994. (Reprinted from The Yankee Nursery Quarterly, Vol 4, #4, 1994) New England Cooperative Extension Systems. University of Massachusetts. Worcester, MA.

Jenny, H. 1941, **Factors of Soil Formation**. McGraw - Hill Book Co. New York, NY.

Lennert, L. 1990, **The Role of Iron in Turfgrass Management in Wisconsin**. USGA TGIF #:17611.

Leslie, A.R. (editor) 1994, **Handbook of Integrated Pest Management for Turf and Ornamentals**. Lewis Publishers Boca Raton, FL.

Lucas, R.E. and M.L. Vitosh, 1978, **Soil Organic Matter Dynamics**. Michigan State Univ. Research Report 32.91, Nov 1978. East Lansing, MI.

Maske, C. 1995, Personal Communication. Maske's Organic Gardening. Decatur, IL.

Makarov, I.B. 1986, **Seasonal Dynamics of Soil Humus Content**. Moscow University Soil Science Bulletin, v41 #3: 19-26.

Morgan, E. 1995, Personal Communication. Lancaster, PA.

Nelson, E.B. 1994, **More Than Meets the Eye: The Microbiology of Turfgrass Soils**. Turf Grass Trends, v3 #2 February 1994. Washington, DC.

Nelson, E.B. 1995, Personal Communication. Cornell University. Ithaca, NY.

Nosko, B.S. 1987, **Change in the Humus for a Typical Chernozem Caused by fertilization**. Soviet Soil Science, 1987 v19 July/August pp 67-74.

Novak, B. 1984, **The Role of Soil Organisms in Humus Synthesis and Decomposition**. Soil Biology and Conservation of the Biosphere. pp 319-332.

Ray, P.M. 1972, **The Living Plant**. Holt, Rinehart and Winston, Inc. New York, NY.

Raven, P.H. and H. Curtis, 1970, **Biology of Plants**. Worth Publishers, Inc. New York, NY.

Roberts, E. 1992, Personal Communication. The Lawn Institute. Pleasant Hill, TN.

Sachs, P.D. 1993, **Edaphos: Dynamics of a Natural Soil System**. Edaphic Press. Newbury, VT.

SSSA# 19. 1987, **Soil Fertility and Organic Matter as Critical Components of Production Systems**. Soil Science Society of America, Inc. Madison, WI.

van Veen, A. and P.J. Kuikman, 1990. **Soil Structural Aspects of Decomposition of Organic Matter by Micro-organisms**. Biogeochemistry, Dec. 1990, v11 (3): 213-233.

Visser, S. and D. Parkinson, 1992, **Soil Biological Criteria as Indicators of Soil Quality: Soil Microorganisms**. American Journal of Alternative Agriculture v7 #1 and #2, 1992 pp 33-37. Institute for Alternative Agriculture, Greenbelt, MD.

Wallace, A., G.A. Wallace, and W.C. Jong, 1990. **Soil Organic Matter and the Global Carbon Cycle**. Journal of Plant Nutrition 1990 v13 (3/4): 459-456.

Waksman, S.A. 1936, **Humus**. Williams and Wilkins, Inc. Baltimore, MD.

Wilson, C.L., W.E. Loomis, and T.A. Steeves, 1971, **Botany**. Holt, Rinehart and Winston. New York, NY.

Chapter 2
From Scratch

A new lawn can be more successfully installed and easily maintained if a few basic considerations are made in advance. Issues such as temperature zones, solar exposure, precipitation, soil texture, slopes and contours, and soil test analysis can all have impact on timing, choices of seed, and other materials used. Attention paid to the soil at this stage can reduce or eliminate many potential problems for both the installer and those who care for the established lawn. Quality soil makes the balance of work easier in both the short and long term.

At new construction sites where topsoil is poor or does not exist, soil improvement is the obvious first step. Unfortunately, improving existing soil at a site is rarely specified in most contracts. The more common practice is to call for imported topsoil and lay down four to six inches of it. This superficial fix can cause a malady called *layering* which disables the capillary movement of air and water through the soil.

Many years ago a scientist named W.H. Gardner found that the movement of water is abruptly inhibited by inconsistent layers of soil. His experiments (see figure 1-9) showed that a layer of topsoil applied to a subsoil with a significantly different consistency becomes an insufficient reservoir of moisture for whatever crop is planted. Presumably, as the topsoil settles and/or compresses over the years, that reservoir shrinks. The top soil may never integrate enough with the subsoil to permit proper capillary movement of water and air.

During heavy rains, the topsoil layer will become saturated with water before any drainage into the layer below occurs. This condition starves the roots of oxygen and stresses the plants. It can also cause denitrification, which results in a loss of available soil nitrogen. When droughts occur, the water holding capacity of three to four inches of topsoil is often not enough to sustain the moisture needs of plants. Starting a site with this problem can be a guarantee of many problems to come.

During the construction of buildings, the native topsoil at the job site is often lost and needs to be replaced. If, however, one were to examine the natural transition from the layer of topsoil to the subsoils beneath it, it would be evident that abrupt changes do not mimic the design that mother nature had in mind.

If reserving the native topsoil is possible, it would help in the reconstruction of the soil's natural structure. This step, however, is not always practical.

At an excavated site, the subsoil is often compacted by the repeated passes of heavy equipment. This disrupts the flow of water and air through soil layers. Although controlling compaction during construction is often difficult, compaction can be limited by fencing off the area designated to be lawn after the rough grading has been completed. If fencing is impractical, a six inch thick layer of straw or hay mulch can mitigate the damage done by vehicle traffic.

Another remedy is to attempt a replication of the natural changes from subsoil to topsoil. As backfilling comes within twelve to sixteen inches of grade, topsoil can be added and mixed with the replacement subsoil so that abrupt changes in the soil's horizons do not occur. This can be accomplished with a rototiller, or by premixing the subsoil with topsoil. As backfilling gets closer to grade, (within eight to ten inches) a greater percentage of topsoil can be mixed with the subsoil. The last four to six inches of backfilling can be accomplished with straight topsoil.

This construction design provides more gradual changes in the soil's physical structure, allowing better movement of air and water. Root systems of plants will have better drought resistance and easier access to soil atmosphere. This program may be more expensive in the short term, but can be much less expensive in the long term.

In areas where backfilling is not part of the operation, some topsoil should be rototilled into the existing soil before the final 4-6 inch layer is applied. This transitional layer will mitigate the abrupt changes from poor soil to quality loam. The practice can also loosen the compacted rough grade layer.

The quality of the topsoil being imported is another aspect requiring scrutiny. Topsoil is often ordered from suppliers, dumped, and spread without any question of where it came from or how rich in nutrients and organic matter it is. Some physical attributes may be noted by the contractor, but it is usually related to the ease or difficulty of handling the material. Knowing the quality of topsoil might be analogous to knowing the quality of the concrete being poured for the footings of a tall building. The consequences of poor quality in either case could result in complete reconstruction at some point down the road. Without a soil test, the long term success of a landscape is at risk.

Imported topsoil is usually altered in the process between excavation and installation. The digging, scraping, dozing, loading, transporting, dumping, and spreading of topsoil causes significant changes to its structure, chemistry, and biology. If topsoil is left sitting in a pile for any extended period of time, more of these changes will occur. Unfortunately, none of these changes improves the quality of the topsoil. Organic matter is diminished, beneficial organisms such as earthworms and mycorrhizae fungi are all but wiped out, and the aggregation of soil particles is significantly lessened. If the topsoil was of poor quality when it was excavated, it will be even worse when it is delivered.

SOIL TESTING

Often, site specifications call for lime, fertilizer, and/or other amendments without first analyzing the existing soil conditions. This practice is like hunting in the dark, discharging rounds of ammunition in the hope that some game will be hit. It is not a practical approach in terms of cost efficiency, nor in addressing any real deficiencies or excesses that exist in the soil. Excess or unneeded applications of fertilizer can also cause pollution. This may, at some point, create legal liability for the owner, the designer who wrote the specifications, and the contractor who applies it the fertilizer.

Conducting a soil test is a simple and inexpensive way to ensure that the proper amounts of soil conditioners are applied. If, however, the soil samples gathered do not represent the overall soil conditions, the information from the analysis report will be less helpful than no information at all (see chapter 5 on soil testing). If imported topsoil is being used on a job, it is a good idea to test a sample. Like anything else, there are good quality materials as well as poor quality materials.

ORGANIC MATTER

The test for organic matter is important, especially in a sample of the topsoil that is intended for use. Topsoil with an organic matter content of less than two percent in the temperate region should be considered an inferior quality material. Topsoils with four percent or more organic matter are superior and should be preferred in site specifications. Muck soils with twenty percent or more organic matter can be too much of a good thing. They are soggy and difficult to work with, and not an ideal growing medium for many cultivated plants.

As we move closer to the equator, high levels of organic matter in soils are more difficult to find and maintain because the warmer annual temperatures increase the biological activity decomposing soil organic matter. However, this is not a reason to accept poor quality topsoil. Many suppliers are now mixing composted organic wastes into topsoil, increasing the percentage of organic matter. Beginning a job with higher quality topsoil, even in the warmer regions of the country, gives plants a better chance for long term survival.

Peat moss is also used as a means to increase the organic matter content of topsoil, and although it does lower the bulk density of the soil and provide porosity, it does not break down into humus very quickly and will take longer to provide many of the benefits of a stable soil organic matter. Peat moss may, however, be a prudent alternative in warmer climates, where maintaining adequate levels of organic matter is more difficult.

COMPOST

An alternative to using topsoil is the incorporation of high quality compost into the native soil. This practice enables one to improve the existing soil environment rather than having to create a new one.

Adding compost will stimulate beneficial soil functions, but it is important to understand that compost is not stable soil humus. Less than one percent of a compost application may actually become stable soil humus (depending on soil conditions, climate, and the way in which the soil is managed). If the top six to seven inches of soil weigh two million pounds per acre and the compost being used is fifty percent organic matter, then it would take forty thousand pounds (twenty tons) per acre to temporarily raise the soil organic matter by one percent. Heavy applications of compost (greater than thirty tons per acre) are not recommended unless they are incorporated into the soil. Like layers of topsoil, layers of compost can also disrupt the flow of water and air through the soil. Tilling or discing in ample amounts of compost can change the quality of a backfilled subsoil into a medium that promotes vigorous plant growth without the occurrence of layering. Another advantage of compost over topsoil is that it usually contains little or no weed seed, negating the need for herbicide. In any soil there are literally millions of dormant seeds just waiting for the right conditions to germinate. The excavation, transport, and installation of topsoil brings many seeds to the surface where warmth and moisture make life possible.

Recognizing a good quality compost is not necessarily easy. Most compost manufacturers test their product on a regular basis and are more than happy to show off the results. Interesting values to look for on a test are organic matter content, pH, percent moisture, conductivity, and existing levels of basic plant nutrients. If a large purchase is planned, lab analysis would be a prudent first step. The lab should be informed that the sample submitted is compost and should be tested as a fertilizer or manure, not as a soil. The results of a soil test on compost would be useless information.

Organic matter in most composts ranges from forty to sixty percent, depending on what type of materials are used in the manufacturing process. A list of the raw materials used should be requested to prevent future conflicts with customers who might object if sludge, manures, or other types of composted wastes are applied to their property. Some composts may have lower amounts of organic matter if significant amounts of soil were added during processing. Others may have much higher amounts if the ingredients used were naturally low in minerals. Organic matter is the component of compost that will offer the most improvement in an existing soil. Composts with low amounts of organic matter will have to be applied in relatively greater amounts to have the same effect as composts that contain considerably higher levels.

The pH of compost should be near neutral. Some variance does occur from the inconsistent pH ranges of raw materials, but the biological activity that creates compost cannot function at extremely high or low pH levels. The range of most composts is between 6.0 and 8.0. It is more rare to find a compost with a pH lower than 6.0 than it is to find one with a pH higher than 8.0. Compost with a high pH can contribute toward neutralizing an acid soil but may create more problems on a soil that is already too alkaline. A slightly acidic compost will rarely have an effect on a very acidic soil but may provide some neutralization on alkaline soils. In most cases, lime or sulfur can be used to correct the pH of compost, but it is wiser to find a neutral compost.

Moisture levels in compost do not make a significant difference in the quality of the finished product or the effect it has on soil, but may have some economic impact. A load of compost weighing ten tons contains five tons of water if the moisture level is fifty percent. It would contain six tons of water at a level of sixty percent and only four tons at forty percent. If the compost is hauled for a long distance, the cost of trucking water becomes a significant expense. Most composts are made outdoors and the amount of precipitation that falls during its manufacturing process can have an impact on the final moisture content. There is a certain level of moisture that is necessary for the composting process to occur. Some manufacturers may need to add water if the piles get too dry. Indoor composting facilities are rare, but have total control over the ultimate moisture content of the final product. Soggy composts with very high moisture levels have relatively lower levels of everything else, including organic matter and nutrients, making it necessary to ship and use more. It can also be difficult to work with very wet compost.

The conductivity test measures the level of soluble salts in composts. This test can be extremely important if the compost is being used in conjunction with new seed. Many plant seedlings are sensitive to excessive salts in the soil. Using too much compost with too high a conductivity can destroy a lawn before it ever begins if the compost is not properly incorporated into the soil. The outcome is usually unnoticeable until a glorious crop of weeds finally springs to life. Conductivity is measured in millimhos (mmhos) and compost with levels in excess of 3 mmhos needs to be diluted with the soil. Dilution can be accomplished with a rototiller or other tools designed for tillage. Given that there are 46,000 pounds of soil in the top six inches of every 1000 square feet, it is unlikely that one could find a compost too salty or apply so much of it that dilution would not solve the conductivity problem. Generally, the level of salts in composts is not dangerous to established lawns, but common sense should dictate proper usage. Compost with a conductivity level below 3 mmhos can be used as a seed vehicle: the compost is pre-mixed with seed and the two are applied together. Many managers use this technique for spot seeding thin patches of turf. Compost holds more moisture than soil and is thought to contain compounds that enhance the seeds' ability to germinate.

The nutrient levels normally found in compost are not high, but the amount usually applied (see table 2-1) is large enough to compensate for the low analysis. It is generally rare to find nitrogen (N) levels in a compost above three percent, and all the other nutrients are usually lower. Phosphate is often about one third the level of N, and potash is often about two thirds of the N value. Micro-nutrients are generally present in trace amounts. Variances can occur if raw materials containing high levels of a certain nutrient or nutrients were composted.

YARDS TO COVER

DEPTH	1000 SQ FT	1 ACRE
1/8 INCH	0.38	18
1/4 INCH	0.75	35
1/2 INCH	1.5	69
1 INCH	3.1	135
2 INCHES	6.2	270
3 INCHES	9.3	405

Table 2-1

If a one inch layer of compost is incorporated into 1000 square feet of soil, and it contains only one percent N, more than 30 pounds of total N have been applied to the 1000 square foot area. This may seem excessive, and would be with conventional fertilizers, but compost will release the nutrient slowly without burning. It also feeds other living organisms in the soil that can provide valuable edaphic functions. Needless to say, more fertilization is not usually necessary.

If an analysis of compost is not available and testing is impractical, a lot that can be learned by noticing certain physical characteristics. Smell is probably the most important. If a pile of compost smells so bad you can't get close to it, you probably shouldn't. There should not be any strong odors coming from a well made compost. A simple test is to dig into a pile with a shovel and extract a sample that is a foot or two beneath the surface. If it is a good compost, the sample should smell something like fresh soil. It certainly should not have any very strong or objectionable odors. Composts with very strong odors are not fully decomposed or stable and probably contain high salt levels. What one person thinks is a very strong odor may be different from another's opinion. Given the subjective nature of this kind of test, it is a good idea to compare the smell of one compost to another or several others.

Another characteristic to notice when digging into a pile is temperature. If the compost is still steaming, then it has not stabilized yet and may be high in soluble salts. This is not usually a problem if the compost is being incorporated into a soil. The stabilization can occur in the soil without any harmful effect on plants. It would, however, be an inappropriate material to use as a seed vehicle or as a topdress on newly seeded ground.

If a high percentage of undecomposed raw materials such as wood chips or leaves is evident, it is a sign that the ratio of ingredients used in the compost making process was improper and the overall quality is questionable. Rocks or large pieces of undecomposed debris, such as branches or thick roots, certainly detract from the quality of a compost. Most manufacturers screen their product, which saves the customer time and aggravation when applying it.

Construction of the soil requires the same care of design and quality materials as any structure that is built to last. The proper structure and fertility of any soil is important if the quality of a landscape is designed for the long term.

RENOVATION

There is a case to be made for herbicides when it comes to renovation. When renovating, it is often necessary to kill or weaken the existing growth to limit competition against the new grass seed. Accomplishing this by tillage can be very damaging to an area. The amount of air introduced into the soil by tilling can significantly reduce the organic matter levels. In fragile soils, lacking high organic matter levels, tillage can put a soil over the edge. Chopped up segments of perennial roots will often sprout new shoots in greater numbers than before. Additionally, millions of dormant seeds are brought to the surface by tillers to germinate into weeds. Sod cutters can be used, but the removal of the top two inches of soil will probably net an equal or greater loss of valuable soil components, and there is still the issue of dormant weed seeds.

On the other hand, if a lawn is in need of renovation, it is probably because the soil is lacking the needed fertility and/or structure to support a vigorous turf. Tilling is an excellent opportunity to amend the soil with compost. Copious amounts can be incorporated into the soil with a rototiller without causing layering (see compost section in this chapter). The addition of compost during renovation is a tool that significantly increases the chance of success of a new lawn; compost should be a high priority when beginning a renovation project.

If compost or other suitable organic amendments are not available, herbicides may actually be more effective and less damaging than tillage to the soil's ecology. They can completely kill the surface growth without disturbing the soil and without relocating dormant weed seeds into a horizon where they can germinate. Natural herbicides are beginning to appear on the market that can accomplish this end without compromising one's organic standards. Insecticidal soaps have been altered by some companies to be effective against annual weeds. These products strip the leaves of plants of their protective coating, resulting in desiccation. They are most effective when used in full sun but may have to be applied more than once to eliminate more stubborn weeds. Corn gluten products that are labeled for pre-emergent weed control are beginning to appear on the market. Some herbicides use synthetic plant growth regulators to alter the plants' growing mechanisms, while others are more persistent poisons. If herbicides are used, it is very important to read the labels carefully and choose a product that will have minimal impact on the ecology of the area. If shallow water wells exist, only the most benign, biodegradable products should be used, or nothing at all. By the time this book is printed, there will probably be other environmentally friendly herbicides to choose from. Regardless of whether herbicides are used or not, the best time to renovate a lawn (for cool season grasses) is in the early fall.

Corn gluten is a natural organic material that releases a substance as it decomposes in the soil, preventing roots from forming on germinating seeds. Unfortunately, it is indiscriminate and will kill newly planted grass seeds as well as germinating weed seeds. Corn gluten would be best used in controlling annual weeds in established lawns. Because it contains ten percent organic nitrogen it would also serve a source of nutrients for the existing plants.

Another alternative to tillage for lawn renovation is to physically weaken the existing growth by mowing very low and by using a power rake or dethatching machine to scarify the surface of the soil, stressing the existing plants as much as possible. Then new seed can be applied through a slit seeding machine which will cut through any existing sod and roots (these machines can usually be rented from tool lending companies for as short a period of time as one day). The addition of a thin layer (no more than ¼ inch) of compost after seeding would benefit the new seedlings. If this operation is done in the early fall, when annual weeds are beginning to run out of steam, the chances of success are significantly increased.

If the area to be renovated is very small, black plastic can kill the existing growth by light deprivation or *solarization*. The length of time required to completely kill existing plants varies with the type of plant. Most plants will completely yellow in a couple of days, but will return to health when re-exposed to sunlight. Some plants can take up to 4 years to kill by this method. Most, however, will succumb after being covered for 2-3 weeks. The best time for this method is toward the end of the summer when the weather is still hot, but the ideal fall planting weather is not too far away. This is an excellent way to eliminate old growth, because the soil is not disturbed.

SEED

The choices of available seed are very broad, and selecting the right seed for the site requires careful consideration. The first determination to be made is what varieties of seed are suitable for the environmental conditions at the site. There should be several, but there are many more that are simply inappropriate. Using a variety of lawn seed that is not suited for the existing conditions is asking for trouble in the future. Customers who request a specific type of lawn such as bluegrass in an area where bluegrass will not do well need to be educated. Perhaps if they understand how difficult and expensive it will be to maintain a lawn that would not naturally grow at that site, they might be persuaded to accept a different grass seed or a blend of several varieties.

Diversity is the key to establishing a lawn that can survive the varying and unpredictable conditions at most sites. If the chosen variety does not get established for some reason, and no other better suited varieties are introduced, mother nature will intervene with varieties of plants that are not normally preferred by the steward or the owner. There are several families of grasses that are suitable for most environments. Using a broad selection can offer a type of insurance policy without sacrificing quality. Most people cannot identify a fescue from a ryegrass or a bluegrass plant and may not even realize that more than one variety even exists. Generally, most customers' criteria for a quality lawn is color, thickness and absence of weeds.

Every year new quality ratings are made available on the many different varieties of seed on the market. This information is valuable to a certain extent, but should not be the definitive source of selection criteria. The ratings only compare seeds of the same varieties. In a situation where the worst rating is still good, it becomes difficult to determine an effective way to use the information. If, for example, a variety of seed is chosen because of its endophyte content or its heat tolerance but it is rated outside the top ten or twenty varieties for quality or performance, it does not necessarily mean that it is a poor choice. There may be only a subtle difference between this selection and those that are rated at or near the top.

Seeds that contain endophytes are another consideration. Endophyte is a term that refers to a group of fungi that live within the cells of the grass plant and reproduce as the plant cells divide. The fungi use some of the plant's resources but, in exchange, give the plant protection against many foliar feeding insects. The fungi apparently produce a group of toxins that have insecticidal properties but do not harm the plant. These toxins are distasteful to grazing insects (and other animals) which usually terminate their feeding on that plant. If feeding continues, death can result. The beauty of this system is that domestic animals inclined to graze on grasses containing endophytes are deterred by the taste before any damage, either to the grass or the animal, can occur. The only way to get livestock to eat grasses containing endophytes is to confine them in an area where nothing else is available. Given that choice, they would rather eat distasteful grass than starve.

Grass varieties that contain endophytes are, unfortunately, not a sure protection. Some varieties do not contain enough endophytes to be effective against an army of reproducing, grass eating, insect pests. Varieties that claim to contain endophytes are examined under a microscope to determine the level of infection. The results are published and most seed dealers have access to that information. Seeds that test to less than seventy percent infection are considered to be ineffective for insect protection. This threshold is based on the theory that in a worst case scenario, at seventy percent infection, up to thirty percent of a lawn could be lost to insect attack.

Even if a seed variety has a very high infection of endophytes, there is still no guarantee of protection. If the seeds are stored improperly or for too long, their level of infection could drop dramatically. Endophytes are perishable. Like perishable foods, they will last longer under refrigeration. Seeds with endophytes stored in a warm environment do not have nearly the shelf life that the same seed in a refrigerator or freezer would have. Tests have shown that the endophytes in refrigerated seed can last five years or longer. Seeds stored in a warm to hot environment can lose much of their infection in six to twelve months. Most seed labels have a date on them that usually indicates the harvest date or when the seed was packaged. If you are shopping for endophytically enhanced seed, pay attention to the date on the label. After twelve to thirteen months the endophytes may be ineffective unless the seed was stored in a refrigerated facility. For more information on endophytically enhanced grass seed, see chapter 4.

New research is being conducted with isolated strains of endophytes that also provide disease suppression in turf plants. Commercial availability of these types of grasses should be seen within the next year or two.

SOD

Transplanting patches of turf from one place to another has been done successfully for centuries. Sod production as an industry, however, began in the United States in the 1920's. As of 1985, the industry had grown to a volume of $360 million a year. The benefit of using sod is to have early establishment of turf in situations where planting from seed may be impractical. In areas where the potential for erosion is great or in sports field applications where there simply is not enough time to establish turf from seed, sod becomes a viable alternative. Sod is often purchased as a ready-to-use commodity for customers who simply do not wish to wait for lawns to establish from seed.

The sod industry has been accused of many environmental ills, including topsoil depletion, excessive water use, and pollution. Most of these claims, however, are unsubstantiated. The fact is that sod production, because of the amount of root growth, actually produces soil. The high tech slicing equipment used to cut sod results in a net loss of topsoil that is less than that experienced by farmers growing row crops where tillage and erosion deplete the topsoil to a far greater extent. Water usage by sod growers is generally less than what a homeowner would use to establish turf from seed, because, given the cost of irrigation, the professional will use water as efficiently as possible. The same is true when it comes to fertilizers and pesticides. Sod growers generally use high quality, disease resistant varieties of grasses which further reduce the need for pesticides.

The two major problems with sod are the lack of genetic diversity that sod growers use, and the soil conditions into which sod is installed. Sod is generally planted solely from bluegrass because of its quality and the ability of its roots to knit together so well. This enables the sod pad to hold together even though the grower cuts sod very thin. Unfortunately, this one cultivar may not be ideal for the environment where it is to be installed and if it does not do well, there are no other varieties to fill in. Some sod growers mix fescues in with the bluegrass, adding some diversity.

The more common problem with a sod lawn is that it is often installed onto poor soil which is unable to support the vigorous growth needed for sod to adapt to its new environment. The stress associated with transplanting sod is already high. Failure is a predictable outcome when one tries to re-establish plants in a compacted, infertile soil with little or no organic matter. In some cases, fertilizers and other amendments will temporarily allow the sod to establish itself and thrive, but failure is, oftentimes, only postponed.

Soil preparation for sod should be the same exercise as for seed preparation. Eventually, the sod will establish itself into the same lawn that would exist if it were planted from seed. Common sense dictates that overall conditions should be the same. In cases where nothing but subsoil exists, topsoil can be imported or compost can be used to amend the existing conditions. Using seaweed extracts as a transplanting aid for sod is an inexpensive and worthwhile practice that helps the plants overcome stress and develop new roots faster. Sod producers plant in rich topsoil for quick establishment and vigorous growth. If the soil where the sod is transplanted differs significantly, plant roots can be stressed beyond a tolerable level. Washing sod is a new technique designed to remove much of the soil embedded in the root systems, so that the soil where the sod is transplanted is the only medium and serves as the sod's native soil.

If used correctly, sod can be as vigorous a lawn as any other. If conditions are inappropriate, however, sod can be a nightmare to maintain. The customer who spent a fortune installing sod does not want to hear that it needs to be replaced. Unfortunately, if sod was installed inappropriately by a hit-and-run contractor, the steward of the lawn is left with the headaches.

A popular new alternative to conventional sod is a wildflower sod, or carpet, as it is trademarked. Installing this type of ground cover is an attractive and maintenance free alternative to the rigors and problems associated with turf (O'Brien 1995). The successful establishment of wildflowers from seed has met with mixed results, because the establishment time can allow for weed encroachment. The sod, on the other hand, establishes quickly and can suppress many weeds.

TIMING

Early fall is usually the best time to install a new lawn, especially in the climate zone that is appropriate for cool season grasses. Precipitation is generally more reliable, the soil is much warmer, biological activity is peaking, and competition from weeds is at an annual low. Installing turf from seed or sod during this window of opportunity usually results in far fewer failures than spring installations.

Unfortunately, most customers want new lawns installed in the spring. This can present many problems that are both short and long term. Springtime precipitation in the northeast is often unreliable, especially in the northern sections where the soil does not reach appropriate temperatures for planting until May or June. By that time the spring rains have usually subsided. Unless irrigation is available, new seed can take a long time to germinate on its own, giving annual and perennial weeds an excellent opportunity to become established (see chapter 4). The stress from weed competition, heat, and inadequate amounts of moisture can lead to other problems in a lawn, where young seedlings are less able to withstand these conditions. Temporary lawns can be installed using a hearty, quick germinating variety, such as annual rye, to compete with weeds and shade the soil until fall. Then the area can either be over-seeded with a special seed planting machine or turned under for renovation. This alternative may be more expensive in the short term, but could turn out to be a lot less expensive than dealing with a permanent lawn that failed because it was planted in the spring.

IRRIGATION

Generally it is not recommended to push new seed into germinating with irrigation. The very shallow roots are vulnerable to excessive heat from the sun and can perish easily if the surface of the soil dries out quickly. On the other hand, if natural rains begin the germination process and dry, hot weather immediately follows, irrigation is imperative to prevent the obvious consequences. Automatic irrigation can be both a blessing and a curse on newly seeded lawns. The convenience of being able to provide moisture to a new lawn at consistent intervals is superlative, but excessive use of the tool can stress seedlings into other problems. Automatic systems do not take into consideration any natural conditions. They can come on at an ideal time one day and be completely unnecessary on the next. If the sky is overcast, the soil may only need ten minutes of irrigation. However, on a really hot, dry afternoon the system may need to come on two or three times to keep the surface from drying out. Obviously, if it is pouring, the system doesn't need to come on at all. Established lawns can withstand the vagaries of automatic irrigation systems better than new seedlings, but even established lawns can be stressed by improper use. If irrigation is used at the early stage of growth in a lawn, close attention needs to be paid to the environmental conditions.

It is a good idea to plant seed into moist soil. If it is too wet, however, it can be difficult to work with. After seeding, irrigation should be used at a base rate of about ten minutes (or one tenth of an inch of water) per day in the afternoons. Constant attention should be paid to the soil moisture level after germination begins and adjustments made if necessary. Irrigation should be disabled on rainy days. Too much irrigation during colder weather can lead to disease problems. Like any other tool, irrigation is only an advantage if it is used properly.

MULCHING

Mulching is a excellent means of protecting both the seed and the soil in a newly installed lawn. When the surface of the soil is covered, precious moisture is preserved. This not only speeds up germination but also dampens the impact of heavy rains. It also disrupts the tendency of water to channel into paths that cause erosion and carry away new seeds.

Unfortunately, mulch can have a downside. If mulch is applied too heavily, it can prevent young seedlings from reaching needed sunlight before they exhaust the limited amount of energy they have within the seed. Hay mulch can contain varying amounts of seed that can contaminate a lawn with unwanted varieties of grasses. In a lawn with a very diverse selection of seed this may not be a concern. But if a customer wants a pure bluegrass lawn, then the hay may create a problem.

Paper mulch is commercially available and offers the same protection as hay without the added seed. Most paper mulches are made from scrap newspaper which is shredded and impregnated with some fertilizer. Paper mulch is usually applied through a hydroseeder that can dispense seed, mulch, and fertilizer evenly and simultaneously, over a broad area in a very short period of time. Distributing this type of mulch by hand is tedious and difficult to spread evenly. Researchers at the University of Pennsylvania have found that by pelletizing paper mulch, anyone with a seed or fertilizer spreader can apply it evenly and with very little effort. This product should be commercially available well before this book goes to print.

If mulch is applied correctly, it should not have to be removed. The decaying organic matter can provide many benefits to the soil. If thick mats of mulch are inhibiting the seed from growing, however, or harboring potentially damaging insects or pathogens, the mulch should be gently removed as soon as the new grass begins to grow.

Some managers in the Northeast do not believe mulch is necessary in the fall. The consistency of precipitation and the cooler temperatures are usually at a level where the soil surface remains moist without the need for mulch. If heavy rains occur, however, unmulched seed can be washed away.

FERTILIZING

Proper fertilization cannot be accomplished without a soil analysis (see chapter 5). Any fertility program is more or less like shooting in the dark if the existing nutrient levels in the soil are not known. It can also be a waste of money if one is adding nutrients that the soil clearly doesn't need, causing imbalances that are difficult to correct. Imported topsoil should also be tested. If deficiencies are found in an analysis, the base fertility of the soil should be corrected. Nutrients should also be added in anticipation of what the turfgrass crop will remove from the soil. Soil fertility should be maintained at a maximum, not a minimum, and excessive fertilization must be avoided.

Choosing fertilizers or amendments for correcting deficiencies can be difficult (see chapter 6). There are many different brands and grades of fertilizers made from a diverse variety of ingredients based on several different philosophies. The philosophy in this book is that the plant is only a component of a much larger system and that fertility must apply to the entire system, not just the plant.

Making choices based on this idea narrows the selection process to a manageable level. Natural materials that are either organic or mineral in nature are generally suggested. Soluble salts are not necessarily taboo, but their use must be tempered with common sense and should not be the sole source of nutrients. New seedlings are especially vulnerable to damage from high salt fertilizers. Nitrogen is important for germinating seeds, but overdosing is a clear and present danger. Low nitrogen, organic fertilizers are very compatible with the needs of the soil and the needs of germinating seeds. Concentrated fertilizers designed to cover large areas with very low volumes put concentrated fertility in fewer locations on the soil's surface and are spread further apart. The key ingredient missing in these types of products is carbon in a form that can be used by soil organisms. A detailed discussion of fertilizers and amendments is provided in chapter 6.

OVERSEEDING MACHINES

Overseeding machines enable one to plant seed just under the surface of the soil. The manufacturers of these tools claim that the improved soil contact with the seed increases the percent of seed germinating and reduces the mortality of seed after germination. There are those who would disagree, opting for the old fashioned roller to press the seed into the soil's surface. The differences between the two methods may be insignificant in most instances, but the machine may have an advantage in certain soil types. The big advantage to the overseeding machine is that it can plant new seed into existing sod. This can eliminate the need for tillage in many instances, and can enable one to add new life to an aging lawn without complete renovation (see chapter 4). If new seed is being introduced to bare soil, it may not be worth the effort to travel any great distance and rent a machine.

ROLLING

The old fashioned way of tamping seed into the soil is with a roller. Surprisingly, some professionals feel that the roller is still one of the best tools to be used for installing a new lawn. The big advantage of using a roller is that it promotes more complete contact between the seed and the soil, without burying the seed too deeply. The better contact the seed has with the soil, the sooner it will germinate and the likelihood of it being dislodged by rain or wind is reduced. The roller can also be used to find soft areas in fresh topsoil that may eventually settle into depressions in the finished lawn. Rolling out a prepared seedbed before seeding can reveal areas that are less compacted than others. Correction at this point is much easier that after the lawn is established.

Water is usually added into the drum of the roller to give it weight. The amount of water used should vary depending on the type of soil one is working in. The roller should be heavier when working in light, sandy soils than it would be for heavy, clay soils. For practical reasons, less weight should be used when working on slopes. Your customer would probably not be impressed if a runaway roller ran over the family cat or entered the house through the dining room sliding glass door. Water should not be left in the roller for long periods of time as it may cause rust that will eventually destroy the tool.

SEAWEED

Seaweed has been used in agriculture to enhance plant growth for over a thousand years. The plant growth regulators contained in seaweed perform a myriad of apparent miracles, especially on young plants. Extracts of seaweed preparations have been commercially available for a number of years, and most are relatively inexpensive to use. Research over the years has shown significant value in using seaweed extracts to increase the speed of seed germination and enhance the rooting capabilities of the plant. Seaweed has also been shown to increase the drought resistant qualities of many different turfgrasses. Many managers who use hydroseeding equipment add seaweed to their mixture of seed, mulch, and fertilizer.

Sources:

Adams, W.A. and R.J. Gibbs, 1994, **Natural Turf for Sport and Amenity: Science and Practice**. CAB International. Wallingford, United Kingdom.

Albrecht, W.A. 1938, **Loss of Organic Matter and its Restoration**. U.S. Dept. of Agriculture Yearbook 1938, pp347-376.

Arshad, M.A. and G.M. Coen, 1992, **Characterization of Soil Quality: Physical and Chemical Criteria**. American Journal of Alternative Agriculture v7 #1 and 2, 1992 pp 25-31. Institute for Alternative Agriculture, Greenbelt, MD.

Bear, F.E. 1924, **Soils and Fertilizers**. John Wiley and Sons, Inc. New York, NY.

BioCycle Staff (editors) 1989, **The Biocycle Guide to Yard Waste Composting**. JG Press, Inc. Emmaus, PA.

BioCycle Staff (editors) 1991, **The Art and Science of Composting**. JG Press, Inc. Emmaus, PA.

Bormann, F.H., D. Balmori, and G.T. Geballe, 1993, **Redesigning the American Lawn: A search for Environmental Harmony**. Yale University Press. New Haven, CT.

Brady, N.C. 1974, **The Nature and Properties of Soils**. MacMillan Publishing Co. Inc. New York, NY.

Bunce, R.G.H., L. Ryszkowski, and M.G. Paoletti, 1993, **Landscape Ecology and Agroecosystems**. Lewis Publishers. Boca Raton, FL.

Casagrande, R.A. 1993, **Sustainable Sod Production for the Northeast**. Department of Plant Sciences, University of Rhode Island. Kingston, RI.

Chu, P. 1993, Personal Communication. A&L Eastern Agricultural Labratories. Richmond, VA.

Craul P.J. 1992, **Urban Soil in Landscape Design**. John Wiley and Sons, Inc. New York, NY.

Franklin, S. 1988, **Building a Healthy Lawn: A Safe and Natural Approach**. Storey Communications, Inc. Pownal, VT.

Golueke, C.G. 1972, **Composting: A Study of the Process and its Principles**. Rodale Books, Inc. Emmaus, PA.

Hall, R. 1994, **Turf Pros Respond to Biostimulants**. Landscape Management, Oct. 94. Advanstar Communications. Duluth, MN.

Leslie, A.R. (editor) 1994, **Handbook of Integrated Pest Management for Turf and Ornamentals**. Lewis Publishers Boca Raton, FL.

Lucas, R.E. and M.L. Vitosh, 1978, **Soil Organic Matter Dynamics**. Michigan State Univ. Research Report 32.91, Nov 1978. East Lansing, MI.

Maske, C. 1995, Personal Communication. Maske's Organic Gardening. Decatur, IL.

Merner, M. 1995, Personal Communication. Earth Care Farm. Charlestown, RI.

Neal, J.C. 1992, **Plan Before You Plant**. WeedFacts, July 1992. Cornell University. Ithaca, NY.

Nelson, E.B. 1994, **More Than Meets the Eye: The Microbiology of Turfgrass Soils**. Turf Grass Trends, v3#2 February 1994. Washington, DC.

Nelson, E.B. 1995, Personal Communication. Cornell University. Ithaca, NY.

O'Brien, J. 1995, Personal Communication. Winding Brook Turf Farm. Kennebunk, ME.

Sachs, P.D. 1993, **Edaphos: Dynamics of a Natural Soil System**. Edaphic Press. Newbury, VT.

Schultz, W. 1989, **The Chemical Free Lawn**. Rodale Press. Emmaus, PA.

Senn, T.L. 1987, **Seaweed and Plant Growth**. Department of Horticulture, Clemson University. Clemson, SC.

Waksman, S.A. 1936, **Humus**. Williams and Wilkins, Inc. Baltimore, MD.

Wilkinson, J. 1995, **Compost Preferred Over Topsoil as Soil**

Amendment. Landscape Management April, 1995, V34 #4. Advanstar Communications. Cleveland, OH.

Chapter 3
Cultural Practices

We humans are a little strange when it comes to our lawns. We feed one so it will grow thick and lush, only to mow it down. We apply expensive nitrogen to make the lawn grow green but then we remove most of it when we bag the clippings and send them to the landfill. We stress our lawns by mowing them as close to the ground as possible with dull blades, and then we wonder why they're having so many problems coping with the rigors of the natural world.

Sound familiar? Cultivating a beautiful lawn is a practice that usually has only esthetics in mind. The time has come, however, to introduce some common sense into the equation. Surprisingly, an even more beautiful lawn can be maintained when more sensible cultural techniques are practiced.

SHARP BLADES

If it were necessary to have a mole or wart removed for medical reasons, a natural choice would be to have it taken off by a professional with a sharp surgical instrument — as opposed to someone with a butter knife or a spoon. The latter choice would obviously be a more stressful one, possibly threatening your survival. Mowing a lawn with dull blades is analogous to attempting surgery with silverware. It leaves a jagged wound that is harder to heal, more susceptible to infections by plant pathogens, and will allow a greater amount of moisture to evaporate from the plant than a clean cut would. It also pulls on the plant, weakening its attachment to the soil. The stress that turf plants undergo from mowing with a dull blade weakens their defenses to environmental rigors such as heat, cold, drought, traffic, insects and diseases. Additionally, the lawn mower will use as much as 22% more fuel mowing with a dull blade.

So not only are we stressing the lawns we mow, but we are spending more money doing it. The ecological impact of burning more fuel and creating greater amounts of atmospheric pollutants should also be considered here.

Sharpening a mower blade should be done often. Many professionals whose mowers run all day keep an extra set of sharpened blades and change them daily. The routine of keeping sharp blades on the mowers is well worth the effort when it results in a higher quality turf with fewer fuel dollars spent. Regardless of whether you have an extra set or not, blades should be sharpened after every 7-8 hours of use.

MOWING HEIGHT

The part of the turf plant that we remove when we mow is the part that generates, by photosynthesis, the nutrients needed by the roots and the energy needed by the entire plant. Removing too much of the leaves is analogous to sewing someone's mouth shut so he or she can't eat. This may be fine if weight loss is an objective, but the turf plant has limited energy reserves and can easily be weakened by consistently mowing too low. The more surface area on the leaves of the plant, the greater the photosynthetic production of nutrients for the roots, and thus a relative increase in root mass is achieved. Deeper and more extensive roots mean better access to water and nutrients, which generates a healthier and heartier plant. Figure 3-1

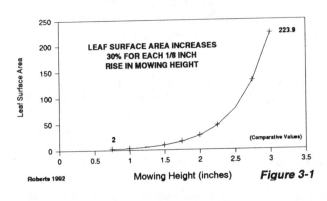

INFLUENCE OF MOWING HEIGHT
ON PHOTOSYNTHESIS
BY TURFGRASSES

Roberts 1992   Mowing Height (inches)   *Figure 3-1*

INFLUENCE OF MOWING HEIGHT
ON ROOT PRODUCTION
(KENTUCKY BLUEGRASS)

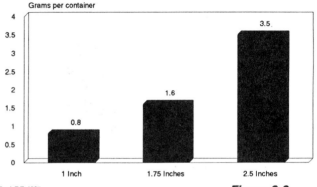

Deal, E.E. 1967

Figure 3-2

shows that for each eighth of an inch the mower is raised, there is a thirty percent increase in the amount of leaf surface area exposed to the sun. When a mower is raised from three quarters of an inch to three inches, the leaf surface area is increased by over 10,000%.

The root systems of turf plants are generally annual: they die off every year and new roots grow from the crown of the plant. The old roots contribute significant amounts of organic matter, distributing it throughout the soil. This organic material provides countless benefits to the turf, including improved water and nutrient retention, lower soil density, and a significant increase in beneficial biological activity.

Container experiments done at the University of Maryland show a significant increase in the amount of organic matter produced from root growth (see figure 3-2) when the mowing height is raised. What is even more impressive is the increase in rhizome development (see figure 3-3). Production of rhizomes (lateral roots that give birth to new plants with new root systems of their own) is raised by more than 1000% when the mowing height is raised from 1.75 inches to 2.5 inches. Overall contributions of organic matter into the soil can be easily and significantly increased simply by raising the mower deck.

INFLUENCE OF MOWING HEIGHT
ON RHIZOME DEVELOPMENT
(KENTUCKY BLUEGRASS)

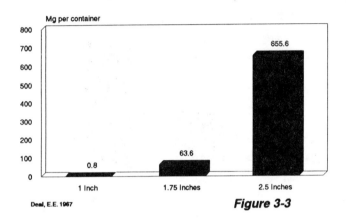

Deal, E.E. 1967   *Figure 3-3*

Another advantage of setting the mower deck higher is that it shades the soil and preserves moisture during crucial times of the year when lawns often go into dormancy from drought. The cooler soil temperature also slows the biological decomposition of organic matter in the soil and preserves more of this vital component of the lawn system.

Research has discovered that the control of crabgrass without chemicals is fundamentally possible simply by raising the height of the mower. Figure 3-4 shows that a mowing height of 3.5 inches suppressed crabgrass to an acceptable level. This particular study compared these results to plots that were treated with four different crabgrass herbicides and found that the 3.5 inch mowing height controlled crabgrass as well as any of the herbicides.

THE ONE-THIRD RULE

Removal of more than one third of the top growth can cause roots to stop growing for up to 28 days. If too much of the leaves is removed, photosynthesis is diminished to the point where the plant must use nutrient reserves in the root system to sustain itself. When new top growth exposes itself to the sun, photosynthesis will begin to produce nutrients for the roots again, but will first have to replenish the reserves used during that period when the leaves were too

INFLUENCE OF MOWING HEIGHT
ON CRABGRASS COVER
1989-1991

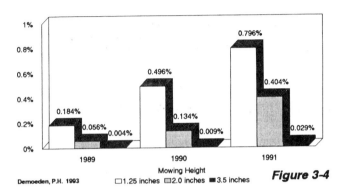

Demoeden, P.H. 1993   □1.25 inches ▨2.0 inches ■3.5 inches

Figure 3-4

short. The energy needed for normal functions plus the restocking of reserves can stop the growth of turf roots for almost a month. Loss of root growth during crucial times of the season can make the difference between a lawn with problems and one without, in both the short and long term. The degree of root growth is relative to how a plant fares through many different types of stresses such as heat, cold, and drought. The root's production of organic matter in the soil is a long term asset that can benefit many future generations of turf plants.

CLIPPING MANAGEMENT

For years the classic response to questions about lawn clippings has been that they must be removed because they can cause thatch, turf diseases, and an unsightly appearance. Research tells us that this advice is wrong. In fact, leaving the clippings behind has a great number of benefits. Clippings contain 58% of the nitrogen that we apply to our lawns. Removing them is equivalent to sweeping up most of the fertilizer that we have just put down. Leaving the clippings behind adds about two pounds of nitrogen per thousand square feet per year.

According to research, returned lawn clippings have a number of other benefits including crabgrass suppression, increased earthworm populations, improved water infiltration into the soil, improved

N UPTAKE BY LEAF TISSUE

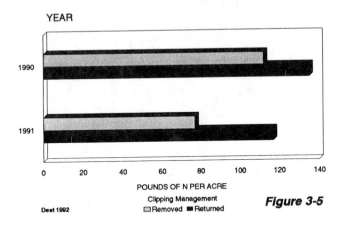

Figure 3-5

turfgrass color, disease suppression, and the reduction of thatch. Clippings can also act as a temporary mulch, preserving soil moisture. Figures 3-5 through 3-12 show the results of recent research on clipping management. What is evident from this research is that the recycling process adds more than just plant nutrients. It energizes many different components of the soil's biological mechanisms. All of this makes sense when one considers that the natural system's

COLOR RATING
1 = Pale Yellow
5 = Dark Green

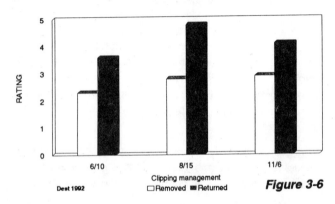

Figure 3-6

EARTHWORM ACTIVITY
1990 and 1991

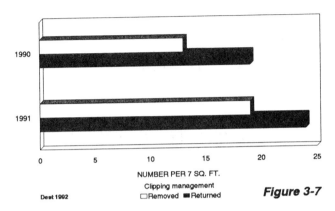

NUMBER PER 7 SQ. FT.

Clipping management
☐Removed ■Returned

Dest 1992

Figure 3-7

design is to recycle residues into nutrients and energy for many soil organisms, including plants.

Mowing without the bag will produce a quality lawn if it is done at proper intervals. Infrequent or inconsistent mowing can produce clumps of clippings that can block necessary sunlight from grass

WATER INFILTRATION
1990 AND 1991

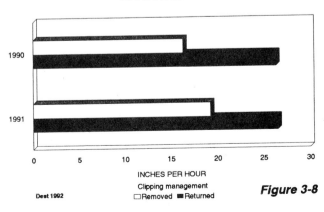

INCHES PER HOUR

Clipping management
☐Removed ■Returned

Dest 1992

Figure 3-8

ROOT WEIGHTS
OF TURF

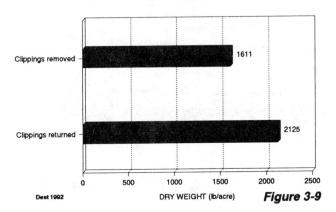

Figure 3-9

plants. The new mulching mowers are designed to chop clippings into smaller particles, shortening the time it takes for them to decompose. They do not work well, however, if one is not mowing often enough. These machines also consume more energy than conventional mowers. Many experts in the field have noted that the clippings from conventional mowers disappear quickly enough and the need for mulching mowers is not really evident.

TOTAL CLIPPING YIELD
1990 AND 1991
(IN POUNDS PER ACRE X 1000)

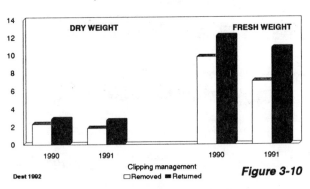

Figure 3-10

WEEDS
1990 AND 1991

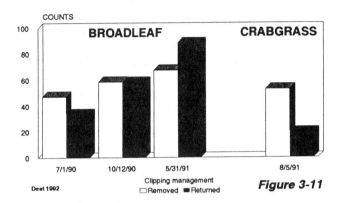

Figure 3-11

If it becomes necessary to remove clippings, it is important to recognize what is being removed from the lawn ecosystem. The nutrients and organic matter contained in grass clippings should be replaced to compensate for the loss. If practical, annual topdress applications of compost should be applied to lawns where clippings are removed.

Clipping disposal can become a problem, especially in munici-

DISEASE RATING
1990 AND 1991

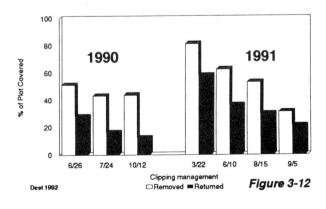

Figure 3-12

palities where they are not allowed in the landfill. Composting is a good idea if one has the time and carbon materials needed to do it right. Composting grass clippings by themselves usually leads to unpleasant odors and irate neighbors.

Another alternative is cold composting. A golf course superintendent in Maine discovered that clippings could be recycled into compost effectively by tilling them into the soil. He chose one site where all the clippings from the entire course are incorporated into the soil. There were no odors and the vastly improved soil could be used in numerous applications around the course.

MOWING FREQUENCY

Mowing frequency should depend on the growth of the plants. Unfortunately, mowing often occurs when the opportunity presents itself, such as every Monday when you service that neighborhood. Growth between Mondays may be more than should be cut off at once, because of abundant rains or recent fertilization. During these periods of rapid growth, mowing frequency should increase so no more than one third of the plant is removed at one time. This may only amount to one or two extra midweek cuttings per year. The extra effort will immensely benefit the health and vitality of the lawn.

Mowing techniques have more to do with producing a quality lawn than all other treatments combined. Fertilizer, pesticide, seed, and other treatments will accomplish little if the lawn is not mowed properly. A tremendous amount of damage and stress can be introduced by improper mowing. Most lawns, especially residential ones, do not serve a specific purpose such as sport recreation. The need is usually only an esthetic one that includes uniform color and height. There is rarely a good reason for mowing a lawn short or for removing the clippings. Lawns mowed at or near maximum mower height during the hottest part of the year can often weather the summer months without going into dormancy, or at least have a much shorter dormant period. Clippings returned to the lawn are rarely noticed and literally disappear in a day or two. The benefits that are eliminated when the clippings are removed can be more easily noticed. Finally, the sharpness of the mower's blade can make a significant difference between a lawn with problems and one without. The stress inflicted upon turf plants when mowed with dull blades can tip the competitive scales in favor of weeds, herbivorous insects, or pathogens and create a need for expensive and toxic controls.

STRING TRIMMING

String trimmers are a great invention. They allow quick and close trimming around trees, stones, statues, even pink flamingos. The string is round, however, and does not so much cut as tear the tops of the grass plants off. Like mowing with dull blades, string trimming can stress plants and lead to other problems. New advances in cord technology have produced a string with edges that do a better job of cutting, rather than tearing, the grass.

EDGING MACHINES

That nice clean edge along the sidewalk or driveway may be esthetically pleasing, but can be creating some problems. Exposed soil and roots are more susceptible to drought and heat, causing grass plants along a trimmed edge to perish and to be replaced by nature's indiscriminate choices. Trimming with a string trimmer may not leave as straight and clean an edge but may provide a much healthier environment for the preferred species of plants.

SPREADER CALIBRATION

Applying the correct amount of material, whether it is lime, fertilizer, soil amendments, or trace elements, is extremely important in achieving balanced fertility. Every spreader should be calibrated from time to time to ensure that the proper amount of material is being applied. Brand new spreaders that one would expect to be at their peak of accuracy are not always calibrated properly. Calibrating a spreader is a relatively simple procedure. The information you need to know is how much material is applied to a specific area at a given setting. The easiest way to determine this is to spread out a tarpaulin or some other catch sheet and spread some fertilizer or other material on top of it. Then measure the area covered, gather up the material, and weigh it. Now you have an accurate measure of how much material was applied to a given area at the current spreader setting. Adjustments can be made to apply either more or less and the calibration can then be re-checked. There are catchers that attach to the spreader and are designed for just this purpose, but may only be cost effective if you calibrate many spreaders often.

DETHATCHING

There are times when a dethatching machine is needed, but not for removing thatch. This tool really should be referred to by one of its other names, such as power rake or vertical mower, because most of the time, it is an inappropriate treatment for thatch. By some estimations, the dethatching machine will only remove about five percent of a thatch layer. A serious side effect of this treatment is an intense physical stress applied to the turfgrass plants at a time when they are already stressed from excessive thatch. The thatch that is removed could have become valuable organic matter if the soil were able to digest it. The two major reasons why excessive thatch exists are 1) too much nitrogen has been applied, stimulating the growth of roots, stolons, tillers, and crowns beyond the capacity of the soil to decompose the material; and 2) pesticides that kill earthworms and other valuable decay organisms have been applied. Odds are that most thatch problems are a result of both causes. When thatch layers reach absurd dimensions, the dethatching machine can be helpful in mitigating the problem. There is, however, no reason why the problem should ever become that severe. Indiscriminate use of the machine, just to pay for its overhead, is not advisable. Overuse can easily do more harm than good. Core aeration is often a more effective treatment for thatch, especially if the soil cores that are removed are broken apart and returned or left behind as a type of topdress material. High frequency, low volume irrigation, applying one tenth of an inch per day during the early to mid-afternoon, has also proven to speed up the decomposition of thatch. Dethatching machines are useful for renovation projects where turning the soil is impractical or undesirable. They can scarify and aerate the surface of the soil while stressing the competitiveness out of much of the existing plant life. Thatch reduction, however, is better accomplished by stimulating the biological activity in the soil with composts, organic fertilizers, and/or bio-stimulants. One excellent use for these machines is the removal of moss, which cannot tolerate wear and tear.

CORE AERATION

Compaction is one of the worst problems that can occur on a lawn. It almost always leads to other, more serious, problems. The core aerating machine is probably one of the greatest advances in turfgrass maintenance tools since the mower. It is the best way to mitigate compaction. There are some new variations of the core aerator, such as high pressure water injection, but the basic premise is the same. Like anything else, this tool can be used to excess and aerating soil too much can have a detrimental side effect–the depletion of soil organic matter. When we make compost, the more air we can entrain into the pile the faster it will decompose. The same thing will happen in the soil if we inject too much oxygen. Aerating lawns as an annual or biannual practice without justification can do more harm than good. Lawns with ample levels of organic matter that are not subjected to heavy traffic should never need aeration. The more we use the aerating machine, the more we may need it, because as the level of soil organic matter is depleted, the ground becomes more prone to compaction.

Aeration should only be done during those times of the year when the turf is growing vigorously. These heavy machines can cause a certain amount of stress, but grass plants should be able to withstand it if they are not already stressed by other environmental factors.

Often there is only a small section of a lawn that needs aeration, such as a path across the lawn that the kids use as a short cut or an area near the driveway where the car accidentally but frequently rolls over the turf. This can be accomplished quickly and easily with a hand aeration tool. A one hundred square foot area can easily be aerated by hand in the time it takes to get Big Bessie off the truck. Aeration only where and when it is needed makes perfect sense. In most other instances we are trying to fix something that is not broken and probably creating problems for ourselves somewhere down the road.

SPRING & FALL RAKING

The tradition of gathering fall leaves with a spring tooth rake into a pile that somehow finds its way to the landfill, right after the kids are done jumping in it, is quickly being replaced by a new game. This game–not quite as much fun for kids–is played with gasoline powered blowers that neighbors use to move leaves onto each other's properties. Many landfills now refuse to take leaves or grass clippings, so, unless people have a section of their property appropriate for the deposition of these wastes, they need to find another way to deal with them.

Unlike grass clippings, the dried and wilted foliage from deciduous trees does not contain much nitrogen. The amount of organic carbon and other nutrients in leaves, however, is significant and can contribute to the health of the soil in numerous ways. Decomposed leaves add valuable organic matter to the soil, benefiting both the tree and the lawn. Thick mats of leaves, especially when they are wet and compressed, are certainly not an advantage for grass plants. Valuable sunlight and atmosphere exchange are severely inhibited. If leaves, however, are chopped into small pieces by one or more passes of a lawn mower, decomposition will be accelerated and the chances of matting are minimal. The time it takes for leaves to disappear after being shredded by a mower is shorter than you may think.

LIME

Time should never be a criterion for liming. Natural conditions that create acid soils usually act very slowly and do not change soil pH significantly over the course of a few years. In most cases, these factors take decades or even centuries to dramatically affect soil pH. The use of acidifying fertilizers and the depletion of soil organic matter are the main causes of rapid pH changes. In an organic fertilization program, lime may rarely be necessary. Raising the pH of the soil above optimum does not improve conditions for the turf plants but does for the organisms that decompose soil organic matter. Repeated applications of lime where it is not needed can accelerate the loss of organic matter, which can eventually lead to other, more serious, problems. There is also evidence that grub damage may increase if soil pH gets too high. The only criterion for applying lime should be a pH test done by a reputable lab (see chapter 5). At-home pH testers can indicate whether lime is needed, but will not provide ample information to determine how much is needed. Labs that provide buffer pH (or other acceptable) tests can determine the amount of lime needed. There should be no lime until it's time, and that time should only be determined by a test.

IRRIGATION

"I spent a lot of money on this system and, by golly, I'm going to use it."

This attitude is the simple reason why irrigation systems should not be installed in home lawns. Excessive watering is often more damaging than persistent droughts. Managing turf for dry conditions by building organic matter levels in the soil, providing a balanced low salt fertility, and mowing high can often accomplish more toward drought tolerance than even the most sophisticated irrigation systems. The tendency to ignore these important cultural practices is more prevalent where irrigation is available. Automatic systems almost always err toward overwatering which, in many cases, can be worse than applying less than is needed. Many professionals who have been practicing organic lawn care for years would prefer no irrigation, given the choice, because the customer almost always misuses the tool. Soil that is saturated with water cannot sustain aerobic conditions. Anaerobic soil inhibits and stresses the activities of all aerobic organisms, including the turf plants. Improper irrigation can also provide improved conditions for the establishment of plant pathogens. In short, the misuse of an irrigation system can do more harm to a lawn than not using it at all.

Homeowners must be educated about the proper use of irrigation. If they understand that improper irrigation, mowing, or any other culturally incorrect procedure makes your job more difficult and your services more expensive, they may be persuaded to learn more sensible methods.

FERTILIZATION

Choosing the correct fertilizer and using it properly is a key component of sustainable turf care. Chapter 6 examines many different materials that are compatible with a functioning soil system. It is important to remember that just because a product is ecologically compatible and environmentally safe does not mean that it can be used indiscriminately or excessively. The truth is that any material, no matter how innocuous it may seem, can be misused to the point where it creates problems. Imbalances in fertility are sometimes caused by the overzealous use of materials that are labeled safe and natural. Chapter 5 looks at the value of soil tests, which should always be considered when developing a fertility program.

WORK IS WORK

Claims are often made that if one were to reduce or eliminate the unnecessary liming, core aeration, dethatching, raking, clipping management, and pest control that are now administered to a customer's lawn, there would be insufficient profit to be made because there would be very little to do. Selling services to customers that they do not need is unprofessional and will eventually harm the steward's reputation. If those services cause other problems of which the steward is cognizant, it is even more unethical. The time lost at one account can surely be traded for time at a new account. After all, efficiency is the key ingredient when one is trying to grow a business (see chapter 7). Seasonal contracts with customers can work better for you and for them when selling ecological lawn care. The customer pays a seasonal charge (perhaps half up front and half at the end of the season) for your services; the less you have to do, the more profit you make.

Sources:

Adams, W.A. and R.J. Gibbs, 1994, **Natural Turf for Sport and Amenity: Science and Practice**. CAB International. Wallingford, United Kingdom.

Albrecht, W.A. 1938, **Loss of Organic Matter and its Restoration**. U.S. Dept. of Agriculture Yearbook 1938, pp347-376.

Beard, J.B. 1995, **Mowing Practices for Conserving Water**. Grounds Maintenance, January 1995. Intertec Publishing. Overland Park, KS.

Bhowmik, P.C., R.J. Cooper, M.C. Owen, G. Schumann, P. Vittum, and R. Wick, 1994, **Professional Turfgrass Management Guide**. University of Massachusetts Cooperative Extension System. Amherst, MA.

Bormann, F.H., D. Balmori, and G.T. Geballe, 1993, **Redesigning the American Lawn: A search for Environmental Harmony**. Yale University Press. New Haven, CT.

Bunce, R.G.H., L. Ryszkowski, and M.G. Paoletti, 1993, **Landscape Ecology and Agroecosystems**. Lewis Publishers. Boca Raton, FL.

Carrow, R.N. 1994, **Understanding and Using Canopy Temperatures**. Grounds Maintenance, May 1994. Intertec Publishing. Overland Park, KS.

Casagrande, R.A. 1993, **Sustainable Sod Production for the North-**

east. Department of Plant Sciences, University of Rhode Island. Kingston, RI.

Craul P.J. 1992, **Urban Soil in Landscape Design**. John Wiley and Sons, Inc. New York, NY.

Deal, E.E. 1967, **Mowing Heights for Kentucky Bluegrass Turf**. Agronomy Abstracts Vol. 59 Nov. 1967 p. 150. American Society of Agronomy, Madison, WI.

Dernoeden, P.H., M.J. Carroll, and J.M. Krouse, 1993, **Weed Management and Tall Fescue Quality as Influenced by Mowing, Nitrogen, and Herbicides**. Crop Science 33:1055-1061. Crop Science Society of America. Madison, WI.

Dest, W.M., S.C. Albin, and K. Guillard, 1992, **Turfgrass Clipping Management**. Rutgers Turfgrass Proceedings 1992. Rutgers University, New Brunswick, NJ.

Elam, P. 1994, **Earthworms: We Need Attitude Adjustment**. Landscape Management July, 1994. Advanstar Communications. Cleveland, OH.

Franklin, S. 1988, **Building a Healthy Lawn: A Safe and Natural Approach**. Storey Communications, Inc. Pownal, VT.

Leslie, A.R. (editor) 1994, **Handbook of Integrated Pest Management for Turf and Ornamentals**. Lewis Publishers Boca Raton, FL.

Maske, C. 1995, Personal Communication. Maske's Organic Gardening. Decatur, IL.

Morgan, E. 1995, Personal Communication. Lancaster, PA.

Nelson, E.B. 1994, **More Than Meets the Eye: The Microbiology of Turfgrass Soils**. Turf Grass Trends, v3#2 February 1994. Washington, DC.

Nelson, E.B. 1995, Personal Communication. Cornell University. Ithaca, NY.

Roberts, E. 1992, Personal Communication. The Lawn Institute. Pleasant Hill, TN.

Roberts, J. 1995, **Spring Fertilization Jump Starts Turf.** Landscape Management, February 1995. Advanstar Communications. Cleveland, OH.

Sachs, P.D. 1993, **Edaphos: Dynamics of a Natural Soil System.** Edaphic Press. Newbury, VT.

Schultz, W. 1989, **The Chemical Free Lawn.** Rodale Press. Emmaus, PA.

Smassanow, E. 1995, Personal Communication. Ballston Spa, NY.

Talbot, M. 1995, Personal Communication. Dorchester, MA.

van Veen, A. and P.J. Kuikman, 1990. **Soil Structural Aspects of Decomposition of Organic Matter by Micro-organisms.** Biogeochemistry, Dec. 1990, v11 (3): 213-233.

Chapter 4
Turfgrass Pests

Lawns can become addicted to chemicals as easily as people can become addicted to drugs. Through common sense practices, this chemical dependency can be broken. Organic lawn care practitioners understand this and strive to reduce or eliminate many inputs rather than just substitute *so-called* organic products for conventional ones.

In the United States there are approximately 40 million acres of turf. Seventy five percent of these 40 million acres are in home lawns. The EPA estimates that 5-10 pounds of pesticides per acre per year are used on home lawns. This amounts to a staggering 200-400 million pounds of pesticides used yearly on home lawns in the United States. The National Academy of Sciences reported in 1980 that lawns received the heaviest pesticide applications of any land area in the United States. The State of Connecticut estimates that 61 percent of all the pesticides used in the state are applied to home lawns.

Aside from the immeasurable impact on the environment and the potential health risk to applicators from constant exposure to these substances, there is a very real and very personal economic impact these chemicals may be having on the lawn steward's net income. Many commonly used pesticides can be reduced or even eliminated simply by changing certain cultural practices. The price paid for some of these products could just as easily be profit.

In the *freedom lawn* (Bormann, 1993), where any species of plants that can endure the height of the mower are allowed to coexist, there are no such things as pests. Plants that thrive under these conditions cannot be referred to as weeds, for they are the preferred species. Insects and pathogens that damage plants can only be considered beneficial, culling out the weaker plants so that the stronger varieties can thrive. This natural system's only input from man (aside from optional applications of lime and fertilizer) is mowing, which only creates a condition to which the system must adapt. A grazing animal would create similar conditions in a pasture. Proper pH and fertility in a freedom lawn often result in a surprisingly high quality turf. After all, what plants are better suited to these conditions than varieties of grasses?

The perfectly manicured lawn with only one variety of grass and no tolerance for pests has been referred to as an *industrial lawn* (Bormann, 1993), and creates conditions that are often impossible for an ecosystem to endure. The requirements for this type of lawn often defy the laws of nature, and result in constant and expensive maintenance to sustain the lawn's existence. The level of maintenance administered to these lawns will often alter the natural system to such an extent that more and more artificial materials become necessary to sustain the integrity of the lawn. There may even come a point at which the lawn can no longer be maintained at its current level of perfection because the ecosystem of the area has been altered too much to support the needs of the turf adequately.

There is a simple equation that must be considered when manipulating nature (see figure 4-1). NS is a Natural System and HI is Human Intervention. AS is an Altered System and M equals Maintenance. What the equation states is that whenever human intervention is added to a natural system, the system is altered to some degree and maintenance is required to sustain that alteration. The degree to which the system is altered determines the amount of maintenance required. If the proper amount of maintenance is not administered, the system will try to revert back to its natural state.

In the *freedom lawn*, the only alteration to the system is brought on by the mower. This subsequently requires continual mowing to maintain the new system. The industrial lawn creates far more alterations and requires a relatively greater amount of maintenance.

Although the lawn is largely a man-made system, especially in the U.S., it can be, nonetheless, a system that functions with balance and ecological grace. The occurrence of turf pests in large

$$\text{NS} + \text{HI} = \text{AS} \longrightarrow \text{M}$$

NS = A Natural System
HI = Human Intervention
AS = An Altered System
M = Maintenance

$$\uparrow \text{HI} = \uparrow \text{AS} = \uparrow \text{M}$$

Figure 4-1

numbers usually carries a message to the turf manager that the system is somehow out of balance. Sometimes the message is simple: *You can't grow that here.* Other times the problems speak of infertility, excessive nutrient(s), compaction, poor drainage, excessive drainage, inadequate levels of organic matter, or incorrect pH. Treatment of the symptom, i.e., the weed, the insect or the disease, does not necessarily recreate balance. It only eliminates the symptom, which nature will often replace with another. Additionally, the applications of pesticides will often eliminate more than just the target organisms. The subsequent depletion of other organisms that may be beneficial to the system can create more unwanted symptoms. This cycle is a relatively classic scenario in lawns which can eventually result in a dramatic reduction of turf quality and biological diversity in the immediate environment. Most of these changes may be unnecessary. The cause of the original problem might have been simple but it is complicated by multiple treatments that have further altered the soil ecosystem.

Grasses are naturally resilient and competitive organisms originally designed by nature to withstand the damage created by large herds of grazing animals. Grown under optimal conditions, grasses can compete with weeds and endure the occasional pathogen or small herd of grazing insects. Soil organisms also react to optimal conditions in a similar manner. Huge populations of soil dwellers compete for resources in a symbiotic orchestration that maintains a balance and harmony throughout the soil system. Infestations of plant pathogens and damaging insects are more difficult to establish in an environment where so much competition exists. Conditions in the soil that harbor pest problems are optimal for the pest, not the plant. Low levels of organic matter, improper mowing height, shallow root systems, excessive thatch, soil compaction, poor fertility, or incorrect pH can all contribute to pest problems by not providing adequate conditions for grasses to be competitive.

THE REAL PEST

Often, the biggest turf pests are the customers who think that their lawn must look like a famous golf course but have no idea why or what is involved in creating and maintaining it. They are the customers who call just as you sit down to eat supper in a full panic about a weed they've found somewhere in their three acre lawn. Unable to relocate it when you arrive at the scene, they swear on their mother's grave that it was here somewhere. These people give new meaning to the word pest. Unfortunately, there is no chemical, biological or botanical treatment for this type of pest. Education is the only cure, and, in many cases the degree of the customer's fanaticism may render the treatment ineffective.

If customers understand the relationship between the amount of human intervention and the cost of maintaining the result (the degree to which the system has been altered), they may be more tolerant of a weed or a bug or some other innocuous cohabitant of their lawn. On the other hand, if the customers are total fanatics who want what they want, no matter what the cost, then there is little choice as to what action the steward of the lawn must take. It is important that a higher profit margin be set for these customers, due to the pest tolerance that you, the professional, must endure.

WEEDS

Weeds are plants that are in the wrong place. In a truly natural setting there are no weeds. The natural tendency of plants is to use every available space on the soil's surface. If there is sun, water, and nutrients in a space with little or no competition for those resources, then there will soon be a thriving plant. The soil system provides this opportunity to protect itself from erosion and to provide the cooling and moisture preserving effects of shade from plants.

Many so-called weeds are cultivated and sold as valuable plants for different locations. An expensive installation of a ground cover that creeps into a lawn becomes a weed at the garden's border. Perennials that propagate underground and spread into lawns become weeds no matter how rare or beautiful they may be.

Weeds may play a greater role in the broad scheme of things. Dandelions, for example, are very beneficial plants. Their deep roots bring leached nutrients back to the surface and are large producers of soil organic matter. Earthworm populations thrive in their vicinity and the weed does not compete with grasses for nutrients, water, or light. Clover is another beneficial plant that has received undeserved bad press. The clover plant is a legume that can fix free nitrogen from the atmosphere and share it with turfgrass. The root systems of clover plants are extensive and contribute significant amounts of organic matter to the soil. These plants are also extremely drought resistant and can stay green long after turfgrass has gone dormant. There is strong evidence that the incidence of insect predators, parasites, and antagonists exists in far greater numbers where there is an increased diversity of plants. Some weeds can also act as bait plants, drawing herbivorous pests away from the more preferred varieties.

Diversity is an important strategy in nature. Depending on only one species of plant to survive and thrive in a given area is too much of a risk for mother nature. Too much could go wrong. The diversity of a natural setting not only provides better survivability but also creates a habitat for a more balanced ecosystem. Allowing only one variety of plant in a habitat limits the number of different species of other organisms that can exist in that environment, which can also limit the amount of natural protection that variety of plant needs to survive. In terms of weed control, a diverse mixture of grasses has a stronger ability to compete with weeds than a single cultivar would. If grasses are to dominate an area without the use of pesticides, they must adapt well to the environmental conditions. Given the diversity of conditions that exists in most settings, it is important to have a variety of different grasses where at least one or two cultivars will thrive if others won't. Diverse combinations of seeds are the key to exploit nature's unpredictable edaphic conditions. Whenever a cultivated crop of grass does not adapt well to existing conditions, mother earth will provide a substitute. Unfortunately, the plant that nature chooses may not be acceptable to the steward and/or the owner of the lawn.

Soil conditions can have a profound effect on the strength and competitive abilities of certain plants. The weeds that exist in turf are often a result of soil conditions, such as compaction (clay soils) or excessive porosity (sandy soils), that are incompatible with the preferred turf cultivars. Intervention at the soil level can often provide a remedy that is effective and long lasting. Charles Walters Jr., in his book <u>Weeds: Controls Without Poisons</u> writes *"A proper calcium level with magnesium, potassium and phosphates in equilibrium will do more to roll back weed proliferation than all the herbicides in the Dow and Monsanto armamentarium."*

Herbicides may eradicate weeds, but they will not change the conditions that caused the problem in the first place. Additionally, many herbicides have been shown to increase pest insect activity by suppressing predators, stressing plants, or both. An increase in populations of herbivorous insects can stress turf to the point where weeds are more easily re-established.

Research has discovered that all living things give off radiation in specific wavelengths (Callahan, 1975). When less than ideal conditions cause problems for plants, those wavelengths are altered and can act as signals to predators such as herbivorous insects. The insect can, in turn, create conditions that favor one species of plant over another. In a situation where there is subclinical illness in turf (i.e., plants that have a health problem but are not as yet showing any symptoms), insects may be signaled by the plants' altered wavelengths and cause further stress to the turf. The activity of the insect can create conditions that favor the establishment of weeds by suppressing the health and vigor of the turf. This phenomenon, however, can be a double-edged sword. Weeds that are in a subclinically ill condition due to the unyielding competition from healthy turf may signal insects to act as a selective, biological herbicide. The general lesson nature teaches us is to strengthen the preferred species rather than weaken the unwanted. Mowing with a dull blade, for example, can exert just enough stress on a stand of turf to trigger either a disease or insect problem which could, ultimately, create the ideal setting for a weed invasion.

The unforeseen circumstances that thin out an area of turf are sometimes unavoidable. Vigilant attention to the injured areas, however, can mitigate problems without resorting to the use of herbicides. If these areas are prepped for new seed as soon as possible, the encroachment of weeds may not occur. Plant and weed residues should be removed to avoid the possible production of allelochemicals that could inhibit the germination of new seed. Some managers create a mixture of seed and aged compost which they rake and tamp into injured areas. This method is very successful; however, compost that is not well cured can have a high salt level which may suppress seed germination. If one uses this method, it is a good idea to have a conductivity test performed on the compost intended for use. The lab performing the test can make recommendations. Generally, a conductivity value above 4 mmhos is too salty.

If all else fails and it becomes absolutely necessary to use a herbicide it is important to investigate the tolerance different species of grasses have to the product you intend to use. If the use of a herbicide further weakens the turf you are trying to help, then the apparent purpose of the product is defeated.

Often, effective weed control in turf is as simple as raising the height of the lawn mower. This action enables the lawn to be more competitive by using the sun's energy for itself and blocking it from fueling unwanted species of plants. For every eighth of an inch that a lawn mower is raised, there is a thirty percent increase in leaf surface area. That increase causes a relative increase in photosynthesis, which feeds a larger and healthier root system. The lateral roots (rhizomes) of many turf varieties often develop new plants that further thicken the stand, providing even more competition. In an experiment done in containers at the University of Maryland (Deal, 1967), (see figure 4-2) rhizome development increased more than ten fold when the mowing height was raised just ¾ of an inch from 2 ¾ to 3 ½ inches. Spring is an important time to mow high, as the plant is in its reproductive stage, creating new tillers, stolons and rhizomes. Mowing high in the spring can control many weeds all season long. Turf roots can produce allelopathic chemicals capable of suppressing weed germination. The greater the root system, the more allelochemicals can be produced.

Crabgrass, considered one of the most insidious of all weeds, is often easily controlled by simply raising the height of the mower. Experiments done at the University of Maryland (Dernoeden, 1993), (see figure 4-3) resulted in statistically equal control of crabgrass by

INFLUENCE OF MOWING HEIGHT
ON RHIZOME DEVELOPMENT
(KENTUCKY BLUEGRASS)

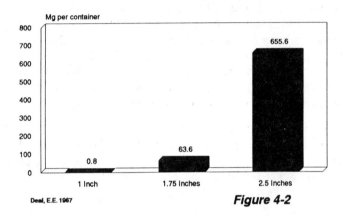

Deal, E.E. 1967

Figure 4-2

mowing at 3 1/2 inches as compared with treatments using four different crabgrass herbicides.

Identifying weeds is as important as recognizing insect pests or plant pathogens, especially if the plan is to use herbicides. Conventional controls work best if they are treating the pest for which they

INFLUENCE OF MOWING HEIGHT
ON CRABGRASS COVER
1989-1991

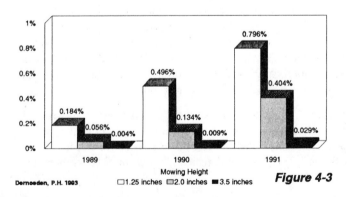

Derneeden, P.H. 1993

Mowing Height
□1.25 inches ▨2.0 inches ■3.5 inches

Figure 4-3

were designed. It is also helpful to understand the conditions in which the pest thrives. For example, crabgrass seems to like sandy, well drained soil that can send cultivated grasses into early dormancy. Dandelions can indicate soil compaction, low pH, or both. Listening to all the different stories that weeds tell is a novel approach to controlling them. In a situation where many different weeds are telling many different stories, however, a treatment may be difficult to prescribe. If symptoms such as weeds are indicating problems in the soil, then a soil test is an easier way to pinpoint those problems. Soil tests will not expose physical problems, such as compaction, but most likely these conditions would be recognized while drawing samples from the area. When a human patient exhibits classic symptoms of a certain condition, a doctor will usually perform a test to confirm the condition before prescribing medication. In a lawn, the weeds may be indicating a specific condition such as infertility or incorrect pH, but a soil test will confirm the diagnosis. It is helpful to understand weeds and what conditions they thrive in, but it is more important to analyze the soil as a first step in developing a weed control plan (see chapter 5).

Books have been published over the years that attempt to isolate various conditions in which weeds tend to thrive. These tomes are very helpful in giving us hints as to what is causing a weed problem. It makes sense, however, first to look at what conditions the preferred species of grasses thrive in, because the optimal conditions for turf plants will limit weed invasion more than anything else. Balanced fertility, correct pH, good soil structure and porosity, ample amounts of organic matter, and proper maintenance procedures are the factors that influence the aggressive nature of turf. If all of these conditions are initially addressed and there is still an invasion of a weed that tells a story, then we must have missed something. At this point the weed books become valuable.

If a particular species of plant haunts a region and is in need of constant control, the best way to learn its strengths and weaknesses is to cultivate it. Raising a small test plot of a particular weed and attempting to grow it well is the easiest way to learn how to defeat it. Applications of different inputs and the use of different cultural practices to make a weed grow will show us the best way to control it in a lawn.

The use of pre-emergent herbicides is well accepted by many managers who do not actually know if it is necessary. The attitude is one of paranoia, caused by the fear of losing the customer or the job should one weed rear its ugly little head. The expense of using pre-emergent herbicides should be considered even if the ecological factors are ignored. Using pre-emergent herbicides is analogous to a person eating antibiotics in anticipation of a bacterial infection. The outcome would be a weakened system that is more susceptible to infection. Pre-emergent herbicides are designed to suppress the germination of weed seeds while having no effect on existing plants. Ecologically speaking, it is difficult to assume that doses of these products do not alter the natural system in some way that creates other unwanted symptoms. If any part of the natural system is stressed, a chain reaction will eventually result in another problem.

Since most turf grasses appear in the spring before weeds, a healthy stand of turf — mowed at the proper height — often acts as a pre-emergent weed control. Peter Dernoden's research at the University of Maryland showed that a tall stand of turf grass suppresses the germination and growth of crabgrass as well as any herbicide (see figure 4-3).

Another simple aid to weed control is to leave the clippings behind when the lawn is mowed. Clippings from many different species of turf plants are thought to contain allelopathic compounds that suppress the germination and/or growth of certain weeds. Furthermore, the distribution of clippings can act as a temporary mulch, prior to decomposition, that not only suppresses weeds but also provides nutrients and preserves moisture for the established turf. More than half of the nitrogen from fertilizers applied to turf resides in the clippings. Redistribution of that nitrogen and the other nutrients that exist in the clippings gives turf the fuel to compete even more aggressively with weeds. Other benefits of leaving the clippings behind include improved water infiltration, higher populations of earthworms, greater root production, and disease suppression. These all have either a direct or indirect influence on the suppression of weeds.

Planting new lawns in the fall instead of the spring is another practical way of controlling many weeds. Competition from weeds is greater in the spring than in the fall when most annual weeds are beginning to die off. There is evidence that when seeds germinate, they release auxins (natural plant hormones) that inhibit the germination of other seeds in their immediate surroundings, giving themselves a competitive edge. This would be as true for weed seeds as it would for grass seeds. This factor makes fall planting, when the germination of weed seed is at a low ebb, more sensible. In the Northeast the reliability of rain is greater in the fall than in the spring. High spring mortality of grass seeds is something we have all witnessed and the replacement seed never seems to do as well, possible because of the auxins released by other germinating seeds.

Another important method of weed control is the proper selection of seed varieties for new lawns. Varieties that struggle to survive under unsuitable conditions are less able to successfully compete with weeds. A reiteration of diversity is appropriate here. Conditions such as sun and shade may be easily identified, but some unnoticed conditions may limit the success of a select species of grass. Diversity in a mix can offer strength over a broad range of conditions and increase the odds of producing a dense sod capable of crowding out most weeds. The similar appearance of many fescues, ryegrasses, and bluegrasses can produce a quality turf without sacrificing vulnerability to adverse conditions.

The soil inherently contains millions of weed seeds deposited by wind, water, and animals. Some of these can stay dormant for hundreds of years until, somehow, they reach the proper soil depth where warmth and moisture will trigger their germination mechanisms. Deep tillage during seedbed preparation can bring many of these seeds to the surface where they can germinate. Shallow soil preparation may be a better alternative if the creation of a seedbed is all that is necessary. Seeding machines that plant seeds without turning the soil will also help to reduce the number of dormant weeds that germinate at the soil's surface. This leads to the subject of regular overseeding.

OVERSEEDING

Senescence is a term used to describe the natural aging process of all living things. Theoretically, the perennial grass plant is supposed to generate new growth from its crown year after year, ad infinitum. In many varieties, it will even generate new crowns. Unfortunately, there are other factors in nature that have a tendency to permanently interrupt this tradition and cause senescence in lawns. There are those who believe that overseeding lawns on an annual or biennial basis can inhibit senescence and thwart the typical invasion of weeds in a declining lawn. The infusion of new seed into existing lawns is, in essence, an injection of youth into a natural aging process. If a lawn in natural decline is normally replaced by nature's choice of seed, why not select a more preferable variety to accomplish the same end? This philosophy is practiced successfully by many professionals, and the money saved from the reduction or elimination of pesticides that would normally be used to control problems in an aging lawn more than makes up for the cost of the seed.

As with anything else, overseeding can be done to excess. If lawns are too thick, they can become more prone to certain diseases: those that thrive in environments where moisture is retained for long periods of time and air entrainment is inhibited. Common sense should intervene when one is about to overseed a lawn that could not look any better than it already does.

DOWN THE ROAD

Organic herbicides are just around the corner. These are weed control products that are biologically or botanically derived and exhibit little or no environmental persistence. At this writing, researchers are investigating the weed controlling properties of corn gluten, a by-product of the corn syrup industry. Corn gluten releases allelochemicals that act as a pre-emergent herbicide by suppressing the growth of roots on germinating seeds. Because it is a food protein, it also provides ten percent nitrogen to the existing lawn. The product will probably be commercially available before this book goes to print.

As innocuous as these new tools may seem, they still address only the symptom, not the problem. They do not correct the conditions that encouraged the weeds to grow in the first place. The development of these products is analogous to the introduction of methadone to heroine addicts. The addiction hasn't changed, only the substance of abuse. Using more environmentally benign materials is always preferred, but is not necessarily the answer to the problem. If a product like corn gluten is used as a tool to accomplish the objective of soil and turf improvement to the point where herbicides are no longer needed, it becomes extremely beneficial. However, if it is used only to doctor symptoms on a regular basis, it can eventually begin to cause other problems.

The need to address the basics is at hand. Regardless how a soil looks or feels, it needs to be tested and treated to obtain a balanced fertility. Beginning with a well balanced and fertile soil environment for turf will do more to prevent weed problems than any arsenal of herbicides. Cornell University often prefaces their weed control information with the statement that *"the first line of defense against weeds is a dense sod."* To obtain a dense sod one must provide the necessary conditions.

Conditions that stress turf plants generally favor weeds. Any time the growth of a grass plant is inhibited by stress, another species of plant will gain a competitive edge. Inadequate fertility can be discovered by testing the soil and administering the proper inputs to correct the imbalance. Low levels of organic matter are not as easy to correct, but can be addressed by different methods. These include mowing high for greater root development and applying compost as a topdress. (Note: Applying more than 3/4 inch of compost per treatment is not recommended.) Compaction can be relieved by core aeration, but this activity should only be done during periods when turf is growing vigorously. If core aeration takes place during dormant periods (e.g., summer), the potential for weed encroachment is increased. Stress caused by heat and/or drought is more difficult to control. Mowing high will help because it not only shades the soil, preserving moisture and lowering the soil surface temperature, but also because it allows roots to penetrate the soil to greater depths where they have better access to soil moisture. Seaweed bio-stimulants are inexpensive to use and are very helpful in mitigating the effects of stress. Research has discovered that the natural growth regulators in seaweed products can give turf significantly greater drought resistance and stimulate greater root development. The greater resistance turf has to stress, the better it will ultimately compete with weeds.

SUMMER DROUGHT

Every spring some of us get a false sense of financial stability–until we realize that Uncle Sam hasn't been paid yet. That same feeling of euphoria, followed by frustration, comes when the beautiful spring lawns we've worked on so hard get hammered by summer heat and drought. The stress from high temperatures and low levels of moisture can change a thick, healthy turf into a lawn peppered with problems. The turf's ability to compete with weeds, resist disease, and recover from insect damage are all but gone in just a few short weeks. Aside from irrigation, it seems as though there is no recourse except to stand by and watch its demise.

Fortunately, there are a few things we can do to combat the summer's impairment of a lawn. First and foremost is raising the height of the mower. Tall grass can shade the soil more, significantly reducing the amount of heat the soil absorbs from the sun and the amount of moisture evaporated from the soil surface. Taller plants grow much deeper roots which have both better access to water and improved storage capabilities. Water use is actually increased slightly from the greater amount of leaf surface area of taller plants. The physical process of evapotranspiration of moisture through the leaves, however, can cool the ambient temperature by 7-14 degrees (F). The longer the grass can stay green, the longer the cooling mechanism can remain working.

VAM is an acronym for Vesicular Arbuscular Mycorrhizie. This is a family of beneficial fungi that attach themselves to the roots of perennial plants and reach into the soil's depths for moisture and mineral nutrients. They exchange these with the plant for a small amount of photosynthesized carbohydrate. This symbiotic relationship exists in over eighty percent of all grass species, and can increase the plants' heat and drought resistance significantly. Unfortunately, if fungicides are introduced into a lawn, that relationship is compromised or eliminated. Combating disease with well aged compost or a program of building soil organic matter will not only provide long term disease protection, but will also encourage the useful relationships VAM's have with turf.

Another non-action we can take is to stop bagging grass clippings. Clippings returned to a lawn can provide several benefits. Between the time that they fall and decompose, they act as a temporary mulch that can lower the soil surface temperature. As moisture evaporates from the fallen clippings, the surrounding air is cooled and stress from heat is further mitigated. Clippings encourage earthworm activity, which not only increases the water holding capacity of the soil but, at the same time, reduces thatch. Thatch can decrease a lawn's resistance to drought conditions because it holds very little moisture and encourages shallow rooting of plants. Pesticides that suppress earthworms are also hurting the drought resistance of a lawn. Clippings can produce allelochemicals as they decompose. Some researchers believe that these allelochemicals suppress crabgrass germination. The nitrogen inherent in clippings is a perfect slow release fertilizer that can help grass stay vital during stressful periods. Clippings left behind have also shown disease suppressive properties which can offer some protection during a time of year when plants are more susceptible to infection.

Be on the lookout for heat tolerant cool season grasses. Researchers have discovered that certain varieties of perennial ryegrass exhibit more competitive behavior during periods of high temperatures. Isolating these strains for breeding is sure to follow.

Irrigation, if available, is the ultimate treatment for stress caused by heat and drought. The misuse of this tool, however, can do more harm than good. Researchers disagree on the ideal frequency and duration of irrigation. Some believe that deep and infrequent watering is best, while others feel that high frequency, low volume irrigation is optimum. Very little research has been done on irrigation frequency and volume and the small amount of data available suggests that light watering (one tenth of an inch) on a daily basis is best for relieving heat and drought stress. Common sense dictates, however, that there is no ideal irrigation program that fits every situation. Under certain conditions, such as deep sandy soils with little water holding capacity, low volume, high frequency irrigation may be the most ideal. But this may be inappropriate for heavy soils that do not dry out as quickly.

Monitoring moisture levels with a moisture meter is a good idea, but the optimum amount of moisture varies in different types of soil (see figure 4-4). It is necessary to analyze the texture of a soil to determine the ideal amount of moisture it can hold. If a lawn care company works with many different types of soils in a given region,

SOIL MOISTURE RELATIONSHIPS

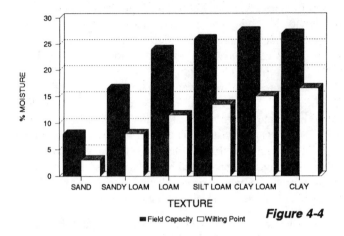

Figure 4-4

it may be expensive to do a texture analysis of each property's soil. This information, however, is very valuable. (See chapter 5 for an inexpensive way to do your own texture analysis.)

Too much water from irrigation can cause more stress to turf than none at all. Waterlogged soil contains little or no oxygen, an essential element to the roots of plants. The stress from suffocating roots is just as detrimental as the stress caused by heat and/or drought. Over watering can result in the leaching of more nutrients, especially nitrates, than any other factor. The loss of these essential minerals can not only stress the plant but also pollute ground water. If pesticides are used on a lawn, improper irrigation can carry toxins into the water supply. The EPA estimates that 10.4% of the community water system wells and 4.2% of rural domestic wells in the U.S. contain at least one pesticide or pesticide degradate at or above acceptable levels. This estimate comes from a study conducted between 1988 and 1990, where approximately 94,600 drinking water wells were sampled. Common sense irrigation is usually the most appropriate.

INSECTS

It is unfortunate that insects have such a terrible reputation in today's society. So much of the insect world is beneficial, and even crucial, to the mechanics of our ecosystem. Well over ninety percent of the insects that exist in our world are neutral or beneficial. That percentage is even higher in turf.

It would be great if all we had to do to control damaging insects was to create a healthy and balanced environment for plants. Since that strategy hasn't worked one hundred percent of the time, it has become a secondary concern to most managers. This is unfortunate, because there are a significant number of instances where a healthy soil environment initiates a chain reaction of biological, physical, and chemical phenomena that control many damaging insects – or limit the amount of damage the insects can cause.

There is evidence that all living things emit radiation in specific wavelengths that can be recognized by other organisms. Insects rely on these signals for both sustenance and reproduction. According to some researchers, the infrared frequencies given off by plants, predators and insects of the opposite sex are received by the insect's antennae. Regardless of wind direction, the insect is able to home in on the source of the radiation.

Plants that are growing in sub-optimum conditions can generate altered wavelengths that may actually attract grazing insects. This theory has been difficult to substantiate, but evidence of radiated signals from plants and reception of similar signals from insects does exist (Callahan, 1975). In nature, optimum conditions for only one species rarely exist, which is one of the reasons why a natural setting contains so much diversity. If insects begin to damage an area because of signals given off by subclinically ill plants, and treatment consists of insecticide applications that may further stress the biological functions of that area, then the turf is, theoretically, rendered more vulnerable to further attack. Treatment of the insect, which is a symptom, without treatment of the conditions in which the plant is growing, is a band-aid approach that can only lead to further treatments down the road.

When insect problems become apparent, the general rule is to identify the pest and find the appropriate poison to eradicate it. Applications of pesticides, unfortunately, often eradicate more than just the pest. In many cases, the insecticide used to control the pest will also suppress some predators. Sometimes, predators that are capable of controlling the target pests are also destroyed. This inhibits or eliminates some of the plant's natural resistance to the pest if a resurgence in pest activity occurs. Other predators, unrelated to the target pest, may also be eradicated; and their absence may be manifested as a new insect problem.

The popular poisons for chinch bugs (*Blissus leucopterus*), for example, will also kill big eyed bugs (*Geocoris bullatus*), a species of insect that is very capable of controlling chinch bugs. If the chinch bugs return, there will not be big eyed bugs to control them. If no insecticide were applied, the big eyed bugs would eventually have brought the chinch bugs under control. Unfortunately, by the time natural suppression occurs, the chinch bugs may have done significant damage to the lawn. In many cases the lawn will come back and, in the long term, a more permanent solution to the chinch bug problem will have been created. It is nothing less than a risk for you as steward of the lawn, however, and for your customer - who faces the expense of reseeding if the chinch bug damage is too extensive.

Another example of predator suppression was discovered in research done by Daniel Potter at the University of Kentucky (Leslie, 1994). The investigators found that predation of sod webworm eggs was significantly suppressed for weeks after a single application of chlorpyrifos (Dursban). These researchers put 500 sod webworm eggs out at 1, 3, and 5 week intervals after treatment with chlorpyrifos, an insecticide used to control many foliar feeding in-

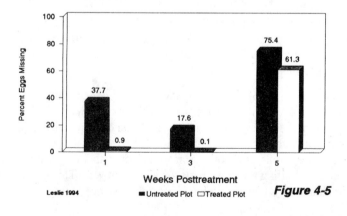

MEAN PERCENTAGE OF SOD WEBWORM EGGS CARRIED OFF BY PREDATORS AFTER ONE APPLICATION OF CHLORPYRIFOS

Leslie 1994 ■ Untreated Plot ☐ Treated Plot *Figure 4-5*

sects and some grub species. The number of eggs that were either eaten or carried off by predators was measured in replicated tests, and the averages are shown in figure 4-5. For more than three weeks predator activity was significantly suppressed by only one application of the insecticide. Known predators of sod webworm eggs are ants, rove beetles, mites, and ground beetles. Insecticides known to affect one or more of these insect groups include chlorpyrifos (Dursban), isofenphos (Oftanol), trichlorfon (Proxol), and bendiocarb (Turcam). Beneficial organisms such as collembola, enchytraeid worms, and saprophytic mites that play a valuable role in recycling organic matter are also affected by one or more of these materials.

Another test done by the same researchers shows suppression of spider and rove beetle populations (both of which are voracious predators) in areas treated with chlorpyrifos (see figure 4-6). As more research is done on the side effects of pesticides, it is becoming clear that a more holistic thought process is necessary to produce and maintain lawns in the future.

IMPACT OF SURFACE APPLICATION OF
CHLORPYRIFOS ON SPIDER AND
ROVE BEETLE POPULATIONS

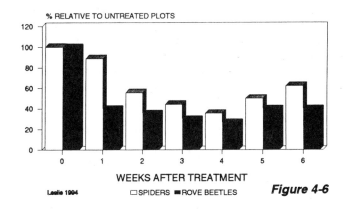

WEEKS AFTER TREATMENT

Leslie 1994   □ SPIDERS ■ ROVE BEETLES   *Figure 4-6*

PLANT DEFENSES

Scientists have discovered that healthy plants are not completely defenseless against pest organisms. Plant species that have no defenses, either their own or from symbiotic organisms such as predators, would have become extinct long ago. Most species of plants can synthesize chemical defense compounds that inhibit pest activity. The synthesis of these organic chemicals depends largely on 1) the availability of the necessary elemental components (i.e. fertility) and 2) the plants' overall health, strength and vitality. In some cases the introduction of a simple primary nutrient such as potassium will cause the host plant to create stronger resistance to certain pests (Heinrichs 1988). Plant resistance to pests is manifested in four basic forms. The first is the manufacture of toxins that affect the biology of the pest. The second is its ability to make itself less attractive either by smell, taste or nutritional value, forcing the pest to go elsewhere for sustenance. The third is the development of tolerances to pest damage, i.e., the ability to thrive in spite of the adversity. The fourth is a physical resistance created by thickening the outer layers of both stems and leaves. Often, a plant may exhibit all four resistances.

It was also discovered that many plants can actually sense imminent insect pest problems and react. When nearby plants are attacked, a natural plant hormone, ethylene, is released, signaling adjacent plants to produce defense compounds in anticipation of attack.

Researchers have studied thousands of varieties of plants that show some type of control of different pests. Unfortunately, there are more than 20,000 different pests that damage crops and fewer than 1000 have been studied, but research continues. It is a relatively safe assumption that other plant varieties with pest control properties exist but remain undiscovered.

Researchers believe that there are as many natural toxins in the environment as there are different organisms. These toxins are usually formed by organisms such as plants, fungi, or bacteria, but some may be mineral in nature. Antibiotics like penicillin, for example, are made by soil fungi and are toxic to many bacteria. These toxins are produced as metabolites of biological activity or as compounds formed from the decay of various organic materials. They serve to inhibit survival of a broad range of organisms. Unfortunately, the production and targeting of these toxins is relatively indiscriminate. Some species of organisms produce compounds that are toxic to themselves, thus providing their own control for overpopulation.

Substances that are toxic to one organism may be nutritious to another. The best balance of these natural toxins in the soil is both directly and indirectly related to the level of soil organic matter. A portion of the natural toxins that exist in the soil are produced from the decay of plant matter. The rest is from the abundance of toxin-producing organisms that live in soils with high levels of organic matter. Many of nature's toxins have been isolated, synthesized and concentrated by scientists into lethal substances called pesticides. Introducing these substances into the environment in unnatural concentrations often causes an ecological chain reaction with unpredictable consequences.

Plants will display a variety of reactions to grazing pest organisms. The amount of organic nutrients released into the soil by roots generally increases, creating a relative increase of microbes in the root zone. Microbial activity can, in turn, increase the amount of available mineral nutrient for the plant. Most plants respond to above ground damage by increasing root growth and the storage of nutrients in the root system. Apparently, reducing the amount of nutrients located in the shoots and leaves makes the plant tops less nourishing and hopefully less attractive to grazing insects. The stored nutrient in the root system can increase the plants' ability to recover from pest damage. Unfortunately, this concentration of energy and nutrients in the roots may also attract below-ground pests. Chinch bugs can, for example, injure the tops of turfgrass plants and, unintentionally, make the roots more palatable for grubs (scarab larvae). Plants can also exhibit a significant increase in the production of alkaloids, substances that are often toxic or distasteful to insects.

ENDOPHYTES

If reseeding does become necessary, a more permanent solution to infestations of chinch bugs, bill bugs, sod webworms, and many other foliar feeding insects is the use of endophytically enhanced grass seed. Endophytes are fungal organisms that live symbiotically within the cells of the grass plants and reproduce during cell division. They create a bitter tasting toxin that repels most insects and kills many of those that continue to feed. There are many different varieties of seeds that contain endophytes and the level of infection varies widely. For a lawn that is truly resistant to foliar feeding insects, endophyte infection should be at least 70% or higher.

Common sense dictates that the level of uninfected seed is relative to the potential amount of damage that can occur. If the seed has only 50% infection, then it is possible to lose half of the lawn to insect damage.

Varieties of seeds that are bred with endophytes include perennial ryegrass and many different types of fescues. Unfortunately, no varieties of bluegrasses or bent grasses have been found yet that contain endophytes.

If endophytically enhanced seed is stored for an extended period of time, the endophytes may die. The length of time the seed can be stored depends on the temperature of the storage facility. A refrigerated facility can keep the endophytes viable for many years but a standard, uninsulated, warehouse situated in New England, for example, would only preserve the endophytes for approximately 12 months.

Endophytes exist only in the above ground portion of the plant and cannot provide protection from root feeding insects such as scarab grubs. Researchers at the University of Rhode Island, however, have found that freshly germinated seedlings of endophytic varieties resist the Japanese beetle grubs. This resistance is greatest in tall fescues but also exists in endophytically enhanced perennial ryegrass and other fescues. The size of the grub was also a factor in these findings. Small grubs were most affected, whereas the most mature grubs were hardly affected at all. Another university is attempting to isolate the chemical basis of the resistance, which may eventually result in a biological grub control insecticide.

Grass seed infected with endophytes has shown other benefits, including improved performance. Some research has suggested that endophytes produce substances similar to plant hormones. The use of plant hormones (a.k.a. plant growth regulators) is discussed in chapter 6.

GRUBS

The Rhode Island study also found that *"grubs are generally incapable of damaging tall fescue turfgrass in this [Rhode Island] area."* This finding has been apparent to many turfgrass managers for some time, which leads us to the conclusion that reseeding with mostly tall fescue on grub damaged lawns is, possibly, an effective non-chemical treatment for grubs. The effectiveness of this treatment depends on other factors, such as climate zone, fertility, and soil structure. Disturbing the soil with a tiller before seeding has an advantage and a distinct disadvantage. The tiller will act as a physical killer to grubs, literally beating them to death, but the tool will also introduce a significant amount of oxygen into the soil which can destroy a good portion of the organic matter component. In a rich soil the trade may be worth it, but in an already poor soil, the loss of fertility may jeopardize the health of the new seedlings to a point where maladies other than grubs may affect the crop. Tilling in good quality compost may be an effective way to counter this problem. Compost, if incorporated into the soil, can be used at doses up to 2 cubic yards per thousand square feet. Care must be taken, however, not to create a layer of soil that makes an abrupt change in consistency from the layer beneath it (see chapter 2). Another problem with the tiller is the amount of dormant weed seeds brought to the surface by deep tillage.

Slit over-seeding is another alternative that will not disturb the soil significantly, nor cause the destruction of organic matter. This tool will physically kill many of the grubs also. A core aerating machine will also adversely affect a grub population. It is not often, however, that one would find many grubs in heavy, compacted soils, and introducing too much oxygen into the soil could cost in soil health what is saved in grub control.

Be on the lookout for a new biological insecticide called Bt Serovor japonensis (a.k.a. Bt buibui). This strain of Bt (Bacillus thurengiensis) bacteria has shown much promise in controlling the grubs of Japanese beetles, Oriental beetles, Masked chaffers, and Green June beetles. Bt is a bacterium that produces a toxin lethal to certain insects when ingested. There are many different strains of Bt, all of which are relatively specific to different pests. There is at least one strain of Bt that is currently registered and labeled for use on turf pests such as sod webworms and armyworms. The *buibui* strain is specific to scarab grubs and should not affect nontarget organisms nor should the toxin it produces persist in the environment for more than a few days. Because of its short life in the environment, it needs to be used at the most vulnerable part of the grub's life cycle. Researchers found that Bt buibui works better when the grubs are smaller, (coincidentally, so do most other insecticides) which is usually in August. This is also the time when turf is stressed the most from heat and drought, adding to its vulnerability to grub damage. The toxin is less effective in the spring when grubs are closer to pupation. The spring window of opportunity is also quite narrow, there being only about two weeks from the time of surfacing from winter soil depths to pupation. This product is being researched and registered by Mycogen Corporation and will, hopefully, be available in the spring of 1996.

Another promising biological control being developed is a commercially prepared fungus capable of attacking and destroying such grubs as the Japanese beetle and Masked chaffers. Products such as these are the wave of the future. They have the potential to be more effective than chemicals and more compatible with the environment at the same time.

The botanical insecticide *neem* is also being tested as a control for grubs. Neem is actually an insect growth regulator that interrupts the insect's maturation process, usually during molting. Unfortunately, the product has been largely ineffective on lawn grubs because it cannot penetrate the soil down to where the larvae reside. Eventually, producers of the product hope to devise a vehicle that will carry the product to greater soil depths. Neem is also being tested on other lawn pests such as chinch bugs, bill bugs, sod webworms, and armyworms. Products containing neem compounds, labeled for use against these insects, may appear on the market before this book goes to print.

INDIRECT GRUB DAMAGE

There are many cases where the population of grubs is not large enough to actually cause damage to the lawn, but damage is caused from skunks and other animals who are foraging for grubs by digging through the turf. The immediate response by many turf managers is to apply an effective larvicide as soon as possible. Unfortunately, this practice is often a complete waste of time and money. Skunks, raccoons, and other animals who hunt grubs are very adept at finding them through the sod. Once they have damaged a particular area, the chances that there are any grubs left to treat is remote. Their activity, although unsightly, is largely beneficial. Not only do they eradicate the grubs but their digging acts as a messy type of aeration. Treatment for animal damage should consist of a rake, a roller, possibly some seed and some good organic fertilizer. In a healthy lawn, the evidence of grub hunters should be gone within a few days. Conventional treatment for grubs that are no longer there may stress the biology of the area and inhibit its ability to recovery quickly.

Birds, such as starlings or crows, that appear as pests on a lawn may be performing a valuable service by foraging for insect larvae or adults. There is no guarantee that what they are eating are, in fact, turf pests, but if pests that are specific to turf are abundant, the bird's diet will probably consist largely of that insect. In addition, the bird acts as an ultralight, silent running, microfine aeration machine, pecking tiny holes in the sod where air and water can more easily interface with the soil. Sometimes the birds will cause damage to the lawn by pecking out tufts of sod. Although unsightly, the indiscriminate thinning of the lawn may in the long run be beneficial. If grooming, fertility, water, and patience are applied, chances are good that the lawn will recover stronger than before. If the customer is not willing to tolerate the damage component of this cycle, however, then the bird's target insect must be identified and treated. Eradicating the birds, by whatever means, is counter productive. Unfortunately, controlling the insects may cause a disruption to the ecology of the immediate environment that may, in the long term, cause further problems.

If bird populations become a real problem, it may be helpful to know that researchers from the USDA found that grape flavoring from a food grade chemical called methyl anthranilate is a very effective repellent for most birds. Products like Grape Koolaid can be diluted and sprayed onto problem areas and the damage caused by bird populations can be expected to decrease. Unfortunately, these materials are not registered with the EPA or labeled as pest controls and use by professional applicators is, technically, illegal. Homeowners, however, can apply homemade remedies to their own properties legally.

BENEFICIAL NEMATODES

Another treatment for grubs that is becoming more popular is the application of entomopathogenic nematodes. These near-microscopic worms enter the bodies of grubs and release a bacteria that quickly infects and kills the grub. The nematodes then use the remains of the grub as resources for their breeding activities. Usually, those resources will support the conception of three successive generations of nematodes, after which the nematodes must escape the body of the host and find new larvae to infect.

Nematodes need moisture to survive. If they are introduced into a dry soil, or if the soil dries out after they are applied, they will be ineffective at controlling grubs. If they are applied in the spring and the soil dries out during the summer, they may have to be reapplied in the fall if they are to control the newest brood of larvae. It is best to thoroughly moisten the soil before they are applied. Nematodes will migrate into the moisture.

Nematodes function best in loamy soils where there is plenty of porosity but not so much that the soil dries out too quickly. Clay soils inhibit the movement of nematodes, but grubs are rarely found in heavy clay soils so it is somewhat of a moot point. Sandy soils, on the other hand, can harbor large infestations of grubs but generally do not stay moist enough for nematodes. Unless there is irrigation or the climate is naturally moist, nematodes may not perform well in a sandy soil. If there is adequate moisture, most nematodes can exist for up to three months in the soil without food. Introducing them as protection from grubs before grub activity is present is a common practice. The nematodes can exist in a temperature range of 32 to 90 degrees Fahrenheit. They are, however, most active in soils that are between 65 and 85 degrees. Turf that is mowed too close to the soil during the hottest part of the year may allow the soil temperature to exceed the upper limits of the nematodes' temperature range.

Nematodes can withstand high pressure, which makes it possible to apply them through almost any water dispensing system. They are best applied in the early morning or early evening. Exposure to direct sunlight in excess of seven minutes will sterilize them. They will still be able to infect and kill grubs, but they will not be able to reproduce.

There are two strains of nematodes commonly used in commercial offerings. The *Steinernema sp* is a strain that attaches itself to a soil particle and waits in ambush for a grub to happen along. There is some research that suggests this strain is less effective at controlling grubs. A new strain called *Steinernema glaseri* is being commercially developed; it shows greater promise as an effective, biological grub control. Products containing this strain of nematode may be available before this book goes to print. The *Heterorhabditis sp* is a hunter which can seek out grubs by following their trail of exudates. Each of these strains can be effective under the right conditions and preparations that include both Steinernema sp and Heterorhabditis sp are available.

MILKY SPORE DISEASE

Milky spore disease is another biological control, effective only, however, at controlling the Japanese beetle larvae. Milky spore is a bacterium that is ingested by the grub and subsequently causes death. The bacteria, like the nematodes, reproduce inside the remains of the grub and increase the inoculation of the area. After two to four years, the spread of the disease is usually sufficient to keep the population of Japanese beetle larvae below the tolerance level for turf. Depending on climate and soil conditions, this can last for more than twenty years. Experiments at Cornell University suggest that the best time to apply Milky spore is mid- to late summer when the new brood of larvae have hatched and have begun to feed. In the Northeast and Pacific Northwest spring soil temperatures are often not warm enough.

The main problem with Milky spore is its availability. At this time there is only one producer and its manufacturing process requires locating Japanese beetle larvae that are infected with the disease. Since 1992, inadequate numbers of infected grubs have been found and consequently, very little product has been available. Fermentation of the bacteria was attempted by a different manufacturer, but the product turned out to be ineffective and had to be recalled. There is a future for biological products such as this, but more research needs to be done to improve both quality and production.

MONITORING

The simple philosophy that a problem should be found before treatment is applied is often ignored in the lawn care industry. IPM (Integrated Pest Management) has become just another commercially attractive buzzword like organic, low spray, no spray, and natural. The problem with monitoring, according to many professionals, is that no one is willing to pay for the time and effort that is involved. Customers don't want to pay for someone to wander around their yard looking for who-knows-what. The lawn care companies share these feelings. Unfortunately, what both sides fail to understand is that monitoring or scouting will, most often, pay for itself (and even net a profit).

A great example of this is a project conducted by Cornell University in 1992 at a golf course in Rochester, NY. Workers scouted the entire course for grubs by lifting sections of sod with a cup cutter in a grid pattern (the cup cutter removes a plug that measures one tenth of a square foot). They identified all the problem areas on the course for a labor expense of $360.00. The amount of money that they saved from not having to treat the entire course exceeded $60,000.00 in the first year. As it turned out, the entire course did not sustain any damage from grubs. The scouting program was an immense success.

A program like this would net higher profits no matter what type of treatment is used. Whether a chemical, botanical, or biological material is used to control the grubs, less of it will be purchased and used, less environmental impact will occur, and more profit can be made.

There are other good examples of how monitoring has not only reduced the number of problems a lawn care professional has to deal with, but has also reduced the cost of maintaining certain properties while increasing profits. One lawn care professional I interviewed reduced her insecticide costs for grub control by $14,000.00 just by training her personnel to do approximately ten minutes of monitoring when they were on the job site (Broccolo, 1995). Her staff had to be trained for pest identification and tolerable thresholds, and subsequently paid a higher rate than if they just mowed lawns, for example, but the outcome was higher profits for her company.

Another Cornell University research project (Grant, 1994) monitored grub populations on more than 300 residential lawns in upstate New York and found out some interesting information. They discovered that even in a bad year of grub damage (good for the grubs) only 18% of the total lawn area monitored needed treatment for grub control and that most preventative treatments for grubs are a waste of time and money. If one were able to cut back the amount of grub controls by 82%, the savings would be significant.

Finding problems in the lawn before they become epidemic is always the most prudent practice, for both esthetic and economic reasons. Treating problems that do not exist can very often be a waste of time, effort, and money, and an unnecessary introduction of pollutants into the environment. It can also alter the ecology of the treated area to a point where new problems are created.

IRRIGATION

Often, turf can tolerate damaging herds of insect trespassers either by creating a defense mechanism, by outgrowing the damage, or both. Unfortunately, during the hot, dry part of the year, most grasses are stressed and cannot provide defense from or outgrow even a small amount of insect damage. Michigan State University found (entirely by accident) that the amount of damage caused by many foliar feeding insects was reduced or eliminated by low volume, high frequency irrigation. Their treatment consisted of daily applications of one tenth of an inch of water in the afternoon, during the hottest part of the day. This procedure is also known as *syringing* by some professionals. The result was a reduction of insect damage to below tolerable levels. If irrigation is available, it makes sense to use that to reduce stress, rather than to apply pesticides which can increase the amount of stress to the turf plants.

DISEASES

Like the human body, a plant has the ability to protect itself from diseases. Much of that protection comes not from the plant, but from a component of the growing system, the soil. There is truth to the axiom that a healthy soil promotes healthy plants. In the soil environment there are thousands of different organisms that exist for two common purposes — to survive and to reproduce. The most limiting factors in their existence are resources such as food, water and a proper atmosphere. Given an unlimited supply of these resources, the populations of soil organisms would increase beyond the earth's spatial capacity in a matter of weeks. These organisms must compete with each other for the limited amount of resources in the soil. As resources dwindle in a given environment, certain segments of the biomass may experience local extinction, thus giving surviving organisms a distinct advantage in terms of competition. If those surviving organisms are plant pathogens, then the microbial imbalance can be manifested as plant diseases.

A rich soil, as its name implies, contains a wealth of resources. Most of us imagine a rich soil to be one that contains an abundance of plant nutrients capable of producing excellent crops. The term, however, has a deeper meaning. Resources are in many forms and benefit many different aspects of the soil system. Most of them are linked, either directly or indirectly, to one important soil component — organic matter. Although the fraction of a mineral soil that is organic matter is relatively small, the function of this component is responsible for the lion's share of the system's benefits. The proteins, carbohydrates, lignins, cellulose, fats, waxes, hemicellulose and other compounds that comprise the soil's organic fraction are resources for billions of soil organisms.

Many managers have discovered that the incidence of disease diminishes significantly when the area is biologically enriched with organic matter such as aged compost. Apparently, the amount and type of organisms living in the compost are very competitive with pathogenic fungi. Others have found that soil management practices that encourage the development of organic matter and soil microorganisms also have a similar effect.

The incidence of organisms in soil is relative to the organic matter content. Organic matter levels are controlled primarily by plant growth and climate. Cultivation practices such as tillage, aeration, irrigation, and liming, however, can significantly accelerate the decomposition process (see chapter 3). Plants are the main source of raw materials for the formation of organic matter, and the main influence for the development of microbial biomass. The roots of plants release approximately 20% of the organic compounds produced by photosynthesis into the soil, creating an area of intense biological activity around the roots. This activity serves many different functions that affect the soil, plant and atmosphere. Antagonism and competition directed at pest organisms are only a couple of them.

Cornell University has done a significant amount of research on the suppression of turf diseases with applications of aged compost. They are attempting to isolate the bacterium that is causing the disease suppression, but are finding that many species of microorganisms are responsible. This suggests that healthy soils, with adequate levels of organic matter, are inherently rich in these disease suppressive organisms. Experts who have been involved in organic lawn care for an extensive period of time will testify that turf disease is a relatively rare malady in lawns where the soil has been restored to optimum health. Cornell's research has been conducted primarily on golf course greens, where they would apply ten pounds of compost per thousand square feet 5 to 7 times per year. Their best guess for application rates on residential lawn is 50 pounds per thousand square feet in the spring, and again in the fall. They warn, though, that all composts are not created equal. The more effective composts for disease suppression are those that are aged for two years or more. They have found that yard waste compost is relatively inferior for disease suppression. The University of Massachusetts warns not to use more than 3/4 of an inch of compost at any one application. That rate would amount to more than two yards of compost per thousand square feet.

Research also shows disease suppression from the use of compost teas, but the data is incomplete. Dr. Eric Nelson and other researchers from Cornell University formulated compost tea by mixing one part mature compost with five parts water and allowing it to soak for 3-7 days. The liquid was then filtered and sprayed onto plants infected with pithium root rot. The results in the lab were far more encouraging than those in the field, and funding was exhausted before further study could be accomplished. Dr. Nelson felt that better results could have been observed if they were able to continue with the research, but that using high quality compost solids instead of the tea would always net better disease control.

Many of our cultural practices performed under the guise of maintenance are responsible for altering the system's capacity to defend against diseases. Mowing with a dull blade, for example, is an invitation for plant diseases to inhabit a given area. Turf mowed with a dull blade is torn rather than cut, and the jagged wound left behind is an ideal place for plant pathogens to become established. Additionally, the stress inflicted upon the plant can lower its natural defenses against potential enemies. Mower blades should be sharpened after every 7-8 hours of use. Some professionals will touch up the edge of the blade with a file after only two hours of use. This may seem unreasonable, but compare the actual cost to the price of buying and applying fungicide to a customer's lawn as often as is usually necessary to combat a persistent disease. A secondary but significant price paid for using certain fungicides is earthworm mortality. The decimation of earthworm populations from certain fungicides will eventually cause other problems, such as thatch buildup and soil compaction. Many operators have extra sets of blades that they rotate daily. Some believe it is important to have the blades balanced regularly to preserve the life of the machines. Cleaning the underside of the mowing deck is also an important practice. The spread of plant pathogens and even some insect populations can be checked by removing potential inoculants from the mower after each job.

Other stress-producing practices such as improper mowing, excessive traffic of maintenance vehicles, excessive use of pesticides, clipping removal, excessive applications of lime, and improper fertilization can decrease the resistance of turf plants to many diseases.

Mowing a lawn too short can limit the amount of photosynthesis that occurs in the plant leaves. The synthesis of organic compounds from the energy of the sun is essential for most other plant functions. In addition, twenty percent of these energy compounds are exuded through the roots into the soil, nourishing large and diverse populations of microorganisms capable of, among many other things, disease suppression. Mowing at a greater height is usually beneficial for turf, but there are varieties of grasses that cannot stand erect beyond a certain mowing height. When lodging occurs, the opportunities for disease organisms to become established increase. Air infiltration is decreased and higher levels of moisture are retained. Mowing height should be determined by the general climate and the species of grasses being cultivated. There are very few cases, however, where mowing below a 2-3 inch level is necessary.

Excessive traffic, either by foot or by vehicle, causes compaction of the soil, which reduces the movement of water and the exchange of gases from the atmosphere into the soil and vice versa. This condition reduces the amount of oxygen available to turf roots and causes stress to plants. This can decrease their natural resistance to pathogens. Once disease organisms become established, traffic serves to further spread the problem to other areas of the lawn. Areas subjected to excessive traffic need to be conditioned. The compaction must be relieved, normally by core or solid tine aeration, and a program for building organic matter should be implemented.

Topdressing with a well aged, good quality compost after core aeration is an excellent practice whenever possible.

The excessive use of pesticides is another factor that can contribute to the fostering of turf diseases. The purpose of pesticides is to kill biological entities that are injuring the health or appearance of cultivated plants. Unfortunately, many pesticides do not discriminate sufficiently between pest, beneficial, and neutral organisms. They can alter the biological system enough to cause stress to the preferred species of plants. Whether the product is a fungicide, herbicide, insecticide, nematicide, or rodenticide, there is evidence that other, non-pest, organisms contributing to the well being of the soil and cultivated plants, are affected. The degree to which these biocides are used can influence some of the beneficial functions in the soil or plants, causing stress and presenting opportunities for disease organisms to become established.

The vast majority of fungal organisms in the soil function beneficially. They perform such tasks as the decomposition of raw organic matter and the generation of carbon dioxide — vital to photosynthesis. Some have symbiotic relationships with plants that allow access to water and nutrients otherwise out of reach from the plant's roots. Others are even parasitic or antagonistic to many plant pathogens. The application of most fungicides, however, does not discriminate between these organisms and can destroy far more beneficial fungi than pathogens.

Plant pathologists recommend removing the clippings from diseased areas so the pathogen is not spread into other areas, but research suggests that leaving healthy clippings behind will suppress many disease organisms (see figure 4-7). Apparently, some of the organisms that decompose clippings are antagonistic to many plant pathogens. Additionally, the recycling of nutrients and organic matter back to the soil promotes the growth of healthier plants that are better equipped to defend themselves against diseases. Pathogens can be spread by foot and vehicle traffic, wind, irrigation, and even by birds and insects. The key defense is a soil rich in microbial life, capable of suppressing the pathogen before it can get established.

Proper pH and nutrient management can play a major role in the development of diseases. Stress associated with nutrient deficien-

DISEASE RATING
1990 AND 1991

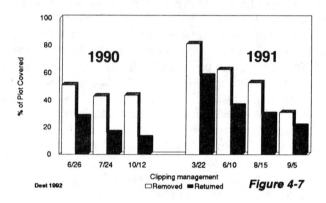

Figure 4-7

cies or incorrect pH can make the difference between a turf that can resist the invasion of pathogens and one that cannot. Testing the soil on an annual or biannual basis is an excellent way to monitor the balance of nutrients in the soil (see chapter 5). Proper fertility is essential for a healthy, disease resistant, stand of turf. Excessive applications of nutrients or lime are often as detrimental to plants as deficiencies are. The notion *if a little is good, more is better* needs to be surgically removed from one's intuition. Different soils have different capabilities to hold nutrients, and the optimal capacity of one soil may be twice that of another. These holding capacities are usually measured and considered by soil testing laboratories making fertility recommendations. Exceeding those recommendations can cause as many (or more) problems as not applying enough.

Dr. Gail Schumann from the University of Massachusetts produced a chart (see table 4-1) outlining cultural and chemical (not shown) controls of specific turf diseases. Seventy five percent of the recommendations involve either increasing or decreasing soil fertility. The chart suggests that too much or too little soil fertility can encourage plant pathogens. Common sense dictates that ideal soil fertility cannot be improved upon. Yet many managers cling to the notion that *more is better*. In the organically maintained lawn many of the nutrients are applied in a form that is unavailable to the plant. The release of these nutrients is facilitated by biological activity in

Disease name	Cultural control
Anthracnose	Fertilize, aerate, raise mower height, less water on leaf blades
Brown patch (rhizoctonia blight)	Avoid excess nitrogen and water; minimize water on leaf blades.
Dollar spot	Fertilize, aerate, minimize water on leaf blades; use resistant cultivars.
Fairy ring	Core and water; mask symptoms with N or Iron; in severe cases, remove soil or fumigate
Fusarium leaf blight, crown and root rot	Avoid drought, minimize water on leaf blades; reduce thatch.
Leaf spot melting out	Avoid excess N and water, minimize water on leaf blades, raise mowing height; use resistant cultivars
Necrotic ring spot	Avoid water and fertility stress, aerate. Reduce thatch; use resistant cultivars
Powdery mildew	Improve air flow, reduce shade; avoid excess nitrogen.
Pythium blight	Avoid excess N; improve drainage. Don't water at night or mow in wet weather.
Pythium root rot	Improve drainage, areate, raise mowing height
Red thread/pink patch	Fertilize, avoid low pH, minimize water on leaf blades. Use resistant cultivars
Rust	Fertilize, aerate, avoid water stress and minimize water on leaf blades. Use resistant cultivars
Slime molds	Minimize water on leaf blades. Hose or rake away mold.

Continued - next page

Table 4-1

(Continued from previous page)	
Disease name	**Cultural control**
Typhula blight (gray snow mold)	Let turf go dormant; mow until growth stops; minimize length of snow cover.
Fusarium patch	Same as Typhula blight control.
Stripe smut	Buy smut-free seed. Avoid excess N in spring; avoid water stress in summer. Use resistant cultivars.
Summer patch	See necrotic ring spot. Raise mower height, lower pH with ammonium.
Take-all patch	Improve drainage, lower pH with ammonium fertilizers; raise mower height; avoid P and K deficiency. Avoid using lime.
Yellow patch	Minimize water on leaf blades; avoid excess N. Reduce thatch.
Yellow tuft	Avoid excess N; minimize water on leaf blades; improve drainage. Mask symptoms with iron.

Schumann 1994

Table 4-1, continued

the soil, regulated by many different environmental conditions such as climate and soil moisture. Coincidentally, the conditions that encourage this activity also encourage the growth of plants. This natural coincidence allows nutrients from organic sources to become available at the most appropriate time for plants, and regulates the release of those nutrients for optimum usage by the plant. In addition, the biological activity stimulated by organic nutrients can compete with, antagonize, or parasitize many turf pathogens. *Note: Where the chart suggests lowering the soil's pH with ammonium products, substitutes such as elemental sulfur, blood meal, or cottonseed meal can be used.*

A researcher at Michigan State University found that light watering of approximately one tenth of an inch (about 10 minutes of irrigation) each afternoon suppressed most turfgrass diseases. The research suggests that stress is the major factor involved in the establishment of an infection, and that the mitigation of stress by providing much needed moisture and by lowering the soil and plant temperatures can ameliorate conditions to such an extent that natural plant resistance is able to combat infection. The research also found that insect, weed, and thatch problems were suppressed in the treated plots. In lawns with irrigation, control of all turfgrass pests may only consist of turning on the sprinkler for ten minutes in the mid- to late afternoon throughout the heat and drought season.

Research has also shown that optimum fertility, especially with regard to nitrogen, can aid in the natural suppression of turf diseases. Natural organic nitrogen is better suited for this task because of its slow release properties and because it encourages the growth of microbe populations that can ultimately compete with plant pathogens.

Choosing disease resistant cultivars is a wise choice, especially in regions where certain turf diseases are common. Most universities have data on different seed varieties and their resistance to common diseases. Diversity is also important in controlling disease. Most pathogens are specific about which plants they infect. If many different varieties exist, the infection of one species may be less noticeable. The interference of immune varieties may also suppress the spread of the disease to other plants.

In the freedom lawn, plant disease is part of the ecology. Plants that do not survive the environmental conditions simply die off, making room for new ones that are better suited for the existing conditions. In an environment where many varieties of plants exist, few if any would be affected by pathogens. Additionally, the diversity of such an environment would promote a relative diversity of other organisms, many of which would be capable of controlling pathogens.

THATCH

There are a lot of misconceptions floating around about thatch. The two most common are: *leaving clippings behind when mowing causes thatch* and *dethatching machines will cure thatch problems.* Thatch is caused when the residues of stems, crowns, stolons, tillers, leaves, and other plant parts intermingled with living roots and shoots accumulate faster than they can be decomposed. Excessive thatch can inhibit water infiltration and promote the volatilization of nitrogen from fertilizers, especially when urea is used. Thatch is usually a result of poor turf management practices. Excessive applications of nitrogen that promote fast growth and the use of pesticides that inhibit the activities of decomposing organisms are the leading causes of thatch accumulation.

Earthworms are probably the most valuable soil organisms for thatch control. They quickly decompose surface residues and enrich the soil with castings while providing aeration, improving water infiltration, and decompacting the soil. Excessive nitrogen can acidify soil, inhibiting the activities of earthworms and other thatch decomposing organisms. Grass clippings contain an excellent slow release nitrogen that favors the existence of decomposition organisms. Removal of clippings when mowing actually favors the accumulation of thatch.

Pesticide use can also play a major role in the creation of thatch. It inhibits the activities of decomposing organisms. A single application of products containing bendiocarb, benomyl, carbaryl, fonofos, or ethoprop can kill 60-99% of the earthworm population in that area. Other compounds such as chlorpyrifos, diazinon, isazophos, isofenphos, and trichlorfon can cause significant mortality of earthworms and other decomposing organisms. Many of these compounds cause the reduction of certain predator groups. The pesticides used to combat disease and/or insect problems related to thatch may only serve to increase it.

Thatch problems are relatively rare in low input or organically maintained lawns because most of the maintenance is directed to the soil instead of the turf. Healthy soils generate huge populations of organisms that can consume thatch faster than it can be created. Composts and organic fertilizers stimulate the biological activity needed to control thatch.

The successful management of thatch can mitigate other problems related to the stress caused by high thatch accumulations.

ALGAE

Algae is often a problem on golf greens, where the turf must be mowed very close and irrigation is at a maximum for maintaining health and color during the hot, dry months of the year. In ornamental lawns, algae usually occurs where there is excessive moisture, high fertility, and low competition from turfgrass. Algae is a photosynthesizing organism and likes full sun, but can also exist in shady areas.

Controlling algae ecologically is similar to managing weeds. A well maintained, thick, tall turf is the best defense against algae. Often, algae begins in areas of poor drainage. Chronically moist conditions can stress turf and lower its ability to compete for space and sunlight. Algae, on the other hand, thrives in excessively wet areas. Problem areas may require drainage tiles as a permanent solution.

Over-irrigation is another cause of algae encroachment. Too much water can stress the grass and provide favorable conditions for algae. Fertilizers applied in excess can also encourage algae. Turf can be stressed by too much fertilizer, especially those with high salt content, whereas algae can tolerate higher levels of nutrients. Mowing high can protect against algae, which tends to grow close to the ground and in thin layers.

Eradication of established algae colonies requires either physical removal or some type of algicide. Household products such as Lysol Disinfectant or Chlorox Bleach with a surfactant are very effective at killing algae, but are not without their problems. The first is that these products are phytotoxic. In others words, they will kill the grass, too, if the dose is too large. This may not be a big problem, because there may not be much grass growing there in the first place. The second problem is a legal one. Household disinfectants and bleaches are not labeled as algicides and technically cannot be used as such. Copper sulfate is relatively successful at defeating algae and some brands are labeled for turf. Greenhouse disinfectants made from quaternary ammonium compounds are found to be most effective, with the least amount of damage to grass plants. Finding a product labeled for turf, however, may be difficult.

The more permanent solution to algae problems is cultural. Creating an environment that is favorable to turf and inhospitable to algae is usually less expensive and more effective in the long term.

MOSS

The occurrence of moss on a lawn usually indicates a wet and cool environment, probably a low soil fertility and pH, and improper mowing. Moss is a slow growing plant that tolerates low pH, little to no fertility, and dense shade. Low mowing is a cultural activity that encourages the existence of moss. Fortunately, moss does not tolerate wear and tear, so removal can be accomplished easily by using a dethatching machine or other tool that will scarify the surface. Preventing moss from reoccurring involves changes to the soil that will support a healthy stand of turf. Adjustments in soil fertility and pH should be done in accordance with a soil test (see chapter 5). Core aeration may be necessary, as well as the introduction of quality composts to boost organic matter and biological activity. Areas subjected to dense shade may require renovation with a grass seed blend containing different types of fescues or other shade-tolerant cultivars. Some areas may be too shady for grasses and might be better off with a shade-tolerant ground cover. Mowing a thick stand of turf at a reasonable height (see chapter 3) will also help to prevent an invasion of moss.

BENEFICIAL PESTS

Beneficial pests include birds, earthworms, moles, skunks, and other organisms whose activities are largely beneficial to their immediate ecosystem but may cause some esthetic impact on the landscape. Unfortunately, eliminating these pests can often result in infestations of other, far more damaging pests. In science, especially turf science, discussions of tolerance are ubiquitous. The amount of tolerance any landscape has for any pest really depends on the owner. If that person's perception of acceptable levels of damage is low (i.e., he or she cannot tolerate very much damage) then that becomes the tolerance threshold of that landscape. The lower the threshold, the higher the expense of maintaining an extremely unbalanced and vulnerable ecosystem. Customers often cannot understand ecology but can usually understand economics. If it is apparent to them that their higher expectations carry relatively higher costs, they may be inclined to tolerate a more natural looking landscape.

Sources:

Adams, W.A. and R.J. Gibbs, 1994, **Natural Turf for Sport and Amenity: Science and Practice**. CAB International. Wallingford, United Kingdom.

ASA# 47. 1979, **Microbial – Plant Interactions**. American Society of Agronomy. Madison, WI.

Baker, R.R. and P.E. Dunn, (Editors) 1990, **New Directions in Biological Control**. Alan R. Liss, Inc. New York, NY.

Barbosa, P. and D.K. Letourneau, (Editors) 1988, **Novel Aspects of Insect – Plant Interactions**. John Wiley & Sons, New York, NY.

Barbosa, P., V.A. Krischik, and C.G. Jones, (Editors) 1991, **Microbial Mediation of Plant – Herbivore Interactions**. John Wiley & Sons, Inc. New York, NY.

Beard, J.B. 1995, **Mowing Practices for Conserving Water**. Grounds Maintenance, January 1995. Intertec Publishing. Overland Park, KS.

Bhowmik, P.C., R.J. Cooper, M.C. Owen, G. Schumann, P. Vittum, and R. Wick, 1994, **Professional Turfgrass Management Guide**. University of Massachusetts Cooperative Extension System. Amherst, MA.

Bormann, F.H., D. Balmori, and G.T. Geballe, 1993, **Redesigning the American Lawn: A Search for Environmental Harmony**. Yale University Press. New Haven, CT

Briggs, S.A. and Erwin, N. 1991, **Pesticides and Lawns**. Rachel Carson Council, Inc. Chevy Chase, MD

Broccolo, L. 1995, Personal Communication. Broccolo Tree and Lawn Care. Rochester, NY

Callahan, P.S. 1975, **Tuning In To Nature: Solar Energy, Infrared Radiation, and the Insect Communication System**. The Devin-Adair Co. Old Greenwich, CT.

Carrow, R.N. 1994, **Understanding and Using Canopy Temperatures**. Grounds Maintenance, May 1994. Intertec Publishing. Overland Park, KS.

Casagrande, R.A. 1993, **Sustainable Sod Production for the Northeast**. Department of Plant Sciences, University of Rhode Island. Kingston, RI.

Cherim, M.S. 1994, **The General Principals of Biological Pest Control**. The Plantsman, June/July 1994. New Hampshire Plant Growers Association, c/o UNH. Durham, NH.

Chet, I. (Editor) 1987, **Innovative Approaches to Plant Disease Control**. John Wiley & Sons, Inc. New York, NY.

Colbaugh, P.F. 1994, **Dealing With Algae**. Grounds Maintenance, May 1994. Intertec Publishing. Overland Park, KS.

Craul P.J. 1992, **Urban Soil in Landscape Design**. John Wiley and Sons, Inc. New York, NY.

Cummings, J.L., J.R. Mason, D.L. Otis, and J.F. Heisterberg, 1991, **Evaluation of Dimethyl and Methyl Anthranilate as a Canada Goose Repellent on Grass**. Wildlife Society Bulletin 19:184-190, 1991.

Davidson, R.H. and W.F. Lyon, 1987, **Insect Pests of Farm, Garden and Orchard:** Eighth Edition. John Wiley and Sons, Inc. New York, NY.

Dernoeden, P.H., M.J. Carroll, and J.M. Krouse, 1993, **Weed Management and Tall Fescue Quality as Influenced by Mowing, Nitrogen, and Herbicides**. Crop Science 33:1055-1061. Crop Science Society of America. Madison, WI.

Dest, W.M., S.C. Albin, and K. Guillard, 1992, **Turfgrass Clipping Management**. Rutgers Turfgrass Proceedings 1992. Rutgers University, New Brunswick, NJ.

DiMascio, J.A., P.M. Sweeney, T.K. Dannegerger, and J.C. Kamalay, 1994, **Analysis of Heat Shock Response in Perennial Ryegrass Using Maize Heat Shock Protein Clones**. Crop Science 34:798-804. Crop Science Society of America. Madison, WI.

Elam, P. 1994, **Earthworms: We Need Attitude Adjustment**. Landscape Management July, 1994. Advanstar Communications. Cleveland, OH.

Franklin, S. 1988, **Building a Healthy Lawn: A Safe and Natural**

Approach. Storey Communications, Inc. Pownal, VT.

Grainge, M. and S. Ahmed, 1988, **Handbook of Plants with Pest Control Properties**. John Wiley & Sons. New York, NY.

Grant, J., M. Villani, and J. Nyrop, 1994, **Predicting Grub Populations in Home Lawns**. Cornell University Turf Times (CUTT) Summer 1994 v5 #2. Cornell University, Ithaca, NY

Hall, R. 1994, **Turf Pros Respond to Biostimulants**. Landscape Management, Oct. 94. Advanstar Communications. Duluth, MN.

Heinrichs, E.A. (Editor) 1988, **Plant Stress – Insect Interactions**. John Wiley & Sons, Inc. New York, NY.

Jackson, N. 1994, **Winter Turf Problems**. Turf Notes, November/December 1994. (Reprinted from The Yankee Nursery Quarterly, Vol 4, #4, 1994) New England Cooperative Extension Systems. University of Massachusetts. Worcester, MA.

Leslie, A.R. (editor) 1994, **Handbook of Integrated Pest Management for Turf and Ornamentals**. Lewis Publishers Boca Raton, FL.

Maske, C. 1995, Personal Communication. Maske's Organic Gardening. Decatur, IL.

Mason, J.R., L. Clark, and T.P. Miller, **Evaluation of a Pelleted Bait Containing Methyl Anthranilate as a Bird Repellent**. U.S. Department of Agriculture, Animal and Plant Health Inspection Service, Denver Wildlife Research Center. c/o Monell Chemical Senses Center. Philidelphia, PA.

Neal, J. 1990, **Waging War on Crabgrass**. Cornell University Turfgrass Times (CUTT), Spring 1990. Cornell University. Ithaca, NY.

Neal, J.C. 1992, **Plan Before You Plant**. WeedFacts, July 1992. Cornell University. Ithaca, NY.

Neal, J.C. 1993, **Turfgrass Weed Management – An IPM Approach**. WeedFacts, August 1993. Cornell University. Ithaca, NY.

Nelson, E.B. 1994, **More Than Meets the Eye: The Microbiology of Turfgrass Soils**. Turf Grass Trends, v3#2 February 1994. Washington, DC.

Nelson, E.B. 1995, Personal communication. Cornell University. Ithaca, NY.

Pfeiffer, E. E. **Weeds and What They Tell**. (Reprinted by) Bio-Dynamic Literature. Wyoming, RI.

Price, P.W., Lewinsohn, T.M., Fernandes, G.W. and Benson, W.W. (Editors) 1991, **Plant – Animal Interactions**. John Wiley & Sons, Inc. New York, NY.

Roberts, E. 1992, Private Communication. The Lawn Institute. Pleasant Hill, TN.

Sachs, P.D. 1993, **Edaphos: Dynamics of a Natural Soil System**. Edaphic Press. Newbury, VT.

Senesac, A. 1992, **Fall Weed Control**. Cornell University Turfgrass Times (CUTT), Fall 1992. Cornell University. Ithaca, NY.

Schultz, W. 1989, **The Chemical Free Lawn**. Rodale Press. Emmaus, PA.

Schumann, G.L. 1994, **Disease Control in Cool Season Grases**. Landscape Management May 1994. Advanstar Communications. Cleveland, OH.

Senn, T.L. 1987, **Seaweed and Plant Growth**. No publisher noted. Department of Horticulture, Clemson University. Clemson, SC.

Smith, C.M. 1989, **Plant Resistance to Insects: a Fundamental Approach**. John Wiley & Son, Inc. New York, NY.

Stuart, K. 1992, **A Life With the Soil**. Orion v 11 #2 Spring 1992 pp 17-29. Myrin Institute. N.Y., NY.

Talbot, M. 1995 Personal Communication. Dorchester, MA.

Vargas, J.M. Jr, 1994, **Management of Turfgrass Diseases**: Second Edition. Lewis Publishers. Boca Raton, FL.

Vavrek, R.C. 1990, **Beneficial Turfgrass Invertebrates**. USGA Green Section Record, November/December 1990 Vol 28(6).

Walters, C. Jr. 1991, **Weeds: Control Without Poisons**. Acres USA. Kansas City, MO.

Chapter 5
Soil Testing

Many of us in the lawn care business tend to apply materials by *dead reckoning*, a term used by airplane pilots that means *flying by instinct, using only a compass*. Fortunately for pilots, this type of navigation works much better for them than it does for stewards of the lawn. We trust that the directions on the bag, box, or bottle of fertilizing material that we are about to apply take into consideration all of the vagaries and idiosyncrasies of the soil to which we are applying it. They don't. Standard fertilizer recommendations are made with the assumption that the existing fertility is balanced. They are not meant to correct imbalances. How could they? The manufacturer of a fertilizer has no idea of the conditions of the soil with which you are working. The only accurate way to determine those conditions is to perform a soil test.

Some professionals fail to understand that the soil is not just a growing medium where turf can be grown hydroponically. It is a biological system that functions in a symbiotic relationship with all plants. The best way to follow the changes that occur in this system from land use is with a soil test.

SAMPLING PROCEDURE

The soil is like an urban community: no matter where we knock, someone different will answer the door. In the soil, it would be rare if two samples could be found that produce the same test results, even if they were drawn a foot away from each other. So it is extremely important to get a good representation of the entire area being evaluated. The test results will only be as useful as the sample is accurate. Figure 5-1 shows an example of a sampling pattern usually recommended to ensure results that are relative to the over-

ONE ACRE LOT

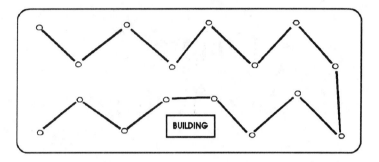

SUGGESTED SAMPLING PATTERN

Figure 5-1

all condition of the area. The number of samples taken should depend on the size of the area. The more samples taken, the better the representation.

Noticeably good or bad areas should be avoided (unless evaluation of a specific spot is needed). The conditions in these areas are extremes of one sort or another and will adulterate the average reading of an area. For obvious reasons, freshly fertilized or limed areas should also be avoided.

Very clean tools should be used for gathering samples. A small amount of rust on a shovel could be interpreted in a test as a good place to start an iron mining operation. An example of an incident that gave misleading results from contaminated tools is the client who used the same shovel to draw samples that he normally used to clean out ashes from his wood stove. The results of the test were so far off that they may have well been from a lawn on the planet Potassium.

Soil sampling tubes are the most efficient and accurate tools for drawing soil, even if sampling occurs only once a year. They significantly increase the speed of the sampling procedure while decreasing labor costs and the chances of contaminating the sample. These tubes are durable, relatively inexpensive, and can be purchased from most horticultural suppliers.

Avoid wet or frozen samples. The proper consistency of a soil sample for analysis is moist but not soaked. The sample should ball up when squeezed, no water should drip out and the ball should crumble easily. Drying out the sample is an acceptable procedure if necessary, but to preserve the original conditions of the soil, samples should not be drawn until the soil is at a proper moisture level. If the soil in question is naturally sandy and dry, do not attempt to moisten it.

The sampling depth for most applications should be about five to six inches. Scrape off any surface debris, such as roots or thatch, from the top of the sample. When all the samples from a given area are drawn, mix them thoroughly and take a representative sample of approximately one cup to send to the lab. Again, to preserve accurate results, send the sample to the lab right away. Avoid letting it sit for an extended period of time.

CHOOSING A LAB

Soil test laboratories do not have nationwide standard procedures for testing soil. Regional methodologies may often be employed by most labs in a given area, but they can opt to follow any procedures they want. *Methods of Soil Analysis*, published by the American Society of Agronomy, is the most widely accepted manual of testing procedures; still the publication often describes many different yet valid ways to test for nutrients. If the same samples were analyzed by several different labs, each using a different method for testing, the results may come back looking as though the samples were taken from several different countries. Additionally, labs may not offer the same type of information as part of their standard test. The University of Vermont, for example, tests for aluminum to determine lime and phosphorus recommendations, a valid but relatively unique procedure.

On a functional level, the most important service a lab can offer is an accurate, reasonably priced test delivered on a timely basis. It is also important, however, to determine the kind of information needed before looking at different labs. It is most cost effective if all the necessary information is offered on the lab's standard test, since optional information can get expensive. Because of the variance in the results one can receive from different labs, it is a good idea to choose a reliable lab and stick with it, especially if one is comparing tests that represent the soil before and after a specific treatment.

Interpreting soil test results is not as difficult as it may seem. It takes a little time and practice, however. Unfortunately, many labs give mostly recommendations, along with insufficient data to make your own accurate interpretation. Those labs cater to customers who only want the necessary information to make their soil balanced and fertile; they are not really interested in learning how to interpret a lab analysis. The ability to interpret a soil test, however, enables one to consider all the variables that can affect the performance of the soil in that specific area, with the net result of possibly saving some money.

Most labs offer recommendations either automatically or as an option (extra cost). They are based on the data derived from the sample. Therefore, the lab recommendations are only as good as the samples taken. Recommendations are based on nutrient uptake of specific plants under average conditions. Normally, a lab will ask for more information such as type of crop, crop use, topography and previous treatments if it is to provide recommendations.

Recommendations for customers who wish to implement organic practices are rarely available, but more and more labs are beginning to respond to the need. So if organic recommendations are optional, ask for them. There is no assurance that the advice you receive will be accurate, because very few lab personnel are trained to make organic recommendations.

To determine nutrient balance and fertility in soil, look for a lab that offers the following information (listed in order of importance):

1. pH and buffer pH
2. Percent organic matter
3. Cation exchange capacity (CEC)
4. Reserve and available phosphorus
5. Soil levels of exchangeable potassium, magnesium and calcium
6. Base saturation.

pH

Many people believe that the initials pH stand for potential hydrogen or power of hydrogen. The H in pH does, in fact, stand for hydrogen but p is a mathematical expression which, when multiplied by the concentration of hydrogen in the soil, gives a value between one and fourteen that expresses the acidity or alkalinity of the soil. Actually, soil pH values are rarely found to be under four or over ten. Values below seven are acidic and those above seven are alkaline. A value of seven is neutral. As values get farther away from neutral they indicate a stronger acid or base. A pH between six and seven is ideal for most plants. Most species of turf plants grow best at a pH of 6.5.

Most labs offer pH in their analysis of your soil, but some do not mention how they are testing for it. Take a look at the A & L sample analysis (figure 5-2): notice that it gives two pH values. The first is a water pH which determines the acidity or alkalinity of distilled water when mixed with an equal volume of the soil sample. This test only determines whether or not there is a need to lime or acidify the soil. The buffer pH or pH_{SMP} test is done with a special solution that determines how much lime to apply. The buffer test is not used if the water pH is near neutral. If a lab only offers one pH value in its analysis and it is not stated how it was found, it is relatively safe to assume it is a water pH. In these cases, the lime recommendation offered by the lab must be relied upon because it is not offering enough information for anyone to determine an appropriate application rate. A few labs indicate salt pH on their analysis report. Salt pH is measured with consideration for seasonal variation of soil soluble salts that can cause changes in pH. Salt pH values are normally 0.5 to 0.6 below what a water pH test would show.

ORGANIC MATTER

Most soils are called mineral soils because of the high level of rock mineral they contain. Soils were first formed on the earth by the weathering of rock into smaller and smaller particles by forces such as rain, frost, wind and erosion. Eventually, rock particles became small enough to be used by organisms as mineral nutrient. As photosynthesizing (autotrophic) organisms evolved, their needs consisted mostly of gaseous elements such as oxygen, nitrogen, hydrogen and carbon dioxide, which were derived from the atmosphere. The organisms' mineral needs were taken care of by the soil. As generations of these autotrophs cycled through life and death, decomposing organisms evolved and ultimately created humus. After millions of years, as more and more organisms appeared, levels of organic matter increased, which increased the production of all organisms from the microbe to the plant and all the other life they supported.

SAMPLE ANALYSIS, A&L EASTERN AGRICULTURAL LABORATORIES, RICHMOND, VA.

%OM	ENR	P1	P2	K	Mg	Ca	Soil pH	Buffer pH	H	CEC	K	Mg	Ca	H
4.5	104VH	83VH	121VH	139VH	187VH	640M	6	6.8	1	6.2	5.7	25	51.3	3.1
7.3	171VH	102VH	160VH	600VH	210VH	2800H	6.3	6.7	2	19.3	8	9.1	72.5	10.5

%OM - percent organic matter; ENR - Estimated Nitrogen Release in pounds per acre (ppa); P1 - Available phosphorus in parts per million (ppm); P2 - reserve phosphorus in ppm; K - Potassium in ppm; Mg - Magnesium in ppm; Ca - Calcium in ppm; Soil pH - Water pH test; Buffer pH - pHsmp; CEC - Cation Exchange Capacity.

Figure 5-2

SOIL DEVELOPMENT

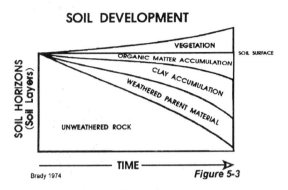

Brady 1974   **TIME**   *Figure 5-3*

Figure 5-3 shows the theoretical formation of different soil horizons over time. Note that the development of organic matter is not
suggesting that the surface of the soil is 100% organic matter. It is
simply the layer in which organic matter will accumulate. The process has a snow-balling effect. Organic matter has its own life cycle,
however, and through oxidation, nitrification, and other natural processes would, on average, amount to approximately five percent in
the top six inches of a mineral soil (see figure 5-4) in the temperate
zone of the planet. This figure varies as climatic and edaphic factors change from location to location.

Organic matter (OM) is a barometer of soil health. The population of organisms supported by soil organic matter is of immeasurable benefit to plants. More OM means more decomposers that
recycle nutrients from plant and animal residues faster; more nitrogen fixing and mineralizing bacteria; more beneficial organisms
that help dissolve mineral, transport water from soil depths and help
control pathogenic fungi; and more humus to increase the water
and nutrient holding capacity of the soil. Humus acts like a sponge
in the soil which expands and contracts as its moisture level changes.
This activity within the soil increases porosity, which improves the
movement of air and water. As all these organisms travel through
their own life cycles, they create even more organic matter.

Burning is an accurate method of testing for OM. What is left
after combustion is ash, which is the mineral portion of the sample.
The percent of OM can then be determined simply by subtracting

Soil Components
Typical analysis of well developed loam

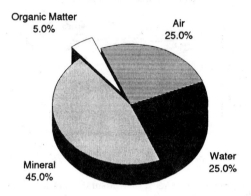

Figure 5-4

the weight of the ash from the total weight of the dry sample before it was burned. A reading close to five percent in temperate regions is a good level. Readings significantly below that figure may be an indication that some sort of soil building program should be implemented. A look at the sample A & L soil analysis (figure 5-2), shows a column just to the right of % Organic Matter labeled ENR. This stands for Estimated Nitrogen Release, and indicates the amount of nitrogen, in pounds per acre, that can be released from the OM content throughout the season under average conditions. To convert this figure to pounds per 1,000 square feet, divide by 43.56 (because there are 43.56 thousand square feet in an acre). A & L Labs uses a colorimeter method for determining percent OM in the soil. The soil is reacted with a chemical and the intensity of color is measured. This method is a valid and accurate way of determining the percent OM and costs slightly less than the combustion test. Most labs will use either method if a specific request is made.

Levels of organic matter naturally differ around the country for various reasons. The climate has a big influence on organic matter levels in different regions. Laboratories should be able to ascertain the average for areas that they service based on their own tests.

CATIONS, ANIONS AND EXCHANGE

To better understand cations (pronounced **cat**-eye-ons) and anions (pronounced **an**-eye-ons), a short review of elementary chemistry is in order. All materials that are on, under, or above the planet's surface, whether liquid, solid, or gaseous, are made up of atoms of different elements that are bonded to each other. The force that holds these atoms together is electromagnetic. It is the same force that holds dust to a television screen. In order for this magnetic force to work, however, there must be both positive and negative charges present. Like charges do not attract.

There are ninety elements that occur naturally on earth. Most of these elements are made up of atoms that have either a positive or negative charge. Some, called inert, have no charge and rarely bond with anything. When the atom of one element bonds with the atom of another, the result is called a compound. The magnetic bonds between elements in many compounds satisfy the attraction each atom has for the other. In many other instances, however, the attraction of one atom does not completely satisfy the magnetic force of the other, leaving a net negative or net positive charge that is still available for another combination. These compounds are called ionic.

Ions are atoms of elements or molecules of compounds that carry either a negative or positive electric charge. The ions of elements such as hydrogen (H), calcium (Ca), magnesium (Mg) and potassium (K) have positive charges and are known as cations. Ions of phosphorus (P), nitrogen (N), and sulfur (S) have negative charges and are called anions. Some elements such as carbon (C) and silicon (Si) can act as anions or cations and bond to either charge.

Molecules of compounds such as nitrate (NO_3), sulfate (SO_4) and phosphate (PO_4) have negative (anionic) charges and can bond with cations such as H, Ca, or K. In the soil there are very small particles, called *micelles* (short for micro-cells), that carry an electronegative or anionic charge. These particles are either mineral (clay) or organic (humus) and are referred to as soil colloids. Although small in comparison to other soil particles, colloidal particles are huge in relation to soil cations such as H, K, Mg or Ca. Cations are attracted to these colloids like dust is to a TV screen.

CLAY

Clay particles, if viewed through a powerful microscope, would appear as flat platelets adhering to each other like wet panes of glass (see figure 5-5). These particles are predominately comprised of silicon, aluminum and oxygen but, depending on the type of clay, can contain a plethora of different elements such as potassium (K), magnesium (Mg), iron (Fe), copper (Cu) and zinc (Zn).

Clay's magnetism comes from the natural substitution of ions in its structure with other ions that don't completely satisfy the avail-

Scanning electron micrographs

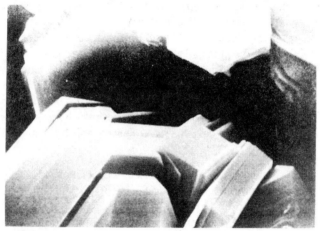

Courtesy Dr. Bruce Bohor, Illinois State Geological survey

Figure 5-5

able magnetic charges. As more of these substitutions occur, the overall negative charge of the particle increases, and there is a relative increase in the amount of cations attracted to it (see figure 5-6). Different types of clays have different abilities for ionic substitutions, and their magnetic force differs accordingly. Clay particles that have greater substitution potential will create more magnetic force and attract and hold more cations. Some clay particles are not colloidal at all.

CLAY PARTICLES
MICELLES

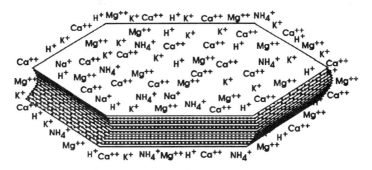

Negatively charged clay particles
shown with typical plate-like
appearance and swarm of adsorbed cations

Figure 5-6

The surface area of clay is also important to consider. If one acre (six inches deep) of clay particles were to be separated and spread out, the surface area would be equivalent to fifty times the area of Illinois. Since most of these ionic substitutions occur on the surface of the clay platelets, there is a relative increase in the soil's capacity to hold cations from the amount of exposed surface area of clay.

HUMUS

Humus particles are also colloidal in nature (negatively charged). Their cation exchange capacity (CEC) is even greater than that of clay per equal unit of weight, but is influenced by soil pH (see figure 5-7).

INFLUENCE OF pH
ON THE CEC OF
ORGANIC MATTER AND CLAY

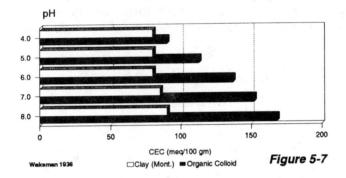

Figure 5-7

Humus gains its magnetic charge from the surface compounds that contain hydrogen (H). In soils with a near neutral pH, H is displaced from humus to participate in a number of different soil chemical reactions. When this occurs, a negative charge that previously held the H ion is left unsatisfied and available for another chemical bond. If base cations such as K, Mg or Ca are present in the soil solution they will be attracted to the humic particle (see figure 5-8). Like clay, humus has a significant amount of surface area.

Clay and humus will often form colloidal complexes together, which not only enhances the overall cation holding capacity of a soil, but also changes the structure of clay soil into a better habitat for roots and organisms. Humus, through complicated chemical bonds, can surround clay particles, thus breaking up clay's cohesive nature that can prevent percolation of air and water through the soil. These chemical bonds also help extend the length of time humus particles can exist in the soil.

Both clay and humus, with their unique structure and electro-static (negative) charge, hold onto a tremendous amount of cation elements in such a way that the ions can be detached and absorbed by plant roots. Hydrogen (H$^+$) ions that are given off by roots are

ORGANIC COLLOID

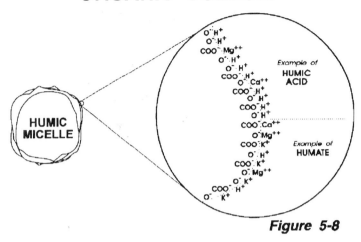

Figure 5-8

traded back to the colloids. This whole process, called cation exchange, is the major source of cation nutrients for plants (see Figure
5-9).

CATION EXCHANGE

The exchange of cations that takes place in the root zone is an
essential activity of the soil system. Minerals such as calcium, magnesium and potassium would be relatively rare and unavailable in
topsoil if it were not for the colloidal nature of clay and humus.
Base cations are magnetically held by soil colloids. When root hairs
grow into proximity with colloidal exchange sites, those bases can
displace hydrogen ions located on the root's surface and can then be
absorbed by the plant. This exchange is essential, not only for the
mineral needs of the plant, but also for the translocation of hydrogen throughout the soil.

HYDROGEN

Depending on soil pH and the level of exchangeable cation bases
(i.e. Ca, Mg and K) in the soil solution, the hydrogen that is adsorbed
to the soil colloid will eventually exchange again; however, this
time with a base from the soil solution. Once the H^+ ion enters the
soil solution a number of reactions can occur. It can combine with
oxygen to form water, or with nitrate or sulfate ions to form strong

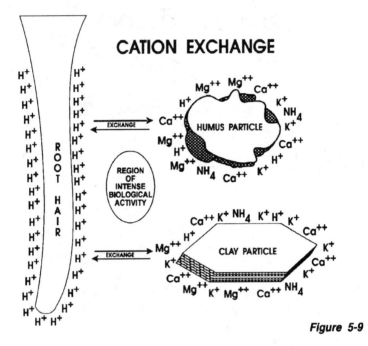

CATION EXCHANGE

Figure 5-9

inorganic acids (nitric and sulfuric acid). These acids can work to liberate more base cations from the mineral components in the soil. H^+ can also liberate and transform phosphate ions into phosphoric acid, which is the form of phosphorus that plants can use.

Soil carbonates react with H^+ ions to form carbon dioxide (CO_2) and water. This process is implemented when lime (calcium carbonate) is added to raise the pH of a soil. Hydrogen can also help form organic acids when reacting with residues of plants, animals and microorganisms. These acids can weather available minerals from rock particles in the soil. This function is especially important in the *rhizosphere*, the zone surrounding the roots of plants. Within the rhizosphere, biological activity is very high and the pH is relatively low. The activity of H^+ ions in this zone releases mineral ions from soil particles that can become available nutrients for the plant. Oxides, abundant components of many minerals, can also combine with H^+ to form water (H_2O).

CEC

The *cation exchange capacity* (CEC) of the soil is determined by the amount of clay and/or humus that is present. These two colloidal substances are essentially the cation warehouse or reservoir of the soil. Sandy soils with very little organic matter (OM) have a low CEC, but heavy clay soils with high levels of OM have a much greater capacity to hold cations.

The disadvantages of a low CEC include the limited availability of mineral nutrient to the plant and the soil's inefficient ability to hold applied nutrient. Plants can exhaust a fair amount of energy (that might otherwise have been used for growth, flowering, seed production or root development) scrounging the soil for mineral nutrients. Soluble mineral salts (e.g. potassium sulfate) applied in large doses to soil with a low CEC cannot be held efficiently because the cation warehouse is too small.

Water also has a strong attraction to colloidal particles. All functions that are dependent on soil moisture are also limited in soils with low CEC. Organisms such as plants and microbes that depend upon each other's biological functions for survival are inhibited by the lack of water. Where there is little water in the soil, there is often an abundance of air, which can limit the accumulation of organic matter (by accelerating decomposition) and further perpetuate the low level of soil colloids.

High levels of clay with low levels of OM would have an opposite effect (a deficiency of air), causing problems associated with anaerobic conditions. The CEC in such a soil might be very high, but the lack of atmosphere in the soil would limit the amount and type of organisms living and/or growing in the area, causing dramatic changes to that immediate environment. Oxidized compounds such as nitrates (NO_3) and sulfates (SO_4) may be reduced (i.e., oxygen is removed) by bacteria that need the oxygen to live, and the nitrogen and sulfur could be lost as available plant nutrients. Accumulation of organic matter is actually increased in these conditions because the lack of air slows down decomposition. Eventually, enough organic matter may accumulate to remedy the situation, but it could take decades or even centuries.

The CEC of a soil is a value given on a soil analysis report to indicate its capacity to hold cation nutrients (see figure 5-2). CEC is not something that is easily adjusted, however. It is a value that indicates a condition, or possibly a restriction, that must be considered when working with that particular soil. Unfortunately, CEC is not a packaged product. The two main types of colloidal particles in the soil are clay and humus and neither is practical to apply in large quantities. Compost, which is an excellent soil amendment, is not necessarily stable humus. Over time compost may become humus, but the end product might only amount to 1-10% (in some cases, less) of the initial application.

Table 5-1 gives an idea of how thick each cubic yard of compost will spread on a 1,000 square foot area. Remember, each percent of organic matter in the soil is equal to over 450 pounds per 1,000 square feet (20,000 lbs/acre). Compost normally contains about forty to fifty percent OM on a dry basis, and weighs approximately 1,000 pounds per cubic yard (depending on how much moisture it contains). If the moisture level is fifty percent, it would take two cubic yards of compost per thousand square feet to raise the soil OM level one percent (temporarily). Large applications of compost to the surface of the soil, however, can do more harm than good. Abrupt changes in soil layers can inhibit the movement of water and restrict the soil's capacity to hold moisture. Obviously, building organic matter in the soil is not something that can or should be done overnight. Natural/organic nitrogen sources, in general, will do more to raise or preserve the level of OM than synthetic chemicals because of the biological activity that they stimulate. Colloidal phosphate contains a natural clay and is often used to condition sandy soils with a low CEC.

Low phosphorus conditions should be present, however, to justify its use.

If a soil has a very low CEC, adjustments can and should be made, but not solely because of the CEC. A soil with a very low

| | YARDS TO COVER | |
DEPTH	1000 SQ FT	1 ACRE
1/8 INCH	0.38	18
1/4 INCH	0.75	35
1/2 INCH	1.5	69
1 INCH	3.1	135
2 INCHES	6.2	270
3 INCHES	9.3	405

Table 5-1

CEC has little or no clay or humus content. Its description may be closer to sand and/or gravel than to soil. It cannot hold very much water or cation nutrients and plants cannot grow well. The reason for the necessary adjustment is not the need for a higher CEC, but because the soil needs conditioning. A direct result of this treatment will eventually be a higher CEC.

During the process of soil building, the steward must be aware of the soil's limitations. Soil with a low CEC cannot hold many nutrients, so smaller amounts of fertilizer should be applied more frequently. Feeding a lawn growing on soil with a low CEC is analogous to feeding an infant. It doesn't eat a lot but must be fed often. As the CEC of the soil improves, larger doses of fertilizers can be applied less frequently.

MILLIEQUIVALENTS (meqs)

CEC is measured in *milliequivalents* (meqs) per one hundred grams of soil. An equivalent is actually a chemical comparison. It is a measurement of how many grams of a substance (element or compound) it takes either to combine with or to displace one gram of hydrogen (H). A meq is simply one thousandth of an equivalent.

It sounds complex but it really isn't. Picture a train with one empty seat. The capacity of that seat is one person. If Joe, who weighs 240 pounds, is polite enough to give up the seat to Ann, who weighs 120 pounds, the capacity of the seat hasn't changed, just the weight of the passenger occupying it. When measuring CEC, each ion is a passenger on the soil colloid. Unfortunately, unlike commuters, ions are far too small to count; therefore, their numbers must be calculated by using known factors such as atomic weight and electromagnetic charge. Hydrogen has an atomic weight of one and has a valence of +1 (i.e., a positive charge of 1). Calcium (Ca), for example, has an atomic weight of forty and a valence of +2. H and Ca are both cations, and they would not combine, so the equivalence here is in terms of displacement. Since Ca has twice the charge as H (it occupies two seats on the colloidal express), only half of its atomic weight is needed to displace the atomic weight of H. Therefore, it would take twenty grams of Ca to displace one gram of H. A CEC with a value of 1 meq/100 gr means that each one hundred grams of soil can magnetically hold either one milligram (mg) of H or twenty mg of Ca (more likely some combination of both). Table 5-2 shows equivalent values of common soil cations.

ELEMENT or COMPOUND	ATOMIC WEIGHT	VALENCE	EQUIVALENCE
Hydrogen	1	1	1
Magnesium	24	2	12
Calcium	40	2	20
Potassium	39	1	39
Ammonium	18	1	18

Table 5-2

The CEC is an overall measurement and is calculated from the amount of exchangeable base cations (i.e., Ca, Mg, and K) and meqs of H found during soil analysis. In a test where exchangeable cations are measured in parts per million (ppm), the equivalence of the cation is multiplied by ten (because the ratio between parts per million is ten times greater than the ratio of milliequivalents per 100 grams) and then divided into the ppm found in the analysis. For example, if 125 ppm potassium were found in the soil test results, its equivalence in meq/100gr would be: 125 divided by 390 = 0.3 (rounded). 125 is the ppm found in the test and 390 is the equivalent of potassium (39) multiplied by 10.

Once the ppm of Ca, Mg and K are calculated into meq/100gr, they are added together. This total constitutes the portion of the soil's CEC currently occupied by the base cations. Meqs of H are calculated from the buffer pH test and then added to the total from the bases to arrived at the soil's overall CEC (see CEC example on the next page).

EFFECTIVE CEC

Labs that offer a CEC value have calculated all of this in advance. If a lab does not run a Buffer pH test, however, it cannot include H in its CEC calculations. The University of Vermont (UVM), for example, offers what they call *effective* CEC (ECEC) which is only calculated from the exchangeable base cations found. Since UVM calculates its lime recommendations from an analysis of exchangeable aluminum, it has no H^+ value to plug into this formula. If calculating the CEC is necessary, its lime recommendation

CEC EXAMPLE IN TEST #1 (from figure 5-2)

BASE	PPM FOUND	Meq/100gr
Potasium	139	.4
Magnesium	187	1.6
Calcium	640	3.2
Total Bases		5.2
Hydrogen		1
CEC		6.2

will act as a H^+ value. For example, if UVM recommends three tons (6,000 lbs) of lime per acre, each 1,000 lbs of lime will neutralize 1 meq of H. Therefore, three tons will neutralize 6 meq of H. According to UVM (and others), the CEC of a soil is pH dependent and should fluctuate with variances in pH. It is UVM's opinion that ECEC is a more accurate measure of cation exchange capacity.

ANIONS

Anions are ions that carry a negative electromagnetic charge. Because they have the same polarity as soil colloids, they cannot be held or exchanged by clay or humus particles. The three anionic compounds most related to plant nutrition are nitrate (NO_3), phosphate (PO_4) and sulfate (SO_4). Phosphate ions bond easily with many different soil elements or compounds, and do not migrate very far before finding a friend to live with. Topical applications of available phosphate, however, can be eroded with normal surface runoff. This runoff causes nutrient loss and possible eutrophication (biological pollution) of waterways.

Nitrates and sulfates are susceptible to leaching. Aside from the issue of ground water pollution, the loss of these nutrients, when applied as inorganic compounds, can be significant. Dissolved nitrates and sulfates in soil solution can be held more efficiently by soils with a higher CEC simply by virtue of the increased water holding capacity. In heavy clay soils where the oxygen supply is limited, however, reduction (the biological or chemical removal of oxygen from compounds) can occur, because bacteria transform the nutrients into gases that can escape into the atmosphere.

Cations, anions and the exchange system in soil is a crucial component in the cycles and chains of life on earth. Their importance is comparable to a vital organ which, by itself, does not sustain life, but without which, life could not exist.

PHOSPHORUS

Most labs report both available and reserve phosphorus and usually use symbols such as VL (very low), L (low), M (medium), H (high) and VH (very high) to indicate how the results of the test compare to what they consider acceptable levels. These symbols are used throughout the soil analysis report.

Phosphorus (P) occurs in the soil as a phosphate (PO_4) ion. Phosphate ions have a negative charge (they are anions) and do not cling to clay or humus particles. Available phosphate can be lost through surface run off but otherwise does not migrate in the soil; phosphate ions can easily combine with other elements in the soil or can be used by soil organisms and plants. Plants use phosphorus as a phosphate combined with hydrogen (phosphoric acid).

Phosphorus tests are inherently inaccurate because there are so many variables in the soil that affect the availability of phosphate. If the lab finds deficiencies of P, however, then an application of some type of phosphate is usually warranted. The problem occurs when the lab finds acceptable levels, but soil conditions are such that it cannot become available. The activity of microorganisms is instrumental in freeing up phosphate by 1) mineralizing organic phosphate from the residues of plants and other organisms, and by 2) chemical reactions with soil compounds that contain phosphate. Good levels of soil organic matter are the key to a healthy population of microbes and adequate levels of available phosphate.

SOIL LEVELS OF EXCHANGEABLE CATIONS

Ca, Mg and K levels are usually tested by standard procedures, but many labs will report them differently. For example, K (potassium) may be reported as K_2O (potash) instead, or all three cation elements may be reported in pounds per acre (ppa) instead of parts per million (ppm). This will significantly change the way application rates of nutrients are calculated. Make sure the lab indicates what measurement units it is using.

BASE SATURATION

Base saturation is simply the balance or ratio of base cations in the soil. Base saturation should be used as a guideline. Labs that offer base saturation percentages will also give normal ranges within which those values should fall. A & L suggests the following ranges:

K = 2 – 7%   Mg = 10 – 15%   Ca = 65 – 75%

Values significantly above the accepted range should not cause concern unless they are creating an imbalance in the form of deficiencies or excessively high pH. Only the deficiencies should be addressed.

Knowing the CEC and base saturation tells two very basic facts about the soil. First, it tells how much potash, magnesium and calcium the soil can hold; second, it tells whether the proper balance of those nutrients exists. Table 5-3 shows where cation nutrient levels should be to achieve balanced base saturation at different CEC's. This table is taken from the A & L Agronomy Handbook for Soil and Plant Analysis which is available from A & L Laboratories for only $5.00. The information contained in the 133 pages of this manual is easily worth ten times that amount.

TEXTURE ANALYSIS

Texture analysis is done by determining the percentage of sand, silt and clay in a given soil. Those findings are plugged into a texture analysis triangle (figure 5-10) to determine soil classification. The triangle is used by extending lines from the appropriate starting points, parallel to the sides of the triangle which are counterclockwise to the sides where the lines began. Like tying your shoes, the triangle is easy to use but more difficult to explain. Here's an example: If a soil texture analysis discovered 40% sand, 40% silt and 20% clay, the first line would begin on the 40 mark of the *percent sand* side of the triangle, drawn parallel to the *percent silt* side. The second line begins at the 40 mark on the *percent silt* side and is drawn parallel to the *percent clay* side. Where those two lines meet is the texture classification of the soil. The third line may be drawn to complete the triangulation, but it is not necessary.

CEC	POTASSIUM 2-5%	MAGNESIUM 10-15%	CALCIUM 65-75%
30	292	360	3900
29	284	348	3770
28	274	336	3640
27	264	324	3510
26	254	312	3380
25	244	300	3250
24	234	288	3120
23	224	275	2990
22	215	263	2860
21	205	252	2730
20	195	240	2600
19	192	236	247
18	187	230	2340
17	182	225	2210
16	176	218	2080
15	170	210	1950
14	164	202	1820
13	158	193	1690
12	152	183	1560
11	147	172	1430
10	141	160	1300
9	135	148	1170
8	129	135	1040
7	123	121	910
6	117	106	708
5	108	90	650
4	85	75	520

From: A&L Agronomy Handbook   **Table 5-3**

A simple texture analysis can be conducted by collecting a soil sample in a glass jar or test tube and mixing it with an equal volume of water. The volume of the dry sample should be measured before water is added. After adding water, shake the container vigorously and then place in a location that will allow it to be undisturbed for twenty four hours. The sand particles will settle to the bottom and the silt above that. Clay will settle on top but can take up to two weeks to precipitate out of suspension, which is why it is important to measure the dry sample before adding the water. If the volume of the original sample is known, it is easy to determine the percentage of sand and silt by measuring each layer and calculating what por-

TEXTURE ANALYSIS CHART

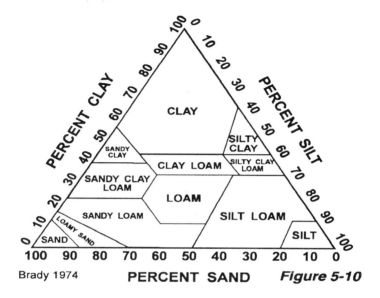

Brady 1974 · **PERCENT SAND** · *Figure 5-10*

tion it is of the whole sample. Once the percent sand and silt is determined, use the texture analysis chart to classify the sample.

Texture analysis is a valuable tool. Knowing the type of soil one is working in allows for more informed decisions about irrigation, core aeration, liming, fertilization, and applications of pesticides.

INTERPRETING THE ANALYSIS

Given the large number of different tests available from an even larger number of laboratories, it would be impossible to outline a blanket method of interpretation for every one of them. If we interpret the analysis for sample #1 (top line) shown in figure 5-2, however, we can get a rough idea of how to apply this method to the test your lab does.

1. The soil pH indicates the need for lime and the buffer pH indicates how much lime to apply (see table 5-4). This table appears on the back of every A&L Soil Analysis Report. Mg levels are very high so dolomite (hi-mag lime) should not be used if other liming materials such as calcite or aragonite are available (see chapter

BUFFER pH	MINERAL SOILS	ORGANIC SOILS
7.0	0	0
6.9	0	0
6.8	1	0
6.7	1.5	0
6.6	2.0	0
6.5	2.5	0
6.4	3.0	1.0
6.3	3.5	2.0
6.2	4.0	2.5
6.1	4.5	3.0
6.0	5.5	4.0
5.9	6.0	4.5
5.8	6.5	5.0
5.7	7.0	5.5
5.6	8.0	6.0
5.5	9.0	6.5

Table 5-4

6). Lab recommendations for lime are often higher than necessary. Cautious applications of 50-75% of the lab's recommendation in conjunction with retesting after six months may be well advised. Applications without incorporation (tilling, harrowing or plowing) should not exceed 2.5 tons of lime per acre (115 lbs. per 1,000 sq. ft.). Too much lime at a time can upset the ecology of a soil. Raising the pH too much can lock up essential nutrients such as iron and create other problems for the lawn.

2. The soil organic matter (OM) level is adequate.

3. The soil CEC is not out of proportion to the level of OM found,

indicating only a small amount of clay is in this soil.

4. The soil phosphorus levels are very high. A very high level of any nutrient is not necessarily good or bad. When excessively high levels of one nutrient are blocking the availability of another then applications of the deficient nutrient are in order. There is no practical way of reducing most nutrients in the soil.

5. The soil potassium (K) level is very high. If potassium were needed, Table 5-3 (from the A&L Handbook) shows how to calculate an application rate. With a CEC of 6.2, the amount of K in parts per million (ppm) should be over 117. Since 139 ppm already exists, more is not necessary. If less than 117 ppm were found, the difference would be applied after being converted to pounds per acre (ppa). Noted on the bottom, right side of the analysis report (not shown in figure 5-2), is the conversion of potassium in ppm to potash in ppa, (multiply by 2.4). **NOTE**: Some application rates may be too much nutrient to put down all at once. Split applications (apply half at a time) might be more appropriate. There is no general rule that applies to all nutrients as far as maximum application rates are concerned. Common sense is usually an accurate barometer but, when in doubt, contact the lab for guidance.

6. The base saturation shows lower than adequate levels of Ca, confirming the need for lime application. Correcting deficiencies in a soil with a very high CEC is more difficult because the capacity is so large. Imagine yourself working a hand pump with two buckets to fill. One holds a gallon and the other is a fifty five gallon drum. Not only does the drum take much more material, but it also takes a lot more energy to fill it. If both containers are filled to capacity, however, and the contents of both are used at the same rate, the advantages of the larger container are obvious.

NITROGEN

Nitrogen (N), which is considered to be the most used soil nutrient, has not been mentioned until now, and it did not appear on our list of important information offered by labs. Nitrogen is a little like New England weather. It changes so rapidly that it is difficult to get an accurate reading that means anything. Most labs offer tests for nitrate nitrogen (NO_3) but, in order to get an accurate result, they suggest that the sample be dried or frozen immediately to stop the biological activity in the sample. *Estimated Nitrogen Release* (ENR) can be calculated from the level of organic matter found in the soil. It is difficult to predict how much of that nitrogen will actually become available, however, because of the large number of variables that affect its release. On the other hand, nitrogen applications should not be based strictly on plant needs. The N that turf receives from organic matter, especially when clippings are recycled, is significant. One third of the N needed by turf is supplied by the clippings and the availability is so efficient that less than five percent of its N is lost even in the worst of conditions. Soil organic matter also provides some nitrogen. Residing in every one percent of organic matter in 1000 ft² of soil, is almost 23 pounds of nitrogen. In a soil with five percent organic matter, there is over 100 pounds of nitrogen per 1000 ft². It sounds like a lot but very little of it is available at any given time. A&L Laboratories give an estimated nitrogen release value (ENR) based on the amount of organic matter found in the sample. Their estimates may seem higher than a steward might want to rely on, but they should not be ignored by any means. Even if only one- to two-thirds of the ENR value is considered reliable, the reduction in nitrogen needs is significant.

Researchers have found that unfertilized turf contains more soluble nitrates during the late summer. A reasonable assumption is that applications of soluble N at this time of the season are more prone to leaching. Natural organic nitrogen is a much more appropriate material to use at this time of year.

Denitrification is a problem in soils with low oxygen levels, such as clay soils, soggy conditions, or excessive compaction. If managed with low soil nitrate levels, denitrification can be reduced or nearly eliminated.

Infusions of soluble nitrate or ammoniated fertilizers in excessive doses can do considerably more harm than good in the soil and can cause pollution in ground water. Moreover, money is wasted on the percentage of these materials that never reaches the plant. Consequences of excess nitrogen for turf include higher disease incidence; excessive thatch development; decreased tolerance to environmental stress conditions, such as heat, drought, and cold; poor root and lateral shoot development; and reduced production and reserves of plant carbohydrates.

Testing for nitrate nitrogen in turf soils may be profitable on large areas where significant applications of fertilizer are proposed. The appropriate timing of the test, however, usually creates a practical problem. Samples for nitrate testing should be drawn after the soil has warmed up and the biological component of the soil has become active again. This may not occur until mid- to late spring in some areas. It is often inappropriate or inconvenient to postpone fertilization this long. If fertilization cannot wait, then applications of nitrogen can adulterate the samples that are drawn later for nitrate analysis.

MICRONUTRIENTS

Although grasses do not have an especially high need for micronutrients, all plants need some. Any deficiency of a nutrient, no matter how small an amount is needed, will hold back plant development. Figure 5-11 illustrates the equal importance of all essential nutrients. Testing for micronutrients can get expensive, but if problems exist that are not explained by a standard test, it may be necessary to spring for it. Many labs hold onto the original sample for thirty days after they have analyzed it so drawing new samples may not be necessary. A simple phone call should get the test performed. Most micronutrients are cations, but labs do not report results in relation to CEC. The levels of micronutrients needed in the soil are so small that virtually any CEC will hold what is necessary.

Great care should be taken when correcting micronutrient deficiencies. There is a very fine line between too little and too much. The lab that does the testing can make recommendations but their recommendations are only as good as the sample taken. Micronutrient tests are easily adulterated by rusty or corroded tools. Because of the high zinc

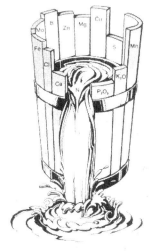

Liebig's "Law of the Minimum"

White 1992 *Figure 5-11*

content, galvanized tools or containers should never be used regardless of what their condition may be.

Iron is a micronutrient turf needs and is rarely deficient in most soils. If the pH of a soil is too high, however, iron becomes unavailable to plants. High levels of phosphates, zinc, manganese, or even thatch can also lock out the availability of iron. Many managers add commercial preparations of iron to compensate for these conditions. Turf will generally respond with improved color and vitality when given small amounts of soluble iron (ferrous iron). If conditions in the soil are such that iron is immediately tied up, however, then much of the iron applied will quickly become unavailable to plants. Many golf course managers will use iron as the weather turns colder to correct chlorosis caused by unavailable nitrogen in cold soils. Iron is also used to treat chlorosis when applications of nitrogen can exacerbate other problems, including certain turf diseases. The introduction of iron does not have an immediately apparent effect on the balance of nutrients in the soil and does not seem to alter the nutrient balance in the plant. Some scientists believe the iron merely coats the leaves, as a paint would, and causes a surface reaction that manifests itself in a dark green color.

LEAF TISSUE ANALYSIS

A soil test may not always provide answers when problems arise. Sometimes an edaphic factor is causing a nutrient deficiency even though there doesn't seem to be a shortage of that nutrient in the soil. Leaf tissue analysis can be performed to definitively determine what the turf is lacking. Most of the plant's physiological activity takes place in the leaves and changes in nutrient absorption by the plant are reflected in the balance of mineral in the tissue of the leaf.

To perform a leaf tissue analysis, 30-40 blades from fresh clippings should be gathered and spread out to air dry overnight. Samples should be packaged in a paper bag or cardboard box with holes punched through the walls to provide ventilation, and placed inside an appropriate shipping container. Send it to the lab as soon as possible. Avoid contamination from soil or other debris. Labs generally provide a sample information sheet which, when filled out, gives them important information needed to provide a useful analysis.

Plant tissue analysis can provide information needed both to solve problems and to prevent them. If, for example, a tissue analysis indicates an excessive amount of nitrogen in the leaves, it is evident that the turf is being overfertilized with nitrogen, which may eventually lead to other problems such as thatch, disease, or insect encroachment. The analysis can also point out deficiencies of seemingly obscure micronutrients such as manganese, copper, or zinc. Unfortunately, leaf tissue analysis is not inexpensive and cannot be done indiscriminately by a professional who intends to remain profitable. It is a useful tool, however, that can be offered to the customer as an optional service.

SUMMARY

Recommendations from most labs for pounds of nutrient per acre or per thousand square feet only apply to plant needs and can prove to be useless or even injurious to the other organisms in the soil. If nutrients are added with consideration for the entire soil system, however, then the whole solar powered, biological turf growing machine can benefit.

It is usually not necessary to fine tune the soil. It does not respond like a high performance engine where subtle adjustments can tweak out another two to three more horsepower. Remember, the results of a soil test are an average of the area being evaluated. If inputs contain the raw materials needed for natural soil system mechanisms, then the system will function correctly.

IMPORTANT POINTS TO REMEMBER:

Take good samples – a lab analysis is useless if poor sampling procedures are implemented.

Choose a lab that gives the type of information needed on a timely basis.

Consider the needs of the soil as well as those of the plants.

Sources:

AAFCO 1990, **Official Publication 1990**. Association of American Feed Control Officials. Atlanta, GA.

AAPFCO 1990, **Official Publication #43**. Association of American Plant Food Control Officials. West Lafayette, IN.

A & L Agronomy Handbook. A & L Laboratories. Memphis, TN; Omaha, NE; Ft Wayne, IN; Lubbock, TX; Richmond, VA; Modesto, CA; Ft Lauderdale, FL.

Albrecht, W.A. 1938, **Loss of Organic Matter and its Restoration**. U.S. Dept. of Agriculture Yearbook 1938, pp347-376.

Arshad, M.A. and G.M. Coen, 1992, **Characterization of Soil Quality: Physical and Chemical Criteria**. American Journal of Alternative Agriculture v7 #1 and 2, 1992 pp 25-31. Institute for Alternative Agriculture, Greenbelt, MD.

Brady, N.C. 1974, **The Nature and Properties of Soils**. MacMillan Publishing Co. Inc. New York, NY.

Chu, P. 1993, Personal Communication. A&L Eastern Agricultural Labratories. Richmond, VA.

Craul P.J. 1992, **Urban Soil in Landscape Design**. John Wiley and Sons, Inc. New York, NY.

Dest, W.M., S.C. Albin, and K. Guillard, 1992, **Turfgrass Clipping Management**. Rutgers Turfgrass Proceedings 1992. Rutgers University, New Brunswick, NJ.

Huang, P.M. and M. Schnitzer 1986, **Interactions of Soil Minerals with Natural Organics and Microbes**. Soil Science Society of America, Inc. Madison, WI.

Jenny, H. 1941, **Factors of Soil Formation**. McGraw - Hill Book Co. New York, NY.

Lennert, L. 1990, **The Role of Iron in Turfgrass Management in Wisconsin**. USGA TGIF #:17611.

Leslie, A.R. (editor) 1994, **Handbook of Integrated Pest Management for Turf and Ornamentals**. Lewis Publishers. Boca Raton, FL.

Lucas, R.E. and M.L. Vitosh, 1978, **Soil Organic Matter Dynamics**. Michigan State Univ. Research Report 32.91, Nov 1978. East Lansing, MI.

Makarov, I.B. 1986, **Seasonal Dynamics of Soil Humus Content**. Moscow University Soil Science Bulletin, v41 #3: 19-26.

Nelson, E.B. 1994, **More Than Meets the Eye: The Microbiology of Turfgrass Soils**. Turf Grass Trends, v3#2, February 1994. Washington, DC.

NRAES, 1992, **On Farm Composting Handbook**. Northeast Regional Engineering Service #54, Cooperative Extension. Ithaca, NY.

Sachs, P.D. 1993, **Edaphos: Dynamics of a Natural Soil System**. Edaphic Press. Newbury, VT.

Senn, T.L. 1987, **Seaweed and Plant Growth**. No publisher noted. Department of Horticulture, Clemson University. Clemson, SC.

Senn, T.L. and A.R. Kingman, 1973, **A Review of Humus and Humic Acids**. Clemson Univ. Research Series #145, March 1, 1973. Clemson, SC.

SSSA# 19. 1987, **Soil Fertility and Organic Matter as Critical Components of Production Systems**. Soil Science Society of America, Inc. Madison, WI.

Waksman, S.A. 1936, **Humus**. Williams and Wilkins, Inc. Baltimore, MD.

White, W.C. and Collins, D.N. (Editors) 1982, **The Fertilizer Handbook**. The Fertilizer Institute. Washington, DC.

Chapter 6
Fertility

The amount of fertilizer applied on home lawns in the U.S. is vast. In 1984 the EPA estimated that more fertilizer was applied to American lawns than the entire country of India applied to all of its food crops. Keep in mind that this is a country trying to feed nearly a billion people. In our quest for the perfect lawn we often provide lawns with a diet more analogous to what the fat lady at the circus might be fed as opposed to what a lean, fit, and healthy human would eat. And we usually serve this nutrition directly to the plants without any consideration for its digestive system, the soil. The benefit of natural fertilizer materials goes far beyond simple plant growth and color. These materials also feed an eclectic assortment of soil organisms that are essential components of a healthy turf ecosystem. Understanding the benefits of certain fertilizer products and the disadvantages of others is important to the lawn care professional. Confusion about all the different fertilizers on the market and the claims they make is understandable. Much of the confusion, however, will be eliminated in this chapter.

Organic does not mean natural, nor does it necessarily mean good. Technically, the definition of organic refers to a complex of chemical bonds between three elements: carbon (C), hydrogen (H), and oxygen (O). Traditionally, the word organic has meant anything that contains carbon compounds derived from living organisms. These different interpretations cast a shroud of confusion upon the world of lawn care professionals. Synthetic pesticides, for example, are almost all organic by the technical definition, but are prohibited by ecological practitioners that certify their services as organic (ELA 1995). Fertilizers that contain ingredients such as greensand or rock phosphate cannot be considered all organic because those ingredients do not contain organic carbon. However, both items are recommended for ecological lawn care. Urea, which is a synthetic form of nitrogen, is technically organic because of its carbon, hydrogen, and oxygen content, but it is prohibited by organic practitioners.

Defining organic when referring to fertilizers might be better accomplished by adding the word *natural*. That term, however, is also misconstrued by some consumers and misrepresented by some manufacturers. A natural organic fertilizer should be defined as a product that contains ingredients derived from plants or animals that have not been chemically changed by the manufacturer. Materials that fit into this definition are derived from plant and animal residues.

Many manufacturers add natural minerals such as rock phosphate or potash salts to enhance the nutritive value of their products. These ingredients are acceptable for use by organic standards, but they are not organic. Natural, inorganic amendments not only change the fertilizer, but in most parts of the United States, change the way in which the product must be labeled. A manufacturer can no longer label the fertilizer products as *natural organic* because the mineral ingredients are not organic.

Figure 6-1 shows the relationship between the four terms most commonly used to define inputs. Both natural-organic and synthetic-inorganic are relatively commonplace terms and well understood. But there are many examples of natural inorganic and synthetic organic materials. Lime, natural potash, phosphate rock and Chilean nitrate are all examples of natural inorganic materials. Urea is a well known example of synthetic organic.

Categorizing any of these materials as good or bad based solely on the terms in figure 6-1 is inappropriate. Judgment should be based on the physical and biological impact each material has on the soil.

This chapter attempts to analyze each elemental plant (and soil) nutrient, and to review some of the materials they are derived from. Emphasis is applied to those materials that are recommended by the Ecological Landscape Association (ELA), a Massachusetts based

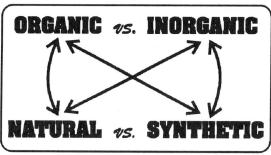

Figure 6-1

organization involved in organic certification of landscape and lawn care professionals. Table 6-1 shows a comparison of different fertility elements and how they relate to the four terms outlined in figure 6-1 (ELA 1995).

NITROGEN

For years lawn care professionals have disputed the benefits of organic versus inorganic nitrogen. There is no dispute that nitrogen is an essential element to plants. There is also no argument that plants can't tell the difference between organic and chemical nitrogen. The controversy is essentially about carbon.

Carbon and nitrogen react to each other a little like siblings. In plants, they function together to form amino acids, enzymes and proteins. In the soil, they can antagonize each other if they get out of balance. Too much carbon can immobilize available soil nitrogen. Carbon in the soil is in the form of organic matter and provides energy, either directly or indirectly, to all heterotrophs (living organisms that use carbon compounds directly from the residues of plants and other organisms). Soil carbon is produced by autotrophic organisms, such as plants and algae, that can fix carbon from the atmosphere by using energy from the sun. The carbon compounds produced by autotrophs eventually become part of a vast warehouse of energy and protein known as soil organic matter. This warehouse functions beneficially in thousands of different ways, but one essential purpose is to provide energy to soil life.

When fresh organic matter (OM) hits the soil, decay begins almost immediately, so long as it is during the seasons that microorganisms are active. What determines the speed at which organic

PRODUCT	ORGANIC	INORGANIC	NATURAL	SYNTHETIC	ALLOWED
Ammonium products	No	Yes	No	Yes	No
Blood meal	Yes	No	Yes	No	Yes
Feather meal	Yes	No	Yes	No	Yes
Leather meal	Yes	No	Yes	No	Yes
Vegetable Protein meal	Yes	No	Yes	No	Yes
Animal tankage	Yes	No	Yes	No	Yes
Dried whey	Yes	No	Yes	No	Yes
Fish meal	Yes	No	Yes	No	Yes
Natural nitrate of soda	No	Yes	Yes	No	Restricted
Urea products	Yes	No	No	Yes	No
Rock phosphate	No	Yes	Yes	No	Yes
Black rock phosphate	No	Yes	Yes	No	Yes
Colloidal rock phosphate	No	Yes	Yes	No	Yes
Calcined rock phosphate	No	Yes	Yes	No	Yes
Soap phosphate	No	Yes	Yes	No	Yes
Raw bone meal	Yes	Yes	Yes	No	Yes
Steamed bone meal	Yes	Yes	Yes	No	Yes
Precipitated bone meal	No	Yes	?	?	Yes
Precipitated milk phosphate	No	Yes	?	?	Yes
Super phosphate	No	Yes	No	Yes	No
Triple super phosphate	No	Yes	No	Yes	No
Ash	No	Yes	Yes	No	Yes
Greensand	No	Yes	Yes	No	Yes
Sulfate of potash	No	Yes	Yes	No	Yes
Sulfate of potash, magnesia	No	Yes	Yes	No	Yes
Muriate of potash	No	Yes	Yes	No	No
Trace elements	No	Yes	No	Yes	Restricted
Compost	Yes	No	Yes	No	Yes
Kelp meal	Yes	No	Yes	No	Yes
Seaweed Extract	Yes	No	Yes	No	Yes
Humates	Yes	No	Yes	No	Yes
Beneficial bacteria	Yes	No	Yes	No	Yes
Ground limestone	No	Yes	Yes	No	Yes
Aragonite	No	Yes	Yes	No	Yes
Gypsum	No	Yes	Yes	No	Yes
Epsom salts	No	Yes	Yes	No	Yes

Table 6-1

matter is decomposed (with adequate air and moisture) is the carbon:nitrogen ratio (C:N) of the organic matter. The C:N ratio is always measured as x parts carbon to one part nitrogen. If the C:N ratio is high (meaning the carbon is high), such as in straw or wood chips, decomposition occurs slowly. Also, the available nitrogen in the soil is temporarily immobilized by decay bacteria for the formulation of their own protein. If the original organic litter has a narrow C:N ratio, such as grass clippings or animal wastes, decomposition will occur more rapidly and nitrogen is made available to other organisms, including plants. Each time the components of organic matter are digested by heterotrophs some energy is used, and carbon is oxidized into carbon dioxide (CO_2) that is released back into the atmosphere.

Figure 6-2 shows how carbon moves from the atmosphere to the soil and back into the atmosphere. Carbon dioxide in the atmosphere is absorbed by plants and transformed into carbohydrates, proteins and other organic compounds. These compounds are essentially storage batteries containing energy that was originally derived from the sun. If the plant is consumed by animals, some of the original energy is used and CO_2 is released back into the atmosphere. If the animal is consumed by another animal, more of the energy is used and more CO_2 is released. Eventually the remaining energy is returned to the soil in the form of animal residues where decay organisms can use it. If plant residues are introduced directly to the

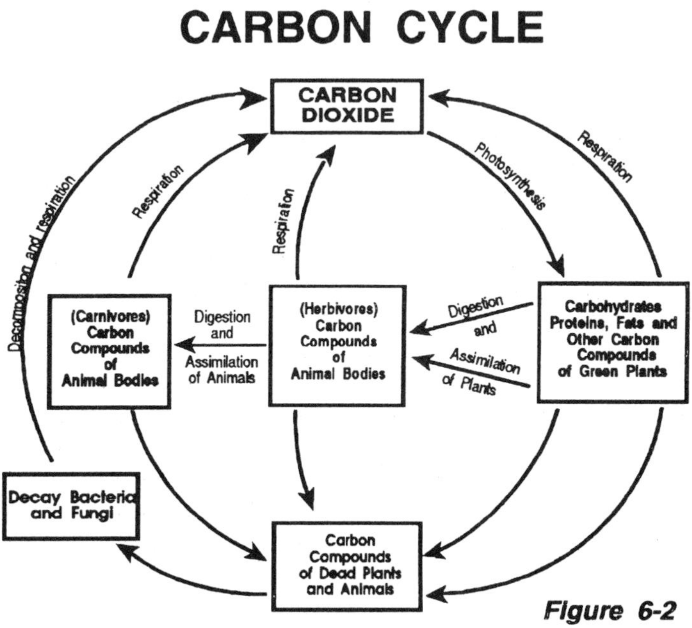

CARBON CYCLE

Figure 6-2

soil without prior consumption, more energy, in the form of carbon, will be available to soil microbes.

Nitrogen (N) serves the microbe as much as (or more than) it serves the plant. If there is only enough nitrogen in the soil for either the plant or the needs of microbes, the microbes will get it first.

When inorganic nitrogen is applied to the soil it stimulates populations of decay bacteria as well as plants. If used judiciously, it can have a synergistic effect with organic matter to increase overall nitrogen efficiency. Large populations of microbes can immobilize a significant portion of the inorganic N by converting it to protein and stabilizing it into a non-leachable, non-volatile organic nitrogen. When those organisms die, they are decomposed by other microbes and the N is slowly mineralized back into plant fertilizer. In order for soil micro-organisms to accomplish this, however, they must have energy in the form of organic carbon.

A problem occurs when inorganic N is applied on a constant, excessive, and indiscriminate basis, causing organic residues to be decomposed too rapidly. Not only is no organic carbon being added to the soil, but the decomposition of the existing organic residues is being accelerated. Figure 6-3 shows the reaction of two different families of soil bacteria (i.e. nitrogen fixers and decomposers) to the introduction of inorganic N fertilizer. The nitrogen fixing bacteria are, in this case, symbiotic to the roots of alfalfa plants. However, non-symbiotic nitrogen fixers react in the same way. The presence of inorganic N makes it unnecessary for these organisms to fix atmospheric nitrogen. They have essentially gone on the dole. The decomposers, on the other hand, are often stimulated into a feeding frenzy, resulting in the release of organic N and the recycling of carbon back to the atmosphere in the form of CO_2 at a significantly faster pace. Another consequence of heavy N applications is the production of excessive thatch. This can lead to other problems including insect pests, greater potential for disease, and decreased drought tolerance. Many inorganic sources of N slowly increase the acidity of the soil, creating the need for lime. The more these materials are used, the more lime will be needed. Broad fluctuations in the soil pH can lead to other problems that require expensive inputs to arrest.

INFLUENCE OF INORGANIC N
ON NATURAL N SYSTEMS
(ALFALFA PLANTS)

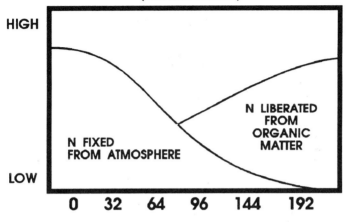

LBS INORGANIC N/A ADDED TO SOIL

Figure 6-3

In 1950, a ton of inorganic fertilizer would, on average, boost yields of grain by forty-six tons. By the early 1980's, the gain from that same ton of fertilizer was only thirteen tons of grain (Worldwatch 1987). The response difference may be due largely to the depleted level of energy that is not being replaced by the inorganic inputs.

A solution to this problem is to use natural organic nitrogen whenever possible, or small amounts of inorganic nitrogen mixed with sufficient quantities of organic matter such as compost, green manures or other sources of organic carbon. Natural organic nitrogen contains organic carbon, which can replenish the soil's energy reserves. Carbon is an essential component in sustaining the cyclical nature of the soil system and can help to balance the effect inorganic nitrogen has on the soil.

Figure 6-4 illustrates the natural cycle of nitrogen in the soil. It is important to note that this cycle would be physically impossible if carbon were not combined with nitrogen at the *Green Plants* stage. The carbon is essential for all the other functions in the cycle to occur.

NITROGEN CYCLE

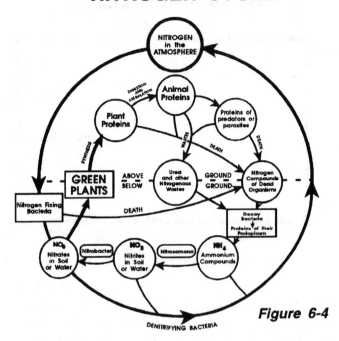

Figure 6-4

Stable compost, with a C:N ratio of approximately 15-20:1, has much to offer in terms of soil conditioning — including large populations of beneficial bacteria, essential nutrients, and plenty of carbon. However, its nitrogen analysis at one to three percent would mean applications of between 1,500 and 4,400 lbs. to receive forty-four lbs. N per acre (one lb N/1,000 sq.ft.). Compost is usually affordable, unless it has to be trucked over long distances, and it can be spread through most top dressing machines. Researchers at Cornell University and elsewhere have recently found that high quality, well aged compost (more than two years) can also suppress many turf diseases. Products that contain a higher C:N ratio than 25-30:1 are probably not appropriate nitrogen sources. If the C:N ratio is too high, the nitrogen content is not sufficient to sustain the growing populations of decomposition bacteria. In addition, other sources of soil nitrogen are temporarily depleted.

Meals ground from beans or seeds usually contain a C:N ratio of approximately 7:1 but if shells are mixed in, the carbon value can get higher. Animal by-products such as feather meal, blood meal or leather meal contain somewhere between three and eight parts carbon to one part nitrogen.

The C:N ratio of raw manures varies considerably depending on the animal it is derived from, that animal's diet, and the type and amount of bedding that is mixed with it. Raw manures are an impractical source of nutrient for turf. They are difficult to apply, are esthetically displeasing, can offend one's olfactory senses, are often replete with weed seed, and contain nitrogen that is unstable. Composting manures prior to application, rather than using them raw, is a very practical solution.

Many companies claim that their products contain organic nitrogen; however, they may be deriving it from urea-based ingredients. Urea is synthetic organic nitrogen with a C:N ratio of 0.4:1 and offers very little carbon to the biological activity in the soil. It has just enough carbon to call it organic.

True natural organic nitrogen is also protein. The mathematical relationship between protein and nitrogen is a ratio of 6.25. In other words, if a product has 6.25 percent protein it also has one

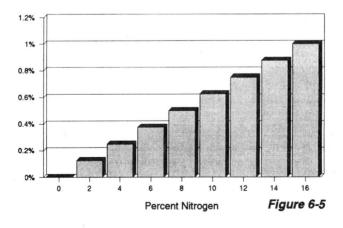

Relationship between
PROTEIN AND NITROGEN

Percent Nitrogen

Figure 6-5

percent nitrogen (see figure 6-5). It is physically impossible for any source of natural organic nitrogen to contain more than 16% N because it would also have to contain more than 100% protein.

Some companies mix inorganic nitrogen into fertilizer blends along with organic carbon from other sources. This combination can increase nitrogen efficiency if enough organic carbon is added. However, there is no set formula that determines the proper ratio. The C:N ratio in a natural soil system averages 12:1. Natural organic nitrogen from plant and animal proteins ranges from three to eight parts carbon to one part nitrogen. No research was found that could quantify the ideal C:N ratio of fertilizers. Common sense dictates that C:N ratios somewhere between 12:1 (soil) and 3:1 (high N animal protein) would be appropriate. Heavy use of a nitrogen fertilizer with an overall C:N ratio of less than 2:1 could eventually lead to some soil problems.

Sources of organic nitrogen vary in C:N ratios, and unfortunately, C:N information is usually not available on bagged, natural organic fertilizers. The only way to find out the C:N ratio of organic fertilizer is either to have it tested or to ask the manufacturer to do so. Some companies may already know the C:N ratio of their products. Table 6-2 indicates the C:N ratio of various ingredients. Feeding nitrogen into the soil is absolutely necessary at times, but applying it without carbon can eventually cause more problems than it is worth. Natural organic sources of nitrogen are derived from proteins in plant and animal residues. The N in animal manures is utilized in large quantities by farmers for crops and by manufacturers who compost or ferment and bag it for sale to consumers at garden centers. Composting and fermentation chemically change the manure into a more stable form of fertilizer, but are accomplished by natural micro-organisms and the fertilizer is still considered a natural organic product. Composted manures are an excellent amendment to soils because of the high percentage of organic matter they contain, but they must be used in larger quantities because of their relatively low nitrogen content. To small scale gardeners, who have a tendency to overdose their soil with fertilizers anyway, this is a preferred material.

Some manure products are being produced by a new process that incorporates partial composting and quick drying. The result is a

INGREDIENT	C:N RATIO
Compost	10-50:1
Blood meal	4:1
Feather meal	4:1
Leather meal	4:1
Vegetable Protein meal	7-8:1
Animal tankage	3-5:1
Dried whey	7:1
Urea	0.4:1
Cow manure	11-30:1
Horse manure	22-50:1
Hen manure	3-10:1
Sheep manure	13-20:1

Table 6-2

dry, granular manure that has a higher nitrogen content. This process of semi-composting, however, will not stabilize all the N into a non-volatile, organic form; strong odors are often painfully evident once the bag is opened.

Other animal residues that contain nitrogen are blood meal, feather meal, hoof and horn meal, meat and bone meal, and leather meal. Some dairy by-products, such as dried whey, also contain some nitrogen. These products differ in nitrogen content but are all much higher than composted manures. Feathers and blood, for example, contain approximately 12-13% N, but blood will release it much faster than feathers. The other animal by-products listed above contain between 5% and 10% N and release it at varying rates, depending mostly on how finely they are ground.

Residues from plants that are high in protein are also useful as sources of nitrogen. Meals ground from beans or seeds such as peanut, cocoa or soy contain between 3% and 7% N. Most of these products are primarily used in animal feeds and priced as protein, however, which can make them prohibitively expensive as fertilizer ingredients. Sometimes the vegetable protein meals used in organic fertilizers have been rejected for feed because of aflatoxins (natural toxins that are a danger to livestock but innocuous in the soil). This rejection makes the material more economically practical for use as a fertilizer.

The only source of natural inorganic (mineral) nitrogen is a deposit of sodium nitrate that occurs in the Atacama Desert, located in Northern Chile. Chilean Nitrate (so called) is mined and purified through a physical process and is shipped around the world. This natural nitrate of soda contains 16% soluble N. Unlike many inorganic salts, Chilean Nitrate does not acidify the soil. It actually has a slightly neutralizing effect on soil pH.

As mentioned earlier, the difference between synthetic inorganic and natural organic nitrogen is carbon. Carbon is the fuel from which all living organisms derive their energy. The carbon cycle illustration (figure 6-2) shows how this essential element is taken out of the air by plants and utilized by every living thing on earth before being returned to the atmosphere as carbon dioxide. Also illustrated is the nitrogen cycle (figure 6-4). It is important to note that at the GREEN PLANTS stage nitrogen is combined with carbon to form proteins. This carbon is necessary for all the other functions in the cycle to occur.

SOURCES OF NITROGEN (N)

Blood meal contains approximately twelve percent N in a form that is broken down easily by soil organisms and made available to plants in a relatively short period of time. It is best utilized when lightly incorporated into the surface of the soil. Unfortunately, this ingredient is as expensive as it is good. Dried blood is used extensively as a feed ingredient because of its very high protein content (approximately 80% crude protein). This use makes the material scarce and costly as a fertilizer. Competing with the feed market makes many sources of natural organic nitrogen untouchable.

Feather meal, like blood, assays to about 12% nitrogen, but it is derived from a very different form of protein. Keratin, a protein that occurs in hair, hoofs, horns and feathers, is very indigestible when fed to animals as protein or introduced to the soil as fertilizer. The structure of keratin is very tight and not easily broken down by soil bacteria. This attribute makes feathers an excellent long term source of nitrogen but not appropriate for the plant's immediate needs. Many companies provide preliminary hydrolysis (i.e., decomposition) of feathers by autoclaving, a process that cooks the feathers with steam and pressure. This step requires energy and raises the cost, while only providing a disproportionate improvement in nitrogen availability. The microorganisms that seem to be most adept at degrading feathers are often found in the bird's manure. Therefore, a mixture of feathers and manure (from the same birds) will improve availability without increasing costs significantly. This practice would only be appropriate for farmers situated on or near feather producing operations. As processes are developed that make feathers a source of more available nitrogen, the costs will continue to rise – not only from the expense of the process, but also because the product becomes more attractive to the feed market as a digestible source of protein.

Leather meal is an excellent source of organic nitrogen, but unfortunately, its use as a fertilizer is laced with controversy over chromium, an element used in the tanning process. Leather meal that comes to fertilizer companies is usually the residue from the planer, a machine that evens the thickness of the hide. The planer shavings contain between 10 – 12% N and sometimes as much as 2.5% chromium. Chromium is used to stabilize the leather by increasing its resistance to decomposition, for a longer useful life. Leather manufacturers used to use aluminum but found that chromium lasted longer. The reaction of both aluminum and chromium in the soil are almost identical. In a pH that is appropriate for most crops, including turf, both elements become unavailable to plants.

Leather and chromium have been studied for more than forty years by researchers in universities, the USDA, and the leather industry. The general consensus among the academics is that it is innocuous to the soil environment when used as a fertilizer. Some disagree, of course. Most of the studies have shown that even under conditions where chromium is toxic to plants, it is still well beneath the toxic level for animals. In fact, some studies indicate that it is beneath the minimum daily nutritional requirement of most animals, including humans. Leather is generally not used as a feed but is allowed as a protein supplement for hogs, which makes it more affordable for use as a fertilizer.

Vegetable protein meals (VPM) (e.g. cocoa meal, soybean meal, cottonseed meal, peanut meal) are usually lower in N than animal by-products, but higher in carbon. Many VPM are used in animal feeds. This can increase the cost beyond a reasonable level for fertilizers. Many are waste components of the feed or food industry, however, making them attractive ingredients for natural fertilizers. Some VPM are tested regularly for aflatoxins (a natural toxin produced by fungi) before being used in feed rations. These toxins can be lethal to animals but are innocuous in the soil. A positive test showing as little as two parts per billion can send a one hundred ton rail car load to the landfill. Fortunately, those rejected VPM can be used as valuable components of natural fertilizers. Many, such as soy meal, cottonseed meal and peanut meal contain 6 – 8% N along with some phosphorus (P) and potassium (K). Ground cocoa shells and coffee wastes are typically around 2 – 4% N. VPM are excellent ingredients for natural fertilizers because of their consistency, nutrient value and organic carbon content.

Wood humate is a dried pulping solid from the paper industry. Wood fibers that are screened as inappropriate for the manufacturing of certain types of papers are digested anaerobically and biologically converted to fertilizer. There are no bleaches, colors, or other contaminates to contend with because the fibers are screened out at a stage of the manufacturing process that precedes the addition of those contaminates. The fibers have been soaked in anhydrous ammonia to soften them and the ammonia is converted into protein by anaerobic organisms. The process is similar to the conversion of ammonia in manures to the proteins in compost. Wood humate is not used as a feed supplement and, therefore, is more moderately priced for use as a fertilizer.

Animal tankage (AT) is the dried, ground remains of a slaughterhouse operation and contains mostly meat and bone meal. An analysis of 9-4-0 (N-P-K) is not uncommon with this ingredient. AT is also used in the feed industry for protein and phosphorus. Aside from its high cost, there is also the problem of putrefaction. When meat begins to break down biologically it can produce strong odors, especially if it is not turned into the soil. These smells can be offensive and attract animals which may cause damage to lawns.

Dried whey is the dehydrated residue of the cheese making industry. Dried whey is usually very expensive because of its value as a feed ingredient, but some whey processing companies are drying the residues from their cleaning operation. These residues usually contain some acids used to separate the whey from the pipes and tanks of a facility, making it unsuitable for animal nutrition and less expensive for fertilizer use. Unfortunately, very few companies are doing this and the availability of this waste resource is limited. As organic waste disposal regulations become more strict, however, more of this product may become available. With a typical analysis of 5-9-1(N-P-K), whey is also an excellent source of phosphorus.

Fish meal has a typical analysis of 10-0-0, but it is not as good as it looks. Again, competition from the feed industry makes fish meal prohibitively expensive to use as a fertilizer. Odors from this product can cause real problems with animal pests, not to mention hired help. The meal is often too dusty to apply through conventional equipment. Fish emulsion, the soluble portion of the protein from fish waste, is often used in agriculture or horticulture, but commonly only as a supplement in a soil fertility program. Actual soil improvement is rarely accomplished with strictly liquid feeding programs because very little organic matter is being applied. Odors are often a problem with the emulsion, too. Some companies have successfully added odor masks, or neutralizers such as citrus extract, to mitigate the problem.

Natural nitrate of soda (NNS) is not an organic source of nitrogen. However, it is natural and is allowed in moderate quantities by the ELA. Called Chilean Nitrate, NNS is a mined product of a desert in northern Chile, the only known deposit of this mineral salt in the world. NNS has an analysis of 16-0-0 and is considered soluble. NNS is commonly used in New England and elsewhere on organic farms as a form of nitrogen that is available to plants in cold soils. The microbial activity needed to mineralize natural organic nitrogen (protein) is suppressed during those times of the year when the soil is cold.

The sodium (Na) content of sodic soils makes NNS incompatible in arid and semi-arid regions. It contains 26% Na. Na, in small quantities, does not cause damage to the soil ecosystem. Plants can use this element, and it is an essential nutrient for most animals and other organisms. The nitrate is used directly by the plant and does not need to be biologically processed. Microorganisms, however, will also use this source of nitrogen for the production of protein and amino acids. Applying NNS along with an organic amendment, such as cocoa meal, peanut meal or compost, will increase the efficiency of both products. NNS should not be relied upon as a sole source of N.

Urea is a synthetic organic source of N made from natural gas. Although urea contains some carbon, it is not enough to provide any significant energy to the soil. Unless urea is coated or processed in some way to slow its release into the environment, or immediately incorporated into the soil, its N can volatilize (i.e., be lost into the atmosphere). Urea contains 46% N. Like nitrate of soda, urea should be used along with an organic amendment to increase its efficiency. Groups that certify landscape services as organic usually prohibit the use of urea.

Ammoniated nitrogen fertilizers are also made from natural gas. These materials offer soluble and available nitrogen directly to the plant. A big disadvantage of using ammoniated products is the acidification of the soil. Changes in pH can occur from repeated use of ammonia products. Ammonia compounds are also unstable, and under some conditions, much of the nitrogen content can be lost into the atmosphere. Ammoniated products vary in nitrogen content, and the final analysis depends on the type of material ammonium is reacting with. Pure ammonia contains 82% nitrogen.

PHOSPHORUS

The occurrence of phosphorus (P) in any form can be traced back to mineral deposits of phosphate rock (apatite). Bone meal contains P that the animal derived from plants, and those plants probably utilized P from some form of rock phosphate. Neither pure bone meal nor rock phosphate are considered organic because they do not contain carbon. They are, however, natural and recommended by groups such as the ELA. The leftover protein residues in raw bone meal (not removed by steam or precipitation processing) are organic, but raw bone meal is not used by many manufacturers because of strong odors that can offend the user and attract animal pests into gardens. Organic phosphorus occurs in manures and in plant residues, but usually in relatively small quantities; plants use less phosphorus during their growth period compared to other macro nutrients. The exceptions are dairy by-products that contain a concentrated amount of available phosphate. Some of these by-products are organic (i.e., contain carbon) and some are not. Organic gardeners or land care specialists who need to correct P deficiencies usually look to natural mineral (inorganic) sources such as bone meal or rock phosphate, rather than to natural organic ones.

Conventional phosphate fertilizer is made by reacting phosphoric acid with rock phosphate to form triple super phosphate. Another popular formula is to combine ammonia with phosphoric acid to form either MAP (monoammonium phosphate) or DAP (diammonium phosphate). All three forms are considered by organic standards to be highly acidifying to soils, and to cause pH related problems. In addition, a high percentage of their total phosphate content is in an available form, making them susceptible to: 1) Fixation, because available phosphate bonds easily to many different soil constituents making them and itself unavailable and; 2) Causing pollution, because surface run off will carry dissolved phosphate into rivers and streams causing eutrophication.

SOURCES OF PHOSPHORUS

Rock phosphate (RP) is a mined raw material used in the production of most of the refined phosphate products on earth. Huge deposits in the southern United States and elsewhere in the world are thought to have been formed by the accumulation of fossil shells on the ocean floor (over a period of millions of years) and brought to the surface by some broad tectonic event.

Phosphate rock is also known as the mineral *apatite*, a chemically impure tri-calcium phosphate. RP is mostly insoluble. Only three of the 30% total phosphate content is considered readily available. Because of its insoluble nature, it has to be finely ground to be of any use in agriculture or horticulture. However, this process makes it dusty and difficult to work with. Applications of RP are usually much heavier than its chemically refined cousins but can last five years or more before another application is needed. Although its release in the soil is slow, it is often more efficient. The level of available phosphate from RP is largely dependent upon microbial activity, which typically coincides with the season of plant growth. In conventional fertilizers, a highly available phosphate is subject to losses from surface runoff or chemical fixation in the soil. It is thought that RP also stimulates the growth of populations of beneficial microbes, increasing the soil system's efficiency. Aside from its phosphate content, RP also contains 33% calcium and has one-fifth the neutralizing value of lime. Because RP is a natural raw material, it also contains some trace minerals.

Black rock phosphate (BRP) like RP is an apatite mineral found in the Carolinas. Its consistency is more coarse, like sand, and it is easier to handle. Black rock gets its name and color from the small amount of (inorganic) carbon it contains. Laboratory tests indicate that BRP has a higher amount of available phosphate (from 4% to 8% depending on the lab) than finely ground rock phosphate. Like RP, BRP contains calcium and a list of trace elements.

Colloidal rock phosphate (CRP) (also called soft rock phosphate) is a waste product from the phosphate mining industry. Rock phosphate is first washed before it is shipped to refineries. The residues from the procedure are stored in large lagoons and are dried by the sun. A material is left that contains 18% phosphate (2% available), 21% calcium and a plethora of trace minerals. Unlike RP and BRP, CRP contains colloidal clay, a very fine clay particle that can help bind sandy soils, enabling them to retain more water and nutrients. Because of the fineness of these particles, CRP can be dusty and difficult to work with.

Calcined rock phosphate is rock phosphate that has been heated. The process weakens the chemical bond between calcium and phosphorus and creates a product with a higher amount of available phosphate. Phosphate is usually calcined for a specific use and is rarely available as a waste by-product.

Soap phosphate (also called organophos) is a calcined rock phosphate that the soap industry used as a whitener in detergents. When it became unlawful to sell detergents with phosphates in most states, however, soap companies were forced to remove it from their products. The recovered waste was then used as a fertilizer ingredient. Very few soap manufacturers are using phosphates as cleaning agents now; consequently, soap phosphate is scarce.

Raw bone meal comes from raw, uncooked bones that are ground and packaged. The protein residues from meat, cartilage and marrow contribute from 5% to 7% nitrogen to this amendment. The phosphate content typically ranges from 12 – 18%. Raw bone meal is also used in the feed industry and can be expensive. Some of the problems associated with using raw bone meal are the odors from the putrefying protein, the pests attracted by the smell, and the increase in labor required because of its moist and caked consistency that makes it difficult to spread.

Steamed bone meal is raw bone that has been put through a process similar to the steam cleaning of surgical tools. Because this step removes much of the protein residue, it produces a bone meal with lower nitrogen, fewer odors, and one that is easier to handle. The steaming process was originally developed to kill pathogens harmful to livestock who were being fed the bone meal. Steamed bone meal is expensive because of the energy needed for the process and the competition from the feed industry.

Precipitated bone meal (PBM) is a by-product of the gelatin industry. Certain protein residues attached to bones are necessary in the manufacture of gelatin. Part of the process requires the separation of phosphate from the other compounds. To do this, lime is mixed with bones which are dissolved in an acid solution. The calcium from the lime reacts with phosphorous from the bones to create a calcium phosphate compound. This compound precipitates out of solution and is dried to be used as an ingredient in feed and fertilizer. PBM contains approximately 45% phosphate, and because of its flour-like consistency, most of that is available. Unfortunately, the fine particles make the product dusty and difficult to work with. A few fertilizer companies are pelletizing it so that it will flow through conventional equipment.

There is no nitrogen in precipitated bone meal. PBM is used in the feed industry as a supplement providing calcium and phosphate, but is not in as much demand as a product containing protein. The product is relatively expensive, but because of its high phosphate content, calculates into much less per pound of P than any of the other bone meals.

Whey meal (see Dried Whey in the nitrogen section.)

Precipitated milk phosphate is made by essentially the same process that produces precipitated bone meal. Manufacturers extracting lactose from milk or whey react lime with the dissolved phosphate to precipitate out a calcium phosphate compound. The product contains approximately 23% total phosphate, of which 19-20% is available. Like precipitated bone meal, milk phosphate is dusty and difficult to work with. If the product were to be pelleted or granulated, it would be an ideal amendment for turf.

Super phosphate is made by reacting sulfuric acid with rock phosphate. The resulting compounds are an available phosphate and gypsum (calcium sulfate). This process creates a product with an analysis of 0-20-0 with 20% calcium and 12% sulfur. It is neutral in its reaction with the soil in that it does not alter soil pH. Unfortunately, this product is prohibited by the various committees that write standards for the production of organic or ecological turf. This is somewhat ironic because the same process occurs in nature when sulfur, oxidized by bacteria, combines with free hydrogen in the soil to form sulfuric acid. When the acid reacts with apatite rock, super phosphate is produced. The concern of the various certification committees is that, if too much available phosphate is applied at once, surface run-off can carry away some of the phosphate, causing pollution.

Triple super phosphate has a typical analysis of 0-46-0 and is made by reacting rock phosphate with phosphoric acid. Like Super Phosphate, Triple Super is also prohibited for use by certified organic practitioners.

Monoammonium and diammonium phosphate (MAP and DAP) are made by reacting ammonia with phosphoric acid. Varying the amounts of each component can create different ratios of nitrogen to phosphorus. MAP typically has a 12-52-0 analysis and DAP is usually graded at 18-46-0. Both are considered acidifying to the soil and are prohibited by ELA standards.

Sodium phosphate is a relatively rare material. It is usually a by-product of some manufacturing process and is often in a liquid form with a phosphate content of about 7% and sodium of about 6%. It is rarely used as a fertilizer because of its low analysis and the sodium content. It is, however, one of the few phosphorus compounds that is considered soluble.

POTASSIUM

Potassium, like phosphorus, is a mineral in its original form. When used by organisms it is changed into an organic form and occurs in the fluid portion of cells. If plant residues are burned the remaining ash contains much of the potassium (and other minerals) that the plant used during growth. The carbon content is released as carbon dioxide and other gases, however, and the remaining material can no longer be considered organic. Natural sources of potassium (K) include rock dusts, greensand, and potassium salts, such as sulfate of potash or sulfate of potash/magnesia. The ashes of various seeds' hulls — such as sunflower, barley or buckwheat — are also rich in potassium. Compost usually contains about 1% potash (K_2O) depending on what it is made from. This may appear to be an insignificant amount until you consider how much compost most gardeners apply to their soil. An application of compost with 1% potash that is spread approximately 1/4 inch thick contains nine pounds of potash per 1000 square feet.

Muriate of potash (potassium chloride) is a natural potassium salt, but is prohibited by organic certification groups because of the chloride content, which they feel can acidify soils and inhibit the activity of many beneficial micro-organisms.

SOURCES OF POTASSIUM

Ash - The term *potash* originally came from an old process where hot water was mixed with ashes and then filtered through sackcloth. The resulting solution, rich in dissolved potassium salts, was then dried and used as fertilizer. Farmers from that era may not have realized that there was more than just potash dissolved in the liquid. Ashes constitute most of the mineral accumulated by the plant over the course of its lifetime. These may include magnesium, calcium and trace minerals, depending on the type of plant and the environment in which it was growing. When using ash as a soil amendment it is a good idea to have it analyzed by a lab to see what one is actually applying. Sometimes applications of ash will create excessive levels of one nutrient while correcting the deficiency of another. Companies that broker ash for agricultural or horticultural use usually have it tested on a regular basis.

Greensand is a natural iron potassium silicate mineral also known as glauconite. It has the consistency of sand but is able to absorb ten times more moisture, making it an exceptional soil conditioner. Greensand contains potassium, iron, magnesium, calcium and phosphorus, plus as many as thirty other trace minerals.

Jersey greensand, so-called from its only known place of origin, New Jersey, was deposited millions of years ago when the Garden State was still under water. It is mined primarily for water purification purposes, but more and more people in the agriculture business are demanding it for the soil. Benefits from greensand are, for the most part, unexplainable. If one were to bring some into an agriculture science laboratory and asked for an analysis, the chemist would most likely tell you the product is worthless. Numerous greenhouse trials, however, show that there is much more to it than what someone might read on a lab report. For years, organic growers have extolled the virtues of greensand without really knowing how or why it has improved their crops. One possible explanation is the mineral content. The introduction of natural minerals has been shown to improve soil by increasing populations of microorganisms. Greensand is an insoluble source of potash and trace elements. If there is an immediate need for available potash, it is suggested that a more soluble form of potash be applied in conjunction with greensand.

Sulfate of potash, also known as potassium sulfate, is a naturally occurring potassium salt that contains 50 – 52% potash and 17% sulfur. Although sulfate of potash is soluble, it is accepted by most organic certification groups as a means to add potash to the soil. Soluble potash should be applied in accordance with the soil's capacity to hold cation nutrients (see CEC in chapter 5).

Sulfate of potash, magnesia commonly referred to as Sul-po-mag or K-Mag (brand names), is also a natural mineral salt and typically contains 22% potash, 11% magnesium and 17% sulfur. Like sulfate of potash, Sul-po-mag is soluble but is an acceptable material to use in the practice of organic land care.

Muriate of Potash, or potassium chloride, is a naturally occurring potassium salt but is prohibited by certification groups. It is considered detrimental to the soil because of the chloride content, which these groups feel inhibits the growth and establishment of beneficial bacteria and lowers the pH of the soil. A factor to consider is that the potential acidity of muriate is theoretically equivalent to sixty seven pounds of lime per one hundred pounds of the material. As the pH of a soil becomes more acidic, populations of bacteria have a harder time surviving. Experiments have shown, however, that a soil environment with potassium from muriate of potash harbors far greater populations of microorganisms than an environment that is deficient in potassium.

TRACE ELEMENTS

Raw ingredients used to make natural fertilizers are inherently rich in trace nutrients. Mother nature likes diversity in the materials she creates. Humans, on the other hand, like to purify everything. Unfortunately, in doing so we tend to overlook the importance of those *contaminants* that we exclude. Trace elements are essential for plants of any kind. However, the subtle differences between not enough and too much can easily injure or kill plant organisms. In most cases mineral soils provide ample amounts of trace elements to plants. Often, when trace elements are deficient, the cause is other factors such as incorrect pH, soil atmosphere imbalances, nutrient imbalances, or inadequate weathering mechanisms in the soil. Because of the plant variety's constant demand for a specific nutrient, mono-cropping can also deplete the soil of certain trace elements. Turf can tolerate both high and low levels of trace elements. Experiments done at Cornell show relatively little response to significant changes in the trace element levels.

Iron is an exception. Turf will usually respond to small amounts of soluble iron with improved color and vitality. Many golf course superintendents will use iron instead of nitrogen to correct chlorosis when applications of nitrogen are inappropriate for one reason or another. Iron is usually abundant in the soil but can become unavailable when soil conditions such as high pH or excessive levels of phosphate, zinc, or manganese exist.

Commercial preparations of trace elements are usually in the form of mineral salts or synthetic chelates. Because plants are very sensitive to excess trace elements, applications of these materials should be in accordance with an accurate soil test. Natural fertilizers made from raw, unrefined materials usually contain a variety of trace elements, which are released at a rate relative to the level of biological activity in the soil. Kelp meal or seaweed extract are also good sources of trace elements.

Plants utilize trace elements in very small quantities for the formation of enzymes and other organic components. Once combined with organic compounds, they are called chelates. The more organic matter content in a soil, the richer it will be in chelates. Organic chelates are a major source of available micro-nutrients in the soil.

Natural sources of trace elements are in the form of both minerals and organic chelates. Most raw minerals such as rock phosphate, greensand, granite dust, and basalt are rich in trace elements, but they are insoluble and rely on biological activity and soil chemical reactions to make them available to plants. Organic sources include composts, manures, and green manures, but the trace mineral content of these sources will vary depending on how much of these elements were in the environment where these sources were produced.

When addressing trace element deficiencies, natural sources may not be appropriate to use. The diversity of elements in natural materials may be fine for maintaining a balanced level in the soil, but these materials do not have enough of any one element to address a specific deficiency. For this reason, most organic certification groups allow synthetic, inorganic sources of trace elements to be used on a restricted basis. The use of concentrated commercial preparations of trace elements is not allowed without justification from a soil test.

Some manufacturers produce synthetic chelates containing specific trace elements which are in a highly available form. Others produce salts or oxides that contain trace elements, also in an available form. Great care must be taken when using these products because there is an extremely fine line between not enough and toxic levels of some trace elements.

OTHER AMENDMENTS

Manure has been used as a means of renewing soil fertility for hundreds of years. It is natural, it contains significant levels of organic carbon, and it provides both soluble and insoluble nitrogen, along with most other essential plant nutrients But, surprisingly, it is unacceptable to use in a certified organic program except in a few circumstances. Raw, uncomposted manure can cause some problems. Its nitrogen, for example, can be volatile. It is estimated that half of the nitrogen from topically applied manure is lost either by volatilization or leaching. Raw manure is impractical to use on turf. It is difficult to spread and smells awful. If manure is converted into compost, however, it becomes the quintessential soil amendment for turf.

Compost used to be referred to as artificial manure back in the early part of this century. If made correctly, it solves most of the problems associated with using raw manure. Compost provides a stable source of nutrients and organic matter with no danger of weed production and no safety or environmental controversy. It is the quintessential fertilizer. In situations where it is the only available source of plant nutrients, the fertility and tilth of the soil improve immeasurably. Many turf problems associated with environmental stress are mitigated or disappear when compost is used. The nitrogen in compost has, through a biological process, been converted into protein which will not leach or volatilize into the atmosphere. The mineral content is organically bound, for the most part, making for easy access by soil organisms. The organic matter from compost adds significantly to the water and nutrient holding capacity of the soil. The drawbacks to compost are in the shipping and handling of the product. Its freight sensitive nature requires a relatively local source, and unless one is using a topdressing machine or manure spreader, the only way to apply compost is manually, with a shovel.

Kelpmeal is a source of naturally chelated trace elements that can increase the health of both the soil and plants. Unfortunately, the product is very expensive to use as a soil amendment unless it is locally available (it is found on coastal shores) and can be easily dried and ground. The more practical method of using kelpmeal is as an animal feed supplement. This improves production from the animal and enriches the manure for use in compost. This may be impractical if the lawn steward is not a part time farmer. A more economical method is to use the concentrated extract from seaweed.

Seaweed extract is produced by dissolving many of the chelated trace elements and growth hormones from the seaweed plant and either bottling it as a liquid or drying it into a soluble powder. Seaweed extract is used for a variety of purposes including improved seed germination, disease and insect resistance, inhibiting senescence, stimulating root growth, and providing essential chelated micro-nutrients that are needed for the production of vital enzymes. The growth hormones in seaweed extract have been shown to increase significantly a turf's resistance to stress. These hormones are produced naturally by most plants, but the production is inhibited by stress such as extremes in temperature, drought or reproduction. If external sources are available, the plant can weather environmental stress conditions that naturally occur, becoming a stronger organism. The plants are then better able to resist problems (such as disease or insect attack) to which weaker plants are more susceptible. Seaweed extract does not usually carry a guaranteed N-P-K analysis on its label because it is not a fertilizer. It is more accurately classified as a bio-stimulant. Seaweed extract can be applied as a foliar or root feed, but is always used as a liquid. It is a relatively inexpensive product and recommended by ELA (ELA 1995).

Humates are naturally occurring components of humus mined from rich organic deposits such as old peat bogs. They are also classified as bio-stimulants. Humates improve the nutrient and water holding capacity of the soil. Their most significant value, however, is somewhat of a mystery. Research has shown that plants can use some organic compounds from humates and exhibit favorable growth responses. Humates occur naturally in a healthy soil. Some researchers have shown that added humates have little or no effect in soils that are already rich in organic matter. Others dispute those findings, showing favorable responses in a variety of conditions. Common sense dictates that there is a maximum response grass plants can exhibit.

Beneficial bacteria are used as an inoculant by many companies that make natural fertilizers and bio-stimulants. There is evidence that the use of these organisms has an enhancing effect, but many experts argue that the natural indigenous bacteria will provide as good, if not better, inoculation if given the fuel needed for growth. The bacteria used in commercial preparations are usually substrate specific, meaning that they are adept at breaking down specific components of organic matter and will not compete for survival very well if that substrate is unavailable. Others argue that the competition from naturally occurring bacteria is too overwhelming for introduced varieties to be effective. Since there are probably no two environmental situations on earth that are identical, it would be difficult to identify instances where these organisms are beneficial and where they are not. The use of beneficial bacteria is, at best, an efficient method of stimulating necessary bio-activity or, at worst, a waste of some time and money.

Ground limestone (calcium/magnesium carbonate) is both a pH neutralizer and a source of calcium and/or magnesium. The carbonate component of lime is what neutralizes soil pH by chemically converting hydrogen ions into water and carbon dioxide. Calcium and magnesium are essential plant nutrients. Lime is a critical component of agriculture and horticulture but it is possible to have too much. Soils with excessive lime foster high populations of bacteria that can use up too much of the soil's energy at once, accelerating the depletion of organic matter. A high pH can also limit the availability of many trace elements in the soil.

Aragonite is a calcium carbonate mineral (like limestone) that comes from sea shells such as oyster shell. It is used in lieu of lime in situations where the soil is already high in magnesium, and dolomite (high magnesium limestone) is the only liming material available. Aragonite has approximately 89% of the neutralizing value of lime.

Gypsum or calcium sulfate is a naturally mined product containing 23% calcium and 17% sulfur. Gypsum is used extensively where calcium is needed and a pH change is not desired. Because gypsum contains no carbonate or oxides it does not neutralize hydrogen. It is also used to alleviate compaction in certain clay soils where a chemical reaction with gypsum causes some granulation. Gypsum is sometimes used to de-salinate soils where road salt has caused damage. There is also some anecdotal evidence that it can provide some insect control for certain turf pests, such as chinch bugs or grubs (university data is not yet available).

Epsom salts (magnesium sulfate), is used where magnesium deficiencies occur in already alkaline conditions. Magnesium oxide (mag-ox) is a more common and a less expensive source, and because of its concentration (60% Mg) mag-ox has only a minimal effect on pH.

BLENDED FERTILIZERS

Soil amendments that offer only one or two primary or secondary macro-nutrients should be used only for correcting deficiencies of those nutrients or for balancing excessively high levels of other nutrients. Mixing natural amendments together as a blended, complete fertilizer is a practical method of offering the soil a broad selection of nutrients that both plants and soil organisms can benefit from and process as needed. Mixing can also mitigate labor costs and energy consumption by reducing the number of trips a spreader travels over a field. Companies that blend fertilizers can customize mixes to suit a particular soil condition or specific crop needs. If nutrients are introduced as raw materials, however, there is some natural control over what is made available and what is not by soil organisms. Blended fertilizers can also be physically processed into a granular consistency for easy, dust-free spreading. There is no particularly ideal ratio of nutrients for turf because different soil and climatic conditions across the country affect the needs of the plants and soil organisms. In terms of the actual amount of nutrients used by grass plants, however, a N-P-K ratio of somewhere around 3-1-2 has been recommended by some labs and extension specialists. This does not mean that ratios which vary slightly are inappropriate nor does it mean that a 3-1-2 ratio is appropriate everywhere. If a soil test analysis indicates that phosphorus and potassium levels are very high, a 1-0-0 ratio may be more suitable.

THE FERTILIZER LABEL

In the U.S., companies that produce fertilizers for sale must comply with labeling laws. These laws are written and enforced by each state, and although uniform guidelines are recommended, the states sometimes differ in their labeling requirements. Most states, however, require that a fertilizer label contain the information that follows (see also figure 6-6):

1. Net weight expressed in pounds and in Kilograms (optional).

2. Manufacturer's name and address.

3. Grade. This is a brief outline of the guaranteed analysis in the format: N-P-K. N represents the total nitrogen, P is the available phosphoric acid or phosphate and K is for soluble potash.

UNIFORM FERTILIZER LABEL

NET WEIGHT
BRAND
GRADE (N-P-K)
GUARANTEED MINIMUM ANALYSIS

Total Nitrogen (N)	?.?%
?.?% Water Insoluble Nitrogen	
?.?% Water Soluble Nitrogen	
?.?% Ammoniacal Nitrogen	
?.?% Nitrate Nitrogen	
?.?% Urea Nitrogen	
Avail. Phosphate as (P2O5)	?.?%
Soluble Potash (K2O)	?.?%

SOURCE OF NUTRIENTS (DERIVED FROM:)
NAME AND ADDRESS OF MANUFACTURER

Figure 6-6

4. Brand name that the manufacturer has given to the product.

5. Guaranteed minimum analysis is the manufacturer's guarantee of the plant nutrients contained in the package or bulk load. The nitrogen value always indicates the total amount of nitrogen. Most states require that the different types of nitrogen (e.g. water soluble and water insoluble, ammoniacal and nitrate) be described just below where the total nitrogen appears. The percentages in this description must add up to the same value given for total nitrogen. Phosphorus is always expressed as available phosphate (P_2O_5) and potassium, as soluble potash (K_2O).

The guaranteed analysis can also include secondary macro-nutrients such as calcium, magnesium and sulfur, or trace elements that are considered essential to plant growth. In many states, bio-stimulants, soil conditioners and long term (slow release) insoluble minerals are not allowed to be mentioned on the label. Fertilizer labels always express the phosphorus content of the product in terms of available phosphoric acid or available phosphate (P_2O_5). P_2O_5 is not phosphoric acid or phosphate, however, and it is not a form of phosphorus that plants use. Phosphoric acid is actually expressed as H_3PO_4, and phosphate is an ion expressed as PO_4. Plants use phosphorus as HPO_4, H_2PO_4 and, in some cases, H_3PO_4. The only condition under which P_2O_5 exists is when phosphate is heated to 650° C. The same is true for K_2O (so-called soluble potash). Heating phosphate and potash is a common way of testing for their content. Consequently, plant food control officials require labeling in this manner.

6. The *derived from* list is a list of materials used to obtain the guaranteed analysis. It does not include any soil conditioners, etc. that may be present in the blend. If the consumer wants to be discriminating about the kind of fertilizer ingredients he uses, however, this is an important section of the label to check.

7. Some states require that the *potential acidity* of the fertilizer be expressed on the label in terms of the amount of lime (calcium carbonate) it would take to neutralize it. A few states want to see the amount of chlorine in the fertilizer on the label.

The aim of all the labeling regulations is to protect the consumer. Unfortunately, the more complex the label becomes, the less consumers will look at it; the label has to be read if it is going to provide protection.

CAN ORGANIC FERTILIZERS COMPLETELY REPLACE CHEMICALS?

The answer is YES. It is done all the time, but the switch must be accompanied by certain changes in cultural practices. The key ingredient to grow anything organically is information. You need to know why you have a problem, as opposed to how to treat the symptom.

The professional landscapers or lawn care specialists will find it somewhat easier to be organic than the food, feed or fiber producers. This is because they are not harvesting nutrients from the soil that inevitably must be replaced. To do the job without synthetic chemicals, however, lawn stewards must have an understanding of the natural soil/plant system. They need to know how the system encourages growth, and at the same time, how it discourages problems. They also need to understand the limitations of their environment. Lawn care specialists who have been organic for many years have discovered that, if the soil system is fed and stimulated correctly, fewer inputs and less labor are required to grow better quality plants. In other words, more can often be accomplished by doing less.

Unfortunately, what most people really want to know when they ask whether organic fertilizers can completely replace chemical fertilizers is not, *"can I do what I'm doing organically?"* They want to know if they can substitute organic fertilizers for conventional ones in a chemical feeding program without modifying their cultural practices. The answer is **yes**, but don't expect a perfect fit.

Sources:

AAFCO, 1990, **Official Publication 1990**. Association of American Feed Control Officials. Atlanta, GA.

AAPFCO, 1990, **Official Publication #43**. Association of American Plant Food Control Officials. West Lafayette, IN.

Adams, W.A. and R.J. Gibbs, 1994, **Natural Turf for Sport and Amenity: Science and Practice**. CAB International. Wallingford, United Kingdom.

Bear, F.E. 1924, **Soils and Fertilizers**. John Wiley and Sons, Inc. New York, NY.

BioCycle Staff (editors) 1989, **The Biocycle Guide to Yard Waste Composting**. JG Press, Inc. Emmaus, PA.

BioCycle Staff (editors) 1991, **The Art and Science of Composting**. JG Press, Inc. Emmaus, PA.

Brady, N.C. 1974, **The Nature and Properties of Soils**. MacMillan Publishing Co. Inc. New York, NY.

Brown, H., R. Cook, and M. Gabel, 1976, **Environmental Design Science Primer**. Earth Metabolic Design. New Haven, CT.

Buchanan, M. and S.R. Gliessman 1991, **How Compost Fertilization Affects Soil Nitrogen and Crop Yield**. Biocycle, Dec. 1991. J.G. Press Emmaus, PA.

ELA 1995, **Ecological Landscape Association**. P.O. Box 1561, Greenfield, MA 01302-1561.

Elam, P. 1994, **Earthworms: We Need Attitude Adjustment**. Landscape Management July, 1994. Advanstar Communications. Cleveland, OH.

Franklin, S. 1988, **Building a Healthy Lawn: A Safe and Natural Approach**. Storey Communications, Inc. Pownal, VT.

Golueke, C.G. 1972, **Composting: A Study of the Process and its Principles**. Rodale Books, Inc. Emmaus, PA.

Hall, R. 1994, **Turf Pros Respond to Biostimulants**. Landscape Management, Oct. 94. Advanstar Communications. Duluth, MN.

Holland, E.A. and D.C. Coleman, 1987, **Litter Placement Effects on Microbial and Organic Matter Dynamics in an Agroecosystem.** Ecology v68 (2), 1987: 425-433.

King, F.H. 1911, **Farmers of Forty Centuries.** Rodale Publishing. Emmaus, PA.

Lennert, L. 1990, **The Role of Iron in Turfgrass Management in Wisconsin.** USGA TGIF #:1761.

Leslie, A.R. (editor) 1994, **Handbook of Integrated Pest Management for Turf and Ornamentals.** Lewis Publishers. Boca Raton, FL.

Minnich, J. and M. Hunt, 1979, **The Rodale Guide to Composting.** Rodale Press. Emmaus, PA.

NRAES, 1992, **On Farm Composting Handbook.** Northeast Regional Engineering Service #54, Cooperative Extension. Ithaca, NY.

Parns, R. 1986, **Organic & Inorganic Fertilizers.** Ag-Access Press. Davis, CA.

Roberts, J. 1995, **Spring Fertilization Jump Starts Turf.** Landscape Management, February 1995. Advanstar Communications. Cleveland, OH.

Sachs, P.D. 1993, **Edaphos: Dynamics of a Natural Soil System.** Edaphic Press. Newbury, VT.

Senn, T.L. 1987, **Seaweed and Plant Growth.** No publisher noted. Department of Horticulture, Clemson University. Clemson, SC.

Veen, A. van and P.J. Kuikman, 1990. **Soil Structural Aspects of Decomposition of Organic Matter by Micro-organisms.** Biogeochemistry, Dec. 1990, v11 (3): 213-233.

Wallace, A., G.A. Wallace, and W.C. Jong, 1990, **Soil Organic Matter and the Global Carbon Cycle.** Journal of Plant Nutrition 1990 v13 (3/4): 459-456.

Waksman, S.A. 1936, **Humus.** Williams and Wilkins, Inc. Baltimore, MD.

White, W.C. and D.N. Collins, (Editors) 1982, **The Fertilizer Handbook**. The Fertilizer Institute. Washington, DC.

Worldwatch 1987, **State of the World**. Worldwatch Institute. Washington, DC.

Part II
IN THE BUSINESS

Chapter 7
Marketing

Pretend you are a winner and most people will believe it.

Like it or not, no matter what your business is, you have to be somewhat of a salesperson to succeed. This doesn't mean you have to be loud, obnoxious, pushy or wear plaid pants. If fact, that stereotype is very hard to find in today's markets. The modern and successful salesperson is a supplier of information to a market that is shopping ever more intelligently. The more credible you are, the better you will fare because long term relationships with customers are based on trust. If customers trust your judgment and ability and don't feel you will ever cheat or deceive them, they will usually remain with you. The level of service they expect must be provided, of course, and it must be within their budget, but it is a comfortable feeling for customers to think that you are:

1. Professional – someone who is an expert at what you do, can communicate clearly with them, and can develop a quality program within their budget.

2. Reliable – someone they can count on to be there when needed and to solve any problems that may arise.

3. Special – In any lasting relationship, whether it is with a spouse, a son or daughter, a friend, a customer, or even a pet, there is a need for each participant to think of the other as special. This is where marketing yourself and/or your company becomes important.

The first step is to convince yourself that you and the people who work for you are special. If that is not possible, it will be difficult to convince anyone else. Once you have elevated your company to the self-imposed rank of special, give yourself a pop quiz with one question on it...Why am I special? Convincing customers of that answer should be the crux of your marketing plan. The big questions in any market are: What are you going to offer in a relationship with a customer that they need but do not already have in the relationship they have now with your competition? And how are you going to let them know about this offer? The answers to these questions is what marketing is all about.

SELLING ICE TO ESKIMOS

Traditionally, this expression describes salespeople who are so good at what they do that they can con Eskimos into thinking that they have a need for ice. The origin of the word *con* in this case is from *convince,* which means to persuade or satisfy by evidence. Convincing a community that it needs something that constantly surrounds it is difficult and often involves dishonesty, which is not being advocated here. Remember, one of the most important components of a lasting relationship with anyone is **trust**. What must be determined is: Do you have something to offer customers that they need? And, do they want it? If the answer to both questions is yes, then hang out your shingle and the calls should come rolling in. Determining if the answer is yes or no, however, can be difficult. Advertising will sometimes provide an answer, but it can be expensive, and if it is not presented well, it may be overlooked by potential clients. If you are already visiting homes and/or commercial properties, it is not too difficult or expensive to conduct a survey. Many people do not like surveys, however, so one that is short and to the point is preferred. If advertising is the only alternative, then posing a question in an ad rather than a statement may be more productive in terms of response. For example:

IF YOU COULD HAVE THIS SPECIAL SERVICE
WHICH WOULD RESULT IN AN EXQUISITE LAWN
FOR THIS SPECIAL PRICE
WOULD YOU CALL THIS NUMBER?

Determining if what you have to offer is wanted by the area you are offering it to is an important step to take. If you find there is very little interest out there for your speciality but you are still convinced that customers need this service, then it is up to you to convince them – to persuade or satisfy by evidence. This involves educating the customer, which can be a time consuming and expensive undertaking. It can also be a profitable one. Education is something that many people want and are willing to pay for. Experts in the field who are willing (and able) to share their knowledge with others are usually in demand. Making a profit from educating people is not unusual. Seminars or newsletters can be used to persuade by evidence that a special service is needed and where this service is available or how customers can provide it for themselves. If you show customers how to do it for themselves, however, you need to be paid for that information, because they won't need you to provide the services.

Gaining exposure in a given area is an important part of marketing and doesn't need to be expensive. Press releases sent to all area newspapers and local radio stations announcing your new company, new employees, acts of charity, or discoveries of new and innovative lawn care techniques will only cost the time it takes to write and send them. Small and inexpensive ads that appear on a regular basis in newspapers or are heard on the radio are proven to be more effective than the big splash, one time, full page advertisements. Public speaking at garden clubs or other organizations can provide a tremendous amount of exposure and respect that can translate into more business. Many garden centers have speakers give seminars to their customers, mainly to attract them into the store, but also to offer education as part of their program. The owner of a garden center would probably be happy to have a qualified speaker on the subject of natural lawn care. Other means of exposure might include exhibiting at home and garden shows, bulk mailings to postal patrons at one or more post office(s), T-shirts or hats with your company name and logo printed on them, advertising on your vehicles, and yellow page listings. You might be able to make a deal with local garden centers or hardware stores to stuff one of your discount certificates into each customer's bag in exchange for your business for supplies or a small commission. Their stamp on the back of each certificate will identify where the customer got it. Gaining good exposure can be as innovative and important as your lawn maintenance skills. Never assume that everyone has heard of you.

Demographics can help develop a marketing plan. How many homes and/or businesses are there in the area that have landscapes in need of maintenance? City hall or a town clerk's office can help with the answer. They won't be able to tell you who has lawns, but they know who pays property taxes (and who doesn't) and the information should be available to the public. How many properties are currently maintained by firms such as yours? This question will be more difficult to answer and may require some surveying on your part. Local landscape, plantsmans, or lawn care organizations may have some useful statistics but you may have to become a member to get access to them. How many new homes and businesses have been built in the last five years? This is another question to ask the town or city clerk. You might also check with the census bureau or the FHA (Federal Housing Administration). The answer will give you a good indication of the potential for growth in a given area. New neighborhoods under construction are an excellent place to cultivate new customers.

After you have discovered where the potential jobs may be, it is important to determine how many of them you can handle. Time spent on each job and time/distance calculations between areas should be performed to determine your potential job load. Taking on more than you can handle will eventually hurt your reputation as someone who is reliable. Once it is determined how many customers you can handle, pricing can be set based on what it costs to provide service and what you perceive to be a comfortable living. It is a good idea to buffer your calculations to cover unexpected expenses. When a price is determined, it is important to compare it to those of the competition. If yours is substantially higher you need to know why. It may be because you are offering something that the competition isn't. If that is the case it is important to promote the service and, perhaps, offer it as an option so that your customers know they are getting something extra for the higher price. If your services are essentially the same as your competition, it will be necessary to refine your operation into a less costly and more efficiently run business. Analyze the cost of every aspect of job performance and determine where costs can be cut. Remember, unless you are special, there is no reason for anyone to pay you more for your services. Since it is assumed that you are special, however, the questions remain:

1. Is what makes you special worth the extra money? and

2. Is your special service needed or wanted by anyone?

Make sure you are comparing apples to apples. It is difficult to offer premium services at conventional, run-of-the-mill prices.

GETTING AND LOSING CUSTOMERS

If you have been in the business of lawn care or landscaping for any length of time, you already know how difficult it is to get new customers and how easy it is to lose old ones. Customers like to feel important no matter where they stand on your priority list. If you can make each customer feel as though he or she is the most important client you have, there tends to be much more loyalty (all other components of service being equal). There are always some customers, unfortunately, who make you regret having taken the job. If it becomes necessary to unload a customer because he or she aggravates you to excess, it should be done as tactfully as possible. Once that customer is out of your hair it may feel good, but if the departing is at all bitter, their word-of-mouth information may haunt you for years to come. Perhaps you can tell the client that you are not properly equipped to handle this job and then recommend your favorite competitor. Or you can explain to the customer the legitimate reasons why your price is rising so much and let them sever the relationship.

Keeping good customers is a constant battle. If anything goes wrong in a landscape or lawn care job, you know who will be blamed. Communication with clients is extremely important. Explaining what you are doing and why, and asking questions about problems or satisfaction levels can make the difference between keeping a customer and losing him or her without notice. If customers are never at the job site, it is important to make contact with them or leave behind an informational flyer and perhaps a brief questionnaire querying their satisfaction level. Statistically, it costs five times more to find a new customer then it does to keep an old one. Never assume a customer is going to remain a customer indefinitely. Keeping good customers is just like courting a potential spouse for the first time. Unfortunately, a customer must always see only your good side whereas a spouse will eventually see the rest.

SALES

Selling your services can be a frustrating experience, especially if you are offering something relatively unique such as organic lawn care. Those of us who are fishermen understand that landing a lunker every time we go out is unlikely. However, we go out anyway, and even if nothing at all is caught on one outing, we look forward to the next. The fisherman understands the single most important concept in sales: *If you don't have your line in the water, you can't catch fish.* In sales, there must be a constant pursuit of customers, whether it is from advertising, word-of-mouth, or knocking on doors. To succeed in almost any business there must be some type of sales. Selling ecological lawn care services can be difficult at first but should become easier after a customer base is established.

A professional in upstate NY waits until summer dormancy to begin his annual sales effort and does so by pointing out that the lawns he maintains in the neighborhood are still green after all the others have turned brown. His tactic is simple but painstaking as he actually goes door to door in an area to tactfully boast about his talents. He doesn't spend a lot of time unless questions are asked. He simply identifies himself, proudly points out the lush lawn at the end of the road, and leaves some literature or a business card. The results are predictably good.

Other methods of gaining exposure include press releases to local papers or radio stations, submitting articles to trade magazines or the local press, and getting yourself booked on radio talk shows that deal primarily with gardening and lawn care. Get a listing in the yellow pages, but don't let the phone company talk you into a large and expensive display ad unless you are absolutely convinced it will pay off. Classified ads in the local paper are often a cost effective way of gaining exposure. Charity work can be very profitable if it is a high profile job and becomes an example of your work to many onlookers or you are given credit in a news article. Your vehicle should don the company logo and a phone number and should be parked strategically everywhere you go. Multilevel marketing can be used to a certain extent by offering your customers a free mowing, or some other treatment for every new customer they refer to you. If your initial sales efforts are thorough and you are noted for quality service, eventually a natural growth will pick up momentum. The need for conscious sales efforts will be reduced because you will be too busy providing service to established customers to go out and look for new ones.

DISCONTENT

If a customer is withholding payment because of dissatisfaction, or just voices his or her unhappiness directly to you, an important opportunity has just crossed your path. It is a common reaction to hide under the rug when customers complain. No one really wants to hear these problems. Hard as we try to be perfect in every way, however, problems do occur. If you eagerly and attentively solve these problems to the customer's satisfaction, chances are very good that a few of the customer's friends and neighbors will hear about it. If problems are viewed as public relations opportunities they are easier to deal with and often result in higher profits.

An example of this principal is a story about two one-man lawn care companies operating in upstate NY. A few years ago the summer was extraordinarily hot and dry, and many lawns failed. Some customers blamed the failure on the lawn care company and called to complain. The first company owner, after receiving a half dozen complaints, took his phone off the hook. The second calmly explained the weather phenomenon to each caller and offered to install a new lawn at cost (some labor included). It wasn't a very profitable year for the second company but the following spring he was pleasantly surprised to see that his customer base had almost doubled. The first company went out of business in the following year.

The importance of keeping customers happy goes far beyond just keeping the customers. Their positive word-of-mouth is the strongest advertising you can get for any amount of money.

NATURAL GROWTH

Mother nature is our best teacher. Wherever we look there are lessons to be learned from the natural world. Growth is probably the most natural phenomenon on the planet. Whether it is the growth of plants or populations of other organisms, there are some basic tenets to be noted.

The growth of anything living depends on the resources that surround it. If there is not enough water and nutrients, the organism will die. Starting a business in an area that cannot support it is the kiss of death. The big advantage that a human has over plants and other organisms is that he or she can perform research and formulate a plan. The success of a plant or animal in the wild can be accidental. But planning for success significantly decreases the need for luck. Thomas Jefferson once wrote: *I'm a great believer in luck, and I find the harder I work, the more I have of it.*

Nature reinvests many of its assets into growth, and although the plant, for example, seems to gain slowly when watched, its overall advances are fast and vast. After all, the great forests of the world were once a single seed. Living systems take what they need to be healthy, strong and live comfortably. It is the only way they can compete effectively with each other. Growth of a business comes in stages, however. It cannot and should not occur overnight. No matter how well we plan, there are always unforeseen circumstances that make it necessary to re-evaluate and repair our system. If growth is too fast, we don't have time to fine tune our system. We become stressed and susceptible to other problems, none of which fit into the image of success. If resources are limited and quick growth is essential for survival, it may be prudent to re-evaluate the business plan.

Nature seems to plan for failure. In most species, reproduction is far in excess of what actually survives. The intuitive instinct in nature is that most offspring will fail but if enough seeds are planted, the species will succeed. Businesses involved in direct marketing have learned that a very small percentage of solicitations will actually result in a productive response. Perhaps only one in forty or fifty will make the sale. This is not discouraging information to them. They know exactly how many pieces of mail to send out to make a profit. The lesson here is not to depend on any one promotion or advertisement or mailing. Nature would never put all of its resources in one place and neither should you. The continuous exhaustion of all possibilities is the only alternative. Thomas Edison failed 10,000 times when he was developing the light bulb. Each failure, however, was viewed by Edison as a step closer to success. Nature will cast its seed everywhere without consideration of the odds that it will germinate and survive. The seed may lodge itself in an inappropriate area and remain dormant for years until the right conditions prevail, and suddenly, a living plant exists and thrives. The indiscriminate circulation of literature or business cards is analogous to sowing seeds. Opportunities exist in many seemingly obscure places. but a seed needs to be there if the conditions for germination are to make a positive change.

It is a rare place on earth where absolutely nothing can survive. It seems that even in the most inhospitable places some type of organism can scratch out an existence. The message mother nature gives is that there is a niche for everyone and everything. The same is true in business: it's just a matter of finding the right niche. Unfortunately, it would not be difficult to exhaust all of one's resources looking for that market. Nature's example of spreading an abundance of seed in hopes that only one will germinate and grow is a good one to follow. Many business persons find their niches completely by accident by spreading their promotion thinly through a broad range of markets. Once a profitable marketplace is found, then the lion's share of energy and resources can be committed to a more specific market.

The growth of a successful business should be like that of a tree. A tree grows slowly, especially in the early stages of its life. However, a tree never stops growing. It begins in a local area and slowly invades surrounding areas both above and below the ground. As the tree reaches farther out the base becomes stronger. If the roots reach a pocket of soil rich in nutrients, the entire tree becomes healthier. The shade from the tree protects it from competition but its purpose is to absorb energy from the sun. The waste generated by the tree is an asset that is recycled into nutrients. The analogies are endless but the message is clear.

Sometimes it is a good idea to go outside, into the woods or a field, and ponder. Look at the natural world, note how its system works and try to glean some ideas that would help you in your quest for success. There are literally millions of ideas out there, and you may need only one.

Sources:

Buss, D. 1994, **Super Selling: 9 Ways to Make Your Sales Soar**. IB Magazine NFIB May/June 1994. Group IV Commmunications, Inc. Thousand Oaks, CA.

Merrill, L.S. 1995, **Keep An Even Keel For Business Success**. Turf Magazine, North Edition, April. 1995 v8#4. NEF Publishing. St. Johnsbury, VT.

Chapter 8

Management

In any business there are key components that need to be managed. These include money, time, human resources, customers, vendors, and growth. Poor or disorganized management techniques in any of these areas can mean a loss of profits, customers, and, eventually, your business.

GETTING AND LOSING KEY EMPLOYEES

Finding good help can be more difficult than finding good customers. Self-motivated, intelligent people are usually running their own businesses. Young graduates of horticulture school are often over qualified for labors such as mowing lawns, and are usually looking for an income befitting a technician rather than a laborer. If the proper training is available and the opportunity to advance is present with the proper incentives, however, it is surprising who will take advantage of it.

The key seems to be in the level of self-confidence the employee has. If people have confidence in themselves, even without any ability, their potential is far greater than someone with low self-esteem. A big ego is not a symbol of self-confidence. It is a mask covering an image problem that employers don't need. Unfortunately, it is difficult, without a barrage of psychological tests, to determine a person's level of self-confidence before you hire them. If one uses a job application form, a simple but productive question to ask is: *Have you accomplished anything in the last five years that was of great personal gratification to you?* Discount all the *I had a baby* answers from either parent. The applicant with little self esteem will not feel comfortable answering this question whereas the egomaniac will ask for another sheet of paper. The confident applicants will generally write one or two accomplishments that they feel good about. Nervousness can be a factor that may adulterate your findings. Some people try to answer questions based on what they think you want to hear. Another good question to ask is *What are your personal career goals or objectives?* This may provide insights as to how much ambition the applicant may or may not have. Ambition is a double edged sword with employees. A laborer without it may not be as driven as you are, but might be content to stay with a company indefinitely. People with serious ambitions may be more productive and innovative, but unless their position and wages are constantly being upgraded, they will eventually find better employment or become your competition.

It is a good idea to hire help on a temporary basis and then promote them to permanent status if they work out. Once employees begin working, it doesn't take long to evaluate their potential. It is important to also evaluate yourself as an employer. Do you convey clear instructions or specifications for each job? Have you thought about contingencies before you leave the job site? Are there any incentives for the employee to do the job as well as you would? It is a good idea to put yourself in the employee's shoes and ask yourself if this is a job you would like to keep for the long term.

There is always the risk that the self-motivated employee, whom you have spent years training and nurturing, will eventually leave to become your competition. If you can provide a similar potential for advancement without the associated risks of running his or her own business, that day may never come. If there is a departure and it is done on good terms, however, a mutually beneficial relationship can still exist. Often employers will change the status of an employee to that of a subcontractor to avoid the costs and paperwork associated with employment. This works out well if the employee has his or her own equipment and does a certain aspect of the company's service well. Agreements can be made that will eliminate the need for, and the concern about, competition between the two parties.

BOSS MANAGEMENT vs LEAD MANAGEMENT

The two basic ways to manage people are either by boss management or by lead management. The boss manager tells employees what to do, how it should be done and uses coercion to force compliance. Usually, the coercion is job security or payroll penalties. Unfortunately, this type of management makes the employer an adversary from the beginning of the relationship to the end. Employees under this type of management generally do the minimum amount of work necessary to satisfy the employer's requirements. There is no incentive offered by the employer for anyone to produce quality work. Even in a system where cash incentives are available, the employee has a difficult time becoming motivated.

In a lead management system, there is mutual respect between the employer and employees and everyone works as a team. The employee feels more like a co-worker than just hired help. The manager employs more than just the physical capabilities of the employees by consulting with them on various aspects of each job. Ideas from interested and motivated employees are often innovative, productive, and profitable. Rewards in a lead management system are generally abundant and coercion is relatively nonexistent. As with most other relationships, trust is possibly the most important factor between the employer and employee. It is crucial that the manager be open and honest with all employees at all times, and in exchange can demand the same in return. If employees do something dishonest once, it is a good idea to make it clear what you expect and give them another chance. If you are dealing with someone who just cannot be trusted, however, he or she should be dismissed immediately. Employees who feel that their employers care about their future will do a better job for them. Nature teaches us that seeds grow faster and stronger in better cultures. Employees can also flourish and be more productive in an environment that encourages the growth of quality habits.

Some people do not have the motivation or ambition to do more than the minimum expected of them, no matter how they are managed. Many employees want to be told what to do and how to do it because they are afraid of making mistakes that may cost them their jobs. Even after months of working for a lead manager, these employees do not break out of their shell and become motivated members of the team. This can be frustrating for the employer, but if the employee is doing what needs to be done and is trustworthy, then it can remain a profitable relationship. Eventually, these employees may develop the confidence needed to join the team as an equal.

AN ORGANIZATION

The difference between a one man band and an organization is not necessarily the number of people involved. An organization is one that can still carry on if any member is incapacitated or leaves. Obviously, if the receptionist, bookkeeper, warehouse manager, laborer, and sales manager are all the same person, it is difficult to have an organization. It is important to understand, however, that over time situations change, and the better prepared you are to expand your organization, the faster you will grow.

Each time you delegate a responsibility to someone else, there is a certain amount of training necessary for that new person to do the job at least as well as you would have. If that person can't do the job, or can but finds a better one elsewhere, or leaves for any other reason, a new person will have to be trained. A worse scenario is when you find someone who can do the job better than you, and he or she eventually leaves. Even you can't train anyone up to that level of efficiency.

Fortunately there is a solution. If a procedure manual is created over time by you and amended by those who work that job for you, then the evolution and perfection of a procedure can be retained for any future employees. A procedure that someone engages in every day seems easy to them, but to someone who has never done it before it may seem terribly complex. If each time a procedure is developed or amended it is written down and stored in a loose leaf notebook that has alphabetized dividers, the method you or someone else learns is forever documented. This is also very valuable for those hard-to-remember tasks that only occur once or twice each year (e.g. tax returns). The office is probably the most appropriate place to keep a procedure manual and most of the information in it will probably pertain to bookkeeping, filing, and other record keeping procedures. Field procedures are more difficult to document and it is unlikely that an employee who doesn't know exactly what to do would be unsupervised in the first place. A field manual, however, may be valuable to a manager who may have forgotten a once-a-year procedure. The manual does not need to be fancy or pretty, but it should be organized so that each procedure is easy to locate. If a computer is available, the methods can be written on a spread sheet or word processor and alphabetized by the computer (NOTE: not all programs can alphabetically arrange data). The computer is very valuable if you want to change something in the manual without rewriting the entire section. Remember to start small and don't try to write the entire manual overnight. Be cognizant of each task you accomplish in your routine and recognize those that would be difficult for a novice to accomplish, or even remember.

COLLECTIONS

Collecting past due bills from customers is always an awkward problem. On the one hand, they have borrowed your money without your permission and have given no indication as to when they intend to pay it back. On the other hand, they may be good customers and you don't want to offend them to the point where they call your competition. When someone owes you money for a job, it is not just your profit that is being withheld. All of the costs from the job that you may have already paid are also captured. The money you used to pay for materials and labor constitutes profit from other jobs. If your net profit before taxes is ten percent, for example, then a customer who owes you $1,000.00 is holding the profit from $10,000.00 worth of business. It is very frustrating when there is more than enough money owed to you to cover your expenses, but because it is not paid, you have to dip into your own savings or your line of credit. It is even more frustrating when you become a delinquent account with your vendors because one or more of your customers won't pay you on time.

It is important never to assume anything when it comes to a delinquent account, even if you know the overall trend of the customer's bill paying habits. It is also important to respond to the past due condition right away, not after the invoice has aged to an alarming point. If after thirty days a customer receives a call or note gently pointing out that an invoice or statement is past due, and inquiring about problems or the unlikely possibility that the bill was lost in the mail, then you have made a few important statements. First, you have told them that you expect to be paid on time. Second, you have indicated that you keep close tabs on your receivables and plan to be in their face until you are paid. Third, you have given them an opportunity to voice discontent, which can be valuable, as discussed in chapter 7. Many people are genuinely surprised or embarrassed that they haven't paid a bill, and quickly locate it under a stack of papers. Others will have a sincere excuse and offer to resolve the problem by a certain date. Some will be in the embarrassing position of having overextended themselves and of being unable to pay in the foreseeable future. When you run into this type of situation, the best possible outcome is to get the customer to agree to a payment schedule that he or she can live with. No matter how small the payment, if it is being sent consistently, then the customer is sincere about paying off the bill.

No matter what transpires in your conversations or correspondence with delinquent accounts, always, always, always write down what was said. If a customer says that you will have a check by Friday and you don't receive it on that day, can you remember exactly which customer it was that said it or which Friday he or she was talking about? The most important thing you can do when chasing receivables is to take notes.

The frustration of dealing with delinquent accounts often tempts one to think of those customers as deadbeats and approach the situation with aggressive and belligerent behavior. Unfortunately, this can be counterproductive for you. Yelling at or threatening the customer, even if you don't care about any future business from that customer, will often make your invoice(s) much less important than other past due bills. Even if your tactics work, the impression you've made on the customer could hurt future prospects if that customer maligns you to friends and neighbors.

The alternative is to empathize with the customer and counsel him or her toward a solution. Chances are you may have been in a similar situation at one time or another; you may remember having much better feelings about a creditor who calmly worked out a solution with you. The important ingredient is the relentless pursuit of a solution. The customer in dire straits will generally want a semipermanent postponement. You, of course, want all your money immediately. Somewhere in between those two positions is a compromise that needs to be mediated by you. It is usually better to get the customer to suggest the solution rather than developing one yourself that the customer hears but is not listening to. Your solution may be agreed to simply as a means to end the embarrassing encounter, but it is not one that will be followed. Let the customer suggest a solution that he or she can stick with. Both you and the customer should write it down. A follow-up letter reiterating your conversation is a good idea. The customer should also understand that the money being withheld is a type of loan, and finance charges need to be assessed. There is a real and tangible cost of money, and anyone who has a line of credit, a mortgage, or just a credit card, is painfully aware of this fact. The customer must understand that withholding your money is an expense for you that needs to be reimbursed.

Collection agencies should be a tactic of last resort. They get a significant percentage of the money owed and often do not collect the entire balance. Using an agency will almost always result in a loss for you and should only be done if nothing else works.

CONTRACTS

A contract is an agreement between two or more people. It does not have to be written down to be valid, but the written contract serves as a record of the agreement if there is a dispute later on. Most companies have a statement of policy that outlines the details of a land care program: what the company provides, how much it costs, and when payment needs to be received. This document serves as a contract whether it is signed or not. The signature is a means of proving that the customer has read and understands the details of the agreement in the event of a later dispute. A purchase order to a supplier is a contract whether it is signed or not. Some vendors want orders signed, but most do not care. Generally, the degree to which a contract is administered is relative to the trust and/or experience one has with the other party or parties involved in the transaction. Eventually, once a comfortable business relationship is established with someone, contractual agreements usually become less formal.

Large projects, because of the amount of money involved and the complexity of the job, need to be spelled out in great detail. Documents called specifications are usually written by architects or engineers to ensure that their design is followed explicitly and that the correct quality of materials is used. On very large jobs, there can be many contractors and subcontractors and the specified guidelines must be available to all parties to ensure that no misunderstandings can exist. Some do anyway.

Contracts are generally straightforward, but the more complex the job, the more details the contract will contain. It should be read carefully and completely, including the boring parts about performance and arbitration. If sections seem unfair, then it is important to ask questions. Often the answer will be that it is standard contractual language. If there are many contractors involved in a job and all of their contracts contain the same language, then it probably is standard language. Sometimes it is not, however, and if your common sense smells a rat, it might be a good idea to have your lawyer look at it.

Any terms or policies that are presented in writing to a customer can serve as a contract. If the customer understands and agrees to those terms, then a legal agreement is made. If the customer has a reputation for being distrustful, it might be a good idea to have the agreement signed. Better yet, find another customer. The agreement should explain in clear and simple terms what the service company intends to provide, how much the customer must pay for these services, and how promptly payment must be made after services are rendered. Language that spells out action to be taken in the event of non-compliance by either party can be added but it may be difficult to cover completely without knowing, in advance, how the agreement will be breached.

The fact is that no matter how inclusive a contract may seem, loopholes can usually be found if someone looks hard enough. A contract is no guarantee that you won't be burned by someone. Even with a written contract, it may cost you more to take someone to court than what is owed to you. This type of frustration can lead one to develop lengthy and detailed agreements in an attempt to protect oneself. Unfortunately, the detailed, omni-protective contract is often daunting to new customers who receive the message, loud and clear, that you don't trust them. It is important not to go overboard in your quest to protect yourself; unfortunately, a small percentage of sleazy customers can taint the relationships you have with others.

If a customer is not paying on time, a warning should be issued that service will stop if the account is not brought up to date. The longer you provide service to a customer who isn't paying for it, the worse the problem gets. All actions you take should be outlined in an agreement or statement of policy that is given to the customer before any work begins.

Some key points to cover in a contract are:

• The basic agreement – what is each party's responsibility?

• Do you offer guarantees or warranties?

• What are your prices?

• When will the work be done and payment due?

• What is the duration of the contract?

• Is the agreement transferable by either party?

• How can the contract can be terminated by either party?

• What are methods of resolving disputes?

• Who is responsible for legal fees in the event of a dispute?

• What is the state in which the laws governing contractual agreements apply?

GROWTH

Growth should be an integral part of your business plan, but growing is not always a pleasurable experience. Always keep in mind your personal limitations when planning growth. One person, no matter how talented or how efficient, can only accomplish so much in each hour of the day. As your company grows, the tasks that need to be accomplished will eventually exceed your capacity to get things done, which will necessitate the hiring of some help. Remember that the addition of an employee will not create a relative increase in your capacity per man-hour. First of all, the employee needs to be trained for a period where little or no productivity will occur. Secondly, the employee may not accomplish tasks at the same pace that you would, or do them as efficiently. Additionally, each employee that you hire will need some degree of management by you, which is time subtracted from you doing other, possibly more productive, tasks.

There are also the expenses of insurance, health care, worker's compensation, etc. that raise the cost of doing business and have to be considered. Filling out government forms for taxes and other employment-related regulations can also be time consuming and costly. Extra tools and equipment will have to be purchased to keep employees productive, and you can bet that the life of the equipment will not be as long in their hands as it would be in yours. These extra expenses will increase your cost of doing business and lower your profit margin, but if you can significantly increase your gross sales, you may increase your overall net profit. For example: If you were working by yourself and reached $60,000.00 in annual gross sales with a profit margin of 40%, your net profit for the year would be $24,000.00. If you hired two employees and increased your gross sales to $130,000 but reduced your profit margin to 25%, you would earn $32,500. So even though your profit margin has shrunk, your net earnings have increased significantly. If your profit margin shrinks to below 19% at the new level of sales, however, then you are no better off than when you were working by yourself.

It is important to track your profit margin at predetermined intervals during the year to see where you stand. Having a good accounting system helps you accomplish this more easily. Many businesses fail simply because they are not netting enough profit to sustain the expense of their existence. Big companies that appear to be rock solid, with a lion's share of the market, are just as susceptible to fail from this problem as the fledgling start-ups. There are many examples of these fallen Goliaths throughout economic history.

Net profit is primarily affected by two factors:

1. How much money is charged for a service and

2. How much money it costs to provide the service.

If a profit margin is inadequate, one or both of these factors has to change. Changing the price of your services is easier than reducing your costs, but may cause the loss of some accounts that are price sensitive. This would be acceptable if you have a waiting list of other customers that are willing to pay a higher price, but if a price increase causes your employees to sit idle because of an inadequate work load, your costs will escalate rapidly. It pays to examine all of your expenses on each job to determine if there are unnecessary costs. This task is made easier by a good accounting system.

When you are ready for growth, there are two basic ways to increase sales:

1. Increase the number of goods or services available to your customers and

2. Increase the number of customers that you are servicing.

The first is probably the easiest and most profitable. If you are already at a site treating a lawn there is no reason why you could not treat trees, shrubs, or flowers. Or you could market products such as fertilizer or tools that the customer needs to accomplish some of the work himself. The addition of tree, shrub or other ornamental services may require some training and/or research on your part to acquire the necessary skills, but will easily pay for itself in short order.

Expanding your customer base can increase your gross, but not necessarily your net. As you travel farther away from your home base to more remote customers, your costs begin to increase significantly. The extra miles put on the vehicle(s), the costs of insurance and fuel are of little consequence compared to the cost of an employee sitting in a truck listening to the radio. At ten dollars per man-hour, six employees riding in trucks cost an employer one dollar per minute just in wages. A thirty minute drive to a job adds sixty dollars to your costs (time out plus time back). When you first begin in a new area, you may have only one or two accounts. The extra travel time may not make it worth being out there unless you are able to accumulate more accounts in that area. On the other hand, it is difficult to build a customer base in any area if you are not there. The ideal situation would be first to develop an area close to home that will be profitable enough to subsidize the initial costs of doing business in more remote locations.

Determining the amount of profit made is an important calculation. It can be done on a per job basis or on a time unit basis, such as per month or per quarter. The profit per job is easy to calculate by subtracting all your costs for materials and labor from the gross revenues. This calculation, however, does not take into consideration any of your general and administrative (G&A) expenses such as heat, rent, interest on loans, vehicle expense, etc. Unfortunately, those expenses are difficult to assay on a per job basis. G&A expenses need to be tracked for a model period of time and then aver-

INFLUENCE OF G & A EXPENSES ON PROFIT

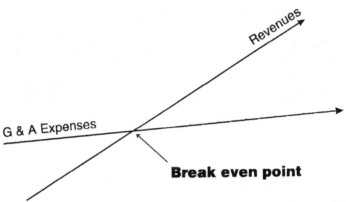

Figure 8-1

aged out to a per week or per month basis. You will find that the G&A expenses do not increase proportionally with the growth of your business. This means that once you grow beyond the break even point, profits, as a percent of gross revenues, will begin to increase (see figure 8-1). If, for example, your company grossed $100,000.00 in one year and had expenses of $50,000.00 in labor and materials and $25,000.00 in G&A, your profit before taxes is $25,000.00 or 25% of gross revenues. If, in the following year, the company grosses $150,000.00 with labor and material costs of $75,000.00 but the same G&A of $25,000.00, then your profit is $50,000.00 or 33% of gross revenues. Chances are the G&A figure will increase some as the business grows, but it is a relatively fixed expense as compared to the cost of labor and materials.

CAPITAL

Capital is the fuel in your tank. Without it you must rely on other people's money to operate — such as the bank's or the vendors' who supply you. Banks can be difficult to negotiate with, especially if you do not have assets that can be used to secure a loan. Vendors who are drafted into carrying your debt because their invoices cannot be paid on time are usually not too happy. If they levy finance charges against you, it could amount to 2 – 3 times what a bank would charge. Eventually the vendor may choose not to extend credit any longer or may stop doing business with you altogether.

Unfortunately, capital is one of the most difficult things to accumulate. A growing but sound business can manage to pay its bills, but is usually not too long on extra cash. Creating a recurring expense which is actually a contribution to a capital fund is one way to slowly accumulate capital. If every time payroll checks are written or some other recurring payment is made, you also put a small amount into your capital fund and forget about it, the fund will eventually grow into a sizable liquid asset. It is not practical to attempt large contributions that will only have to be withdrawn soon to pay operating expenses. The trick is to make contributions that can be sustained throughout the year without having to withdraw them to compensate for normal cash flow fluctuations.

The capital savings fund may be for something specific, such as to replace a piece of equipment that is beginning to show its age. It may just be for cost of operations during a slow part of the year, or used simply as an asset to help secure credit elsewhere. When banks look at financial statements, they are usually very impressed if a company is accumulating capital. It may not make perfect sense to borrow money at an interest rate that is higher than what the capital is earning in a savings account, but it provides a discipline to keep your capital fund growing. Using capital as collateral for a short term loan forces you to keep your capital fund intact. The equity you have in fixed assets such as property or equipment can be used to secure a loan but these assets don't earn interest like a capital savings fund would. Eventually, the capital fund could grow to a level where bank loans are no longer necessary. However, a disciplined system needs to be designed to continually maintain the growth and stability of your capital fund.

LINE OF CREDIT

Credit lines from banks are often essential to compensate for the seasonal vagaries of one's cash flow. Payroll must be made and suppliers must be paid, even if the customers' checks haven't yet arrived. Unfortunately, this situation is as common as sunshine but can be much more distressing than a hurricane. A line of credit from a bank allows for smooth transition through these periods by providing cash that is not, but should be, in your possession. Credit lines for operations should not be used to finance new equipment or for frivolous expenses that the business could not otherwise afford. Great care must be administered when using a line of credit. The temptation to spend money at your disposal is strong, but dangerous. It is analogous to putting a gun in the wrong hands. For a business, misuse of a credit line can easily result in its own demise.

Fortunately (or unfortunately, depending on how you look at it) banks understand this and businesses need to jump through some serious hoops to establish credit for the first time. When approaching a bank for credit it is a good idea to have your ducks in a row before your first meeting.

BORROWING MONEY FROM BANKS

The bankers are in a tough position. They see every loan as a risk. But like any good businessperson, they want to get and keep as many customers as possible. If customers present themselves as a tolerable risk, then the banker is anxious to sign them on. As with most attractive things in life, presentation is very important. A steak dinner with fresh vegetables, a baked potato and fresh baked bread sounds appealing but looks like garbage if it is all piled together on a newspaper.

Financial statements and other reports mentioned in chapters 9 and 10 are documents the bank is going to ask for anyway, so why not bring them with you to your first meeting? A business plan, no matter how simple, can be another impressive and important presentation tool. Bankers love to see a business analyzed to death. They love numbers and love doing business with others who share their passion. Financial reports and other analytical documents show them that you have as much interest in financial success as you do in the success of each lawn you install and care for. The more factual information you can present to them clarifying your direction and needs, the more interested they will be in doing business with you. Often, during this analytical process, you will discover things about your business that may change the way you want to run it, or the direction you should follow.

Lists of customers, contracts, and bid offerings are also items that interest bankers. Training credentials, memberships in trade organizations, publications or business literature, letters of praise from satisfied customers, and/or feature articles about you and/or your company are useful presentation tools to a loan officer. They all serve to illustrate the serious and stable commitment you have made to your business.

Bankers like loans that are designed to generate more revenue. A line of credit, for example, that is used to take advantage of purchase discounts, is appealing to them as is a loan for a piece of equipment that will significantly increase your income. Some type of documentation that accounts for the projected gains, however, needs to be presented to the bank. They need to see, on paper, how you plan to use their money and, more importantly, how you plan to pay it back.

A budget, which is a spending and income plan, is a valuable document to present to a banker. It shows that you have given considerable thought to how the loan will work to generate more income. The budget can be set up like a calendar that shows when and how you plan to spend the money and when you expect to see some kind of return on the investment.

Bankers love organization. The more organized you are the more they will like doing business with you. Organization comes easily to some people but is much more difficult for others. If you are of the latter persuasion, it would be a good idea to make the painful effort to be as organized as humanly possible during your presentation to the bank. This includes having all the necessary documentation in a presentation folder and in the order in which it should be presented. If you are not sure what order that should be, call the bank and ask the loan officer with whom you have an appointment. The material should be neat and legible.

Organization can also refer to your company's structure, as mentioned earlier in this chapter. If you have employees or partners, the bank needs to see how the business will function should anything incapacitating happen to you or anyone else in the business. If you are a one man band, they may require life and/or disability insurance for the loan.

A brief history of your company and a plan for future direction is also a good report to submit to a banker. It doesn't need to be elaborate, but the banker needs to see that you have stable roots attached somewhere and aren't going to take their money and run.

It may seem like a lot of hard work initially to get credit established with a lending institution. It is. But you must understand that banks operate under a tremendous amount of federal regulations that require them to make it difficult for you. Think of it as a type of initiation. Once you are in, and prove to the bank that you are a good loan customer, it's pretty much smooth sailing from there.

Personal appearance is also important. This is not to say one needs to wear a $500 suit, but appearing neat and clean presents an image of someone who cares. From the banker's perspective, customers who don't care how they look (or smell) may not care about sending their loan payments in on time. Once you have established yourself as a good customer, bankers don't generally care at all about your appearance.

Another incredibly valuable card to play with the bank is to set up either a checking or savings account (or both) well before you approach them for a loan. Put as much money as you possibly can in the account(s) and leave it there for as long as you can. The longer you have those accounts established with money in them, the more favorably the bank will look at your loan application. Depositors are already good customers whom bankers value above all else. If your application for a loan is a reasonable request, a banker doesn't want to risk losing you as a customer by denying you credit, especially if he thinks that some other bank might grant the loan. If you have already been banking with a specific institution for a long period of time then you should be all set, unless you have a record of often being overdrawn or have some other problem that sends a clear and negative signal to the loan officer. If that is the case, it would probably be wise to start over at another bank or consciously strive to improve your record at your current location.

When a bank grants a line of credit it is forced to become a silent partner in your business. If a loan customer understands this it can be very helpful both when approaching a bank for a loan and also after the loan has been granted. Bankers are partners in thousands of other businesses. They have, over the years, seen what makes or breaks many different businesses. If a banker is approached by someone anxious to form a partnership and use the bank's knowledge about becoming successful, it is a much more appealing venture to him. It should also be appealing to you to have an experienced business consultant who can offer advice whenever it is needed. Keep in mind that banks usually learned their lessons from customers who defaulted on loans for one reason or another. It is to your advantage that they can pass on this very expensive information to you for free.

SPENDING

Although tempting, it is important not to exhaust too many of your resources on equipment, supplies, facilities, etc. before you develop a market. The classic failure story in business is the company that builds a state-of-the-art manufacturing facility before it develops a market. It is impressive to have modern, high quality tools, but if you do not have customers who require the use of those implements, it is difficult to justify the need for them.

Face it – spending money on new toys feels great. Whether it's for a truck, a mower, a new computer, or a cellular phone, buying new gadgets to make your life easier is fun and uplifting. In fact, some psychologists recommend shopping as a treatment for mild cases of depression. Unfortunately, it can become an addiction that can get you in trouble. The temptation to spend money that you do not have yet is very strong and dangerous. If, for example, funds owed to you are not paid, and a use for those funds has already been applied, you could be in financial trouble.

Patience is the key word. Wait until the money is in hand and all your commitments have been paid off before you go on a spending spree. And don't forget about Uncle Sam!

Sources:

Liffers, S. 1995, Personal Communication. Earth Gro, Inc. Lebanon, CT.

Merrill, L.S. 1994, **What Are Lenders Looking For?** Turf Magazine, North Edition, Dec. 1994. NEF Publishing. St. Johnsbury, VT.

Merrill, L.S. 1995, **Keep An Even Keel For Business Success.** Turf Magazine, North Edition, April. 1995 v8#4. NEF Publishing. St. Johnsbury, VT.

Reynolds, R.R. 1994, **Mowing/Job - Costing.** Landscape Management, May 1994. Advanstar Communications. Cleveland, OH.

Riggs, R. 1995, **Identifying the Ideal Employee.** Greenhouse Business, April 1995, Vol 1, No. 4. McCormick Communications Group. Park Ridge, IL.

Steingold, F.S. 1995, **Shaping Up Contracts**. Grounds Maintenance v30 #3 March 1995. Intertec Publishing Corp. Overland Park, KS.

Vinlove, F.K. and R.F. Torla 1995, **Comparative Estimations of U.S. Home Lawn Area**. Journal of Turfgrass Management, Vol. 1, No. 1, 1995. Hawthorn Press, Inc. Binghamton, NY.

Chapter 9

Business Plan

Anyone who runs a business, any business, must have an objective or a goal. Knowing where you want to go without a plan as to how to get there, however, is impractical. The business plan is made up of the charts and maps with which we navigate our business. Without a plan we must feel our way through the darkness.

A business plan does not have to be an elaborate, hundred page thesis on how you plan to become a multinational corporate giant (unless that is your goal). A S.C.O.R.E (Service Corp of Retired Executives – a branch of the Small Business Administration) counselor once told me to jot down a plan on a piece of paper before I came in to see him. Being pressed for time and having little incentive to write anything elaborate, I wrote:

Work hard & Succeed.

Surprisingly, the counselor looked at it and commended me on a good plan. He suggested that I add some more specifics as time went on, changing the plan into a guide which could be used to focus the company toward a goal. I took his advice and slowly added information as my objectives became clearer. I wasn't writing this plan to woo investors or to borrow money from a bank. It was (and is) only a reminder to me of where I want to go and how I plan to get there. If I find new avenues of opportunity along the way, then I amend the business plan. After 12 years of being in business, my plan still fits on one page of paper.

More ambitious business people would have written a more comprehensive plan at an earlier stage of their business and might have grown at a faster pace than I did. Any plan, no matter how simple, should be written down and looked at periodically, however.

A good business plan should include some or all of the following information:

I. Company information

  A. Description of the business

    1. Name and address

    2. Physical location

    3. Products or services

    4. Personnel and positions

    5. Market

    6. Competition

  B. Goals of the business

  C. Financial needs and use of funds

  D. Projections of earnings

  E. Potential return to investors (if applicable)

II. Services

  A. Description of Services

  B. Comparison to competition

  C. Unique services offered.

III. Market analysis

  A. Description of total market

  B. Competition

  C. Industry and market trends

  D. Target or niche market

IV. Marketing strategy

  A. General strategy

  B. How your product or service fits into the market

    1. Method of marketing

    2. Method of fulfillment

    3. Method of invoicing

  C. Pricing policy

    1. Compare to market

V. Management Plan

   A. Business structure (if applicable)

   B. Board of directors (if applicable)

   C. Officers (if applicable)

      1. Chart organization

      2. Names, titles and responsibilities

      3. Resumés of individuals

   D. Staffing plan

      1. Number of employees

      2. Responsibilities of employees

      3. Source of employees

   E. Facilities Plan

      1. Description of existing or initial facility

      2. Plans for improvements or changes

   F. Operating plan

      1. Business on hand

      2. Prospective business on hand

      3. Plans to generate new business

      4. Projections

VI. Financial Data

   A. Financial statement for the past 3-5 years

   B. First year financial projections

      1. Profit and loss statement

      2. Balance Sheet

      3. Monthly cash flow charts

      4. Projected capital expenditures

   C. Annual financial projections for the next 2-5 years

      1. Profit and loss statement

      2. Balance Sheet

      3. Monthly cash flow charts

      4. Projected capital expenditures

D. Explanation of projections

TOO MUCH WORK! I'M NOT GOING TO DO IT! I DON'T HAVE THE TIME!

This response is all too common and understandable, but this isn't a task that needs to be completed overnight. Nor does it need to be as elaborate as the outline above. The trick is to write one section at a time, as if that were the only section to do. When it is done, take a rest and tackle another section. After the plan begins to take shape it becomes easier, if not enjoyable, to work on. If you are starting a new business and need investor or bank money, this information is critical and needs to be as complete as possible. In this instance, the pressure is on to do the whole plan in as short a time as possible. It is interesting to note that, statistically, those businesses that do complete a business plan succeed significantly more often than those that do not.

The best way to start a business plan is to decide what your objectives are. Is feeding and clothing your family the extent of your goals, or are you obsessed with total control of the Lawnmowlian Empire? Whatever the goal, it is easier to get started if you know where you want to go. The next step is to plan your route. Do you want to follow the tried and true, boring but safe road? Or do you wish to cut a new trail toward your objective, a path with unique perspectives that no one else has thought of? Even though the latter plan may be riddled with risk, if it is well constructed and realistic, it is usually more attractive to bankers and investors than the conventional highway plan.

These are the basics of a business plan. After you know where you want to go and how you plan to get there, the rest is simply filling in the blanks. Some of the blanks, such as market research, are not always easy to complete, but the information is well worth the extra effort. Libraries, universities, lawn and landscape associations, and even telephone books can be a great source of information.

Estimating the market area can be the most difficult blank to fill in. A recent study (Vinlove 1995) found that residential lawn area is relative to population and that the average lawn size is 0.3 acre. This figure will vary if the area is predominately urban, suburban, or rural. Discovering the population of an area should not be difficult. The State Bureau of the Census should be able to tell you not only the population of a given area but also the number of homes. The FHA (Federal Housing Administration) sometimes has actual lawn size figures for a given area.

As you piece together the components of your business plan you may come to realize one of three things:

1. Your plan is more brilliant than you had ever imagined;

2. Your plan will work only if you commit yourself to a lot of hard work for a lengthy initial period; or

3. Your plan is a bogus bomb that has only a slightly better chance of success than a bill in Congress calling for a cut in congressional salaries.

Information will generally point to hard work and time as the factors that determine the plan's success. If the plan is a bomb, it usually needs an adjustment in strategy as opposed to a slam dunk in the circular file. It is certainly better to discover the flaws at this stage, before enormous losses of time, money, and energy occur.

RUNNING IN PLACE

It may seem that no matter how hard you work, you never get anywhere. Like running on a fast moving treadmill or swimming against a strong current, it is a struggle just to maintain the same position. Unfortunately, this perception is often reality and the only thing that makes any difference in gaining, losing or remaining stationary is the level of ambition you have. Ambition does not make the job physically easier, but if you are constantly focused on a goal the satisfaction of each gain becomes a personal triumph that makes work more enjoyable. The more pleasurable a task is, the easier it is to accomplish.

If it bothers you to look at all the companies that appear to be doing better financially than you, don't look. There is something to be said for working with blinders, constantly focused on the task before you. If you never have anyone to compare yourself to, you probably look very impressive. Remember, those large companies that look so impressive also had to start at the bottom rung of the ladder.

If you invest the necessary time and energy in your business plan and truly believe that it will work, then the only important thing to focus on is your own progress. Time line projections are difficult to predict and can mean very little in terms of the success or failure of a business plan. Even if your goals take twice as long to reach as you had originally projected, the fact remains that they are attainable.

SELLING DOCUMENT

The business plan is a selling document designed to convince banks, investors, and yourself that your objectives are attainable. Like the blueprints of a house, the benefit of the business plan is to provide a step by step manual for building a successful business.

Many business people do not attempt a plan until they have experienced their market for a few years. Others continually update their plan as they discover new opportunities. Whatever the situation, there are very few instances in business where a plan is not appropriate.

Sources:

Buss, D. 1994, **Super Selling: 9 Ways to Make Your Sales Soar.** IB Magazine NFIB May/June 1994. Group IV Communications, Inc. Thousand Oaks, CA.

Gumpert, D.E. 1990, **How to Really Create a Successful Business Plan.** Inc. Publishing. Boston, MA.

Merrill, L.S. 1994, **What Are Lenders Looking For?** Turf Magazine, North Edition, Dec. 1994. NEF Publishing. St. Johnsbury, VT.

Merrill, L.S. 1995, **Keep An Even Keel For Business Success.** Turf Magazine, North Edition, April. 1995 v8#4. NEF Publishing. St. Johnsbury, VT.

Reynolds, R.R. 1994, **Mowing/Job - Costing.** Landscape Management, May 1994. Advanstar Communications. Cleveland, OH.

Vinlove, F.K. and Torla R.F. 1995, **Comparative Estimations of U.S. Home Lawn Area.** Journal of Turfgrass Management, Vol. 1, No. 1, 1995. Hawthorn Press, Inc. Binghamton, NY.

Chapter 10

Accounting

Accounting is a subject that many accountants want you to think is complicated. It can be a complex endeavor to keep financial records for large companies with multifaceted operations. Most companies start small, however, and if the complexities of accounting evolve at the same pace as the company, they can easily be learned. In the early stages of developing a small business, accounting should not be a complex and time consuming component of your business. But a good accounting system, learned at an early stage, can be applied to your company at any point – no matter how large or complex your business becomes.

In a double entry system, there are five general categories of accounts. They are *assets, liabilities, capital, revenues, and expenses*. Each of these general accounts has many divisions, called detailed accounts, which enable the user to better track the flow of money. The term accounts may be confusing because it refers to all the places where money goes, not just where it is kept. When money is spent, it is usually considered *gone*, which may make it difficult to envision it *kept* in an expense account. However, if you have ever worked for a company that paid for your business expenses, you had to *account* for every penny you claimed.

ASSETS

An *asset* is something of value you own (not necessarily outright). Cash is an asset, of course, but so is equipment such as trucks, mowers, trimmers, tractors, or trailers. Inventory is also an asset, but unless you maintain a large inventory of materials on a constant basis, it is easier to treat supplies as an expense. Money that is owed to you by customers is your *accounts receivable*, also an asset. Anything owned by you or your company that has worth is an asset.

There are two categories of assets. The first is *current assets* or *liquid assets*, which include cash, accounts receivable, inventory or anything else relatively liquid. The second is *fixed assets*, like buildings or equipment that has worth but would take longer to liquidate.

LIABILITY

A *liability* is money, goods, or services that is owed to someone else by you. If you have employees and withhold income tax and social security (FICA) from their paychecks, then the withheld funds should be noted in a liability account until they are paid to the government. Money owed to a bank or other financial institution for equipment, buildings, etc. is a liability. Money owed to someone for supplies already delivered is a liability that is usually noted as *accounts payable*. If a customer pays in advance for products or services, you owe that customer something - which is a liability. This type of liability, however, is easier to track as a negative entry in accounts receivable (an asset account). Any financial obligations your company has are liabilities.

REVENUE

Revenue is simply income. When a customer pays for services, the money is usually deposited in a checking account. The source of this deposit is from sales (a revenue account). Unfortunately, only a few customers pay for services at the time they are rendered. The revenue transaction takes place at the time when the goods or services are invoiced to the customer. If payment is not made immediately then the revenue is noted and the money is essentially deposited in *accounts receivable* instead of your checking account. When the customer finally pays, the funds are moved from accounts receivable to the checking account.

EXPENSE

Expense is expense. Whether it is for supplies, fuel, paper clips, parking, phone, postage, electricity, payroll, or cost of goods sold, it is always classified as an expense. Most small business owners want to track their expenses in an effort to better manage their return. If, for example, a lawn care company is spending $1,000 on advertising and is only receiving $2,000 in sales from it, then it

becomes apparent that the advertising is not having the desired effect. The ads are either too expensive for the return, or ineffective
for some reason. The point is that it would be difficult to determine
this if you weren't tracking this individual expense account. Expenses are often divided into two general categories: *job costs* and
general & administrative (G&A) expenses. The first is usually the
cost of materials directly related to the job. Items such as seed,
fertilizer, or sod, and the cost of transporting them, are noted here.
All other expenses, including payroll, equipment expenses, insurance, taxes, etc. would fall under G&A.

CAPITAL

Capital is simply a way to separate your personal money from
the assets of the company. When you write a check to yourself, it
can hardly be called a payroll expense unless your business is incorporated. If you own the company as a sole proprietor, it already is
your money. Moving it from a company account to your personal
account (or your pocket) does not constitute an expense. The same
is true in reverse. If your own personal funds are put back into the
company for some reason, it cannot be considered revenue. You
have not sold anything or rendered any services and you certainly
do not want those funds to appear as income on a tax return.

CHART OF ACCOUNTS

The total list of accounts that a business creates for itself is called
the *chart of accounts* and can be as simple or as detailed as a bookkeeper wishes. *Insurance*, for example, can be an expense account
for all insurance-related expenditures. It could also be a general
account for other, more detailed accounts, such as vehicle insurance, building insurance and disability insurance. It depends on
how many individual accounts the bookkeeper wants to track. The
key to accounting is to keep it simple. On the other hand, attention
to detail in whatever task you attempt is usually a big advantage.
The appropriate chart of accounts is different for every business.

It is important to have the *chart of accounts* written down in
order to avoid duplicating accounts using different names. *Freight*
and *trucking*, for example, are the same thing. If *freight* was the
original account and *trucking* was inadvertently added at another
date, the company's shipping expense money may have been divided into these two accounts. Looking at only one of the accounts

will give an erroneous view of this expense. If the accounts are written down somewhere, it is easier to know what account names are available.

The following is an outline of a sample *chart of accounts*. Each section heading is a general account into which all other accounts of that section flow. A general account is a summary of all the detail accounts that flow into it.

> (G) - General Account
>
> (D) - Detailed Account

I. Assets (G)

  A. Current assets (G)

    1. Petty cash (D)

    2. Checking account (D)

    3. Savings account (D)

    4. Marketable securities (D)

    5. Accounts receivable (D)

    6. Inventory (D)

  B. Fixed assets (G)

    1. Autos & trucks (net value) (G)

      a. Original value (D)

      b. Accumulated depreciation (D)

    2. Furniture and fixtures (net value) (G)

      a. Original value (D)

      b. Accumulated depreciation (D)

    3. Buildings and other property (net value) (G)

      a. Original value (D)

      b. Accumulated depreciation (D)

    4. Machinery and other equipment (net value) (G)

      a. Original value (D)

      b. Accumulated depreciation (D)

    5. Office equipment (net value) (G)

      a. Original value (D)

     b. Accumulated depreciation (D)

II. Liabilities (G)

  A. Short term liabilities (G)

    1. Accounts payable (D)

    2. Notes payable (D)

    3. Disability insurance (D)

    4. Taxes payable (G)

      a. Payroll taxes payable (D)

      b. Other taxes payable (D)

    5. Federal income tax withheld (D)

    6. State income tax withheld (D)

    7. City income tax withheld (D)

    8. FUTA (Federal unemployment tax) (D)

    9. SUTA (State unemployment tax) (D)

    10. Sales tax (G)

      a. State (D)

      b. County (D)

      c. City (D)

      d. Other (D)

    11. Property taxes payable (D)

    12. Income taxes payable (G)

      a. Federal (D)

      b. State (D)

      c. City (D)

      d. Other (D)

  B. Long term liabilities (G)

    1. Mortgage (D)

    2. Equipment loans (D)

    3. Other long term indebtedness (D)

III. Revenue (G)

  A. Sales (D)

B. Sales returns or other credits to customers (D)

C. Shipping charges (G)

    1. Freight (D)

    2. UPS (D)

    3. Postage (D)

    4. Packaging (D)

    5. Other (D)

D. Financial income (G)

    1. Interest income (D)

    2. Finance charges (D)

    3. Purchase discounts (D)

E. Other revenues (G)

    1. Recovery of bad debt (D)

    2. Gain from the sale of assets (D)

    3. Rebates or refunds (D)

    4. Commissions (D)

    5. Miscellaneous (D)

IV. Expenses (G)

A. Cost of goods sold (G)

    1. Materials and supplies (D)

    2. Sales commissions (D)

    3. Shipping expenses (G)

    a. Pallets (D)

    b. Cartons, stretch wrap, etc. (D)

    4. Refunds or rebates to customers (D)

B. General and administrative expenses (G)

    1. Payroll (G)

      a. Wages (G)

        1. Hourly (D)

        2. Bonuses (D)

        3. Contract labor (D)

 b. Benefits (G)
   1. Worker's compensation (D)
   2. Other benefits (D)
 c. Taxes (G)
   1. FICA Employer (D)
   2. FUTA (D)
   3. SUTA (D)
2. Maintenance (G)
 a. Trucks and other vehicles (D)
 b. Equipment (D)
 c. Furniture and fixtures (D)
 d. Buildings (D)
 e. Maintenance of other assets (D)
3. Rents and Leases (G)
 a. Trucks and other vehicles (D)
 b. Furniture and other fixtures (D)
 c. Office equipment (D)
 d. Machinery and equipment (D)
 e. Buildings or lots (D)
 f. Other rents or leases (D)
4. Insurance (for assets) (G)
 a. Trucks and other vehicles (D)
 b. Buildings and contents (D)
 c. Machinery and equipment (D)
 d. Office equipment (D)
 e. Other insurance (D)
C. Travel (G)
1. Transportation (D)
2. Meals (D)
3. Lodging (D)
4. Tolls and parking (D)

5. Entertainment (D)

6. Other travel expense (D)

D. Shipping (G)

1. Freight (D)

2. Packaging (D)

3. UPS (D)

4. Insurance (D)

5. Other shipping expenses (D)

E. Taxes (G)

1. Sales tax (D)

2. Property tax (D)

3. Other taxes (D)

F. Consultation (G)

1. Legal (D)

2. Accountants (D)

3. Other (D)

G. Office supplies (D)

H. Telephone (D)

I. Postage (D)

J. Utilities (D)

K. Licenses and permits (D)

L. Memberships, Dues, Subscriptions (D)

M. Advertising (D)

N. Promotions (G)

1. Brochures and other sales literature (D)

2. Other promotional expenses (D)

O. Public relations (D)

P. Bad Debt (D)

Q. Losses from damaged goods (D)

R. Financial expenses (G)

1. Bank charges (D)

2. Sales discounts (D)

3. Interest on loans (D)

S. Other expenses (D)

V. Capital (G)

1. Capital contributions (D)

2. Retained earnings (D)

3. Current earnings (D)

4. Draw (D)

The chart of accounts need not be as elaborate as this one, or it could be much more detailed. It depends on the company's needs and the time constraints of the bookkeeper. It should be at least as detailed as the tax returns you file, so that all the information you need can be extracted easily.

DOUBLE ENTRY

Any time the amount of money is changed in one of these accounts, it must be changed by an equal amount in other accounts to create a balanced transaction. This is called *double entry accounting* and it's a valuable protection for you. If someone else is handling your books, it is very difficult for them to steal from you if you are using a double entry system. It also protects you from your own mistakes because in a double entry system, errors will come to the surface sooner. Double entry transactions occur only between two or more detailed accounts – never between general accounts. General accounts only provide summary information. If, for example, you did several transactions in the category of travel expenses (some for lodging, some for meals, some for transportation, and a few for entertainment), all of the transactions would occur in those detailed accounts. However, when your accountant calls and asks for your travel expenses, he is only interested in knowing what is in the general account, which is a summation of all the detailed accounts in that section.

Anyone who uses a checking account is practicing double entry accounting, probably without even being aware of it. The money in your checking account is an asset. When a check is written for fertilizer, for example, the amount of money in the asset account is decreased and the expense account for supplies is increased by an equal amount. If the check is written to you, then the transaction is between an asset and a capital account (unless your business is incorporated). Or, if a piece of valuable equipment is purchased, then the transaction is between two asset accounts (i.e. a decrease in the check book balance and an increase in an equipment account). Each transaction is a balance between two accounts. Simple checkbook journals treat everything as an expense (an issued check) or revenue (a deposit). They do not divide your transactions into more detailed accounts. This may be fine when you first start out in a small business but may become inadequate as your company grows.

DEBITS AND CREDITS

The most confusing component of double entry accounting is the system of debits and credits. A debit can indicate either an increase or decrease, depending on the type of account in which it is used. The same is true for a credit. In an asset or expense account, a debit will increase the amount in the account, whereas a credit will decrease the amount. When a deposit is made in your checking account (an asset account), for example, it is recorded as a debit to the account. When a check is written, it is a credit. If the check is paying for supplies or another expense, then a debit is used to record an increase in that expense account.

The opposite occurs in liability and revenue accounts. A debit in these accounts decreases the account balance, whereas a credit increases it. If you have a line of credit from a bank, for example, and draw down some needed funds, it is recorded as a credit, increasing your liability to the bank. When the funds are deposited into your checking account, they are recorded as a debit, increasing your checkbook balance. In this example the double entry transaction is between a liability account (line of credit) and an asset account (checking). At some point, when the bank is repaid, the checkbook will be credited (decreasing the balance) for the amount paid back and the liability will show a debit (decreasing the amount owed).

In a capital account a debit and credit can mean either an increase or a decrease in a corporate chart of accounts; in simple accounting, however, debits and credits will normally be used as they are with assets. When some of your own money is infused into the company checking account, the *capital contributions* account is *credited* (and the company's checking account is debited), increasing the amount of money you have given back to the company. When the company pays you, the capital *draw* account is *debited* (and the checkbook is credited), increasing the amount the company has paid you.

A simple but steadfast rule in double entry accounting is *for every credit there must be an equal debit, and vice versa.* If you already know, for example, that writing a check is a credit to your checking account, then you can conclude that the other side of the transaction will be a debit no matter what type of account it is with. If a deposit to checking is recorded as a debit, then the source of the funds must be recorded as a credit whether it is from sales, capital, bank loans, accounts receivable or your mother. Figure 10-1 shows the relationship that debits and credits have with each type of account.

	INCREASE	DECREASE
ASSETS	Debit	Credit
LIABILITIES	Credit	Debit
REVENUES	Credit	Debit
EXPENSES	Debit	Credit
CAPITAL	Debit	Credit

Figure 10-1

LEDGERS

Ledgers are simply books that record money transactions. A checkbook journal is a ledger. It records when each check was written, how much it was written for, what it paid for, and the current balance in the account. The simple checkbook that can slide into your back pocket is easy to use but postpones the time-consuming work of detailing the company's expenses until tax time. Unfortunately for most people involved in landscaping or lawn care, tax time is already a very busy time of year. The bigger checkbooks with disbursement columns are more time-consuming to use when issuing checks, but save time at the end of the year and can give a clearer picture of the business's cash flow at any given moment.

Computer checking is probably the least time-consuming in both the short and long term (once you've mastered the system), but requires considerably more of an investment than a checkbook. In general, the more detailed a ledger you maintain, the easier it is to gather financial information about your company. The computer accounting system enables the user to take a financial snapshot of the company at any given moment, with very little effort. Manual ledgers are more time-consuming to maintain, but can offer the same basic picture.

A checkbook balance does not report your accounts receivable or accounts payable. It does not show the balance between your assets and liabilities, nor does it provide a picture of sales or inventory. The checkbook shows all your expenses, but unless you have disbursement columns, you have no way of knowing how much you are spending in each category. It is difficult to ascertain if you are making a profit or not until all the figures are tallied up. By then, unfortunately, it may be too late to change anything. The level of detail that is right for a small business depends on the needs of the person(s) running it. A company with ample working capital and fixed profit margins that has a whole year's work lined up in advance, with customers who always pay on time, probably does not need an elaborate double entry accounting system. Unfortunately, few of us have those luxuries.

Setting up ledgers does not have to be difficult. For most small business, a general ledger is all that is needed. One of the new check writing systems with disbursement columns can act as a general ledger. Each column can represent an account or group of accounts from the company's chart of accounts. The amount of the check needs to be entered into the appropriate column when the check is written and each page needs to be totaled (posted) when the last check of the page is written. These systems work well for small businesses, enabling them to track revenues and expenses easily. Unfortunately, the number of columns available in the checkbook may not be sufficient for the number of accounts you may want to track. When more detail is needed, additional ledger books are necessary.

Tracking income can be as important as tracking where money is spent. A simple receivables ledger records each invoice and breaks down the total invoice amount into columns such as mowing, fertilizing, trucking, etc. At the beginning of each month, it is a good idea to start a new page. This ledger will tell you what time of year your sales are strong and in what area your strength lies. Deposits can also be recorded in this ledger to determine the seasonal nature of your cash flow. If set up correctly, this ledger can track the total amount in your accounts receivable at any given time.

The checkbook with disbursement columns makes an excellent payables ledger. If check writing systems with an adequate number of columns are not available, however, it may be necessary to find a payables ledger to record your checks in. There are two ways to set up a payables ledger. The first is to accrue payments as your invoices come in. When a bill is received, the indebtedness is recorded into the ledger, noting the company owed, the amount owed, the due date, and what the expense is for. The second way is to simply record the payable when it is paid, inserting the same information except for due date.

Ledger books are available from most office supply companies and come in a wide array of formats. Many are designated for receivables, payables, general ledger or payroll. Some have fold-out pages that offer a multitude of columns for companies wanting more detailed accounting.

The general ledger is a summary of all your other ledgers. Some companies update their general ledgers only once per year, while others do it weekly. The general ledger can include all the company's detailed accounts or just the five general account categories. The level of detail is up to the individuals who need access to financial information about the company.

As your business becomes bigger and more complex, it may become necessary to use a computer accounting system. There is a period of learning these systems that can be frustrating at times, but once mastered, ledgers and reports can be generated quickly and easily. The information still has to be entered into the machine just as it would in a manual ledger. Once entered, however, the computer can use the data to create any type of report or ledger, and you can update the reports as often as you would like.

POSTING

Posting simply means to add (or subtract) the results of transactions into your ledger. When all the checks you wrote are subtracted and the deposits are added in, the current balance is posted into your checkbook. If a company keeps separate ledgers for accounts receivable, accounts payable, cash, and/or inventory, these are all totaled up individually and posted into a general ledger. The general ledger is a summary of all the other ledgers. Posting can occur frequently, as it does in a checkbook (each time a check is written or a deposit is made), or it can be done as infrequently as every month. The more often it is done, the easier it is to see your financial position at any given moment. It is easy to imagine how uncomfortable it would be to post your checkbook only once a month. In computer accounting, the software usually will not include any unposted transactions in the financial reports. Therefore it is necessary to post regularly if the reports are going to contain current and accurate information.

BALANCED BOOKS

In accounting, the concept of a balanced set of books is analogous to an inventory of one's financial condition. The balance is between assets, liabilities, and equity (capital). The assets group would include cash, inventory, accounts receivable and the value of any fixed assets, such as buildings or equipment. Liabilities listed would include accounts payable, debts to banks or other lenders, money owed to various tax bureaus, and any other miscellaneous indebtedness. The difference between assets and liabilities is equity (your net worth). If your liabilities happen to be greater than your assets then your equity is in the red (a negative number). If there is any doubt about the outcome of your net worth, the proving equation is *liabilities + equity = assets*.

Although this balance sheet may have information that seems less than useful to the owner, it is valuable. It gives a clear picture of the ratio of debts to assets. This is important to know if you plan to stay in business for the long term. It is interesting to note that the balance sheet is one of the first documents that banks and other lending institutions will ask for when approached for credit. The balance sheet is a statement of current financial condition and is usually presented as shown in figure 10-2.

Balance Sheet			
Asset Accounts	Amount	Liability Accounts	Amount
Cash		General payables	
Securities		Bank loans	
Receivables		Taxes due	
Real Estate		Other debts	
Vehicles			
Inventory			
Personal property			
Other assets			
Total		Total	
Equity = Total assets minus Total liabilities			

Figure 10-2

The balance sheet does not indicate income (profit or loss). This information comes from an income statement. The income statement is an equally simple equation between revenues and expenses. Revenues include sales, even if monies have not yet been collected. It also includes any *passed-on* expenses, such as freight, postage, taxes, or handling charges. If your company assesses finance charges to customers who do not pay on time, those revenues would be represented here.

The expense side would include any cost associated with running the business. The list of these costs can be fairly extensive and may include categories such as cost of goods sold, payroll, equipment expenses, insurance, shipping, taxes, etc. The income statement may appear in figure 10-3.

REPORTS

Reports such as balance sheets and income statements may seem like a waste of valuable time, but they are important, especially if you are striving for specific financial objectives. Running a business without these reports is like sailing a boat in the ocean without

Income Statement		
Revenue accounts	Current Period	Year to date
Sales		
Interest income		
Finance charges		
Purchase discounts		
Commissions		
Other income		
Total Income		
Expense Accounts		
Cost of goods sold		
Labor		
Taxes, FICA, etc.		
Fuel, repairs		
Equipment lease		
Office expenses		
Building expenses		
Insurance		
Licenses, permits		
Advertising		
Bad debt loss		
Interest expense		
Utilities		
Other expenses		
Total Expenses		
Net Profit		

Figure 10-3

a compass. These reports should be made on a monthly basis and the income statement should have a column for the current month and a column for year-to-date.

If your books are done on a computer and up-to-date information is entered on a regular basis, then generating these reports can be as easy as making a couple of key strokes. If your bookkeeping is done manually, it is a good idea to generate blank copies of these reports so that each month the dollar amounts can be filled in easily. The time spent doing these reports is usually time saved at the end of the year when tax returns need to be filled out, and money saved if your accountant can find needed information quickly and easily. It is also time saved when you have to run to the bank or credit union for an equipment loan or short term cash and they need to see up-to-date financial statements.

Another important report is *cash flow*. This shows at which times during the year your company is cash poor; it also shows when lucrative times arrive. This information is helpful in planing capital expenditures or credit needs. The report is generated easily by recording the ending statement balance of your checkbook every month. If bank money or personal capital is used to run the business, it should be discounted so that the company's true position is shown. When plotted on a graph, the cash flow chart may look like figure 10-4.

CASHFLOW

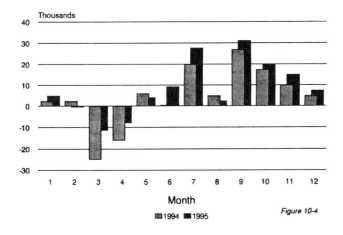

Month

■1994 ■1995

Figure 10-4

END OF YEAR

At the end of the year, profit or loss is calculated from the totals of the revenue and expense accounts and noted in a capital account, usually called *retained earnings*. The revenue and expense accounts are then changed to a balance of zero so the new year can begin with a clean slate. Assets and liabilities are carried over into the new year as is, unless there is a need to depreciate certain asset accounts for tax purposes.

SUMMARY

Double entry accounting is not difficult to learn but requires a fair amount of patience. Your need for a good accounting system will make it easier to develop one. In the long run, a computer accounting system will be the least time consuming and the most accurate for bookkeeping. A relatively large initial investment of time is needed, however, to thoroughly understand these systems. Many companies doing millions of dollars of business every year still do their books manually, but most have an in-house bookkeeper or someone who comes in part time. The type of accounting system used is not nearly as important as the need for one. Running a business without one is like walking through the woods on a moonless night without a lantern or a flashlight. It can be done, but not without frequent painful encounters with large obstacles.

Sources:

Grizzaffi, A.A., CPA, 1995, Personal Communication. West Lebanon, NH.

Chapter 11

You Are The

Expert

There is a remote possibility that the information in this book is erroneous. There is no way to know for sure. Even if the PhD's rave about it, there is a chance it's all a crock. Only time will tell.

Most people believe what they want to about a subject or an issue. If a politician upholds the sanctity of most people's beliefs, he is usually elected (or re-elected). Those beliefs are normally derived from common sense.

Common sense can be a very valuable asset, but only if it is based on good information. A lack of information or misinformation can render common sense illogical and useless, much like the soil test results from a contaminated sample. The accumulation of information from a diversity of sources is usually a good representation of the available knowledge on any given subject. Sampling the soil from one spot will not necessarily represent the fertility of the entire area, nor will one book or magazine represent the wealth of available wisdom.

If common sense is based upon good information, it elevates the user to the rank of expert. The uniqueness of every site – from differences in the soil, the climate, the lay of the land, to all of the other edaphic factors – injects a certain amount of illegitimacy into manuals or handbooks on horticulture. The only true expert is the well-informed individual who cares for the site.

In a profound sense, the ecology of any given area has an enigmatic personality which the author of a book cannot know intimately and cannot, therefore, fully understand. It is the steward who has the relationship with the environment. If well informed, he or she is clearly the expert.

If this tome has served to strengthen the common sense asset of the expert, then it was worth both the reading and the writing.

Glossary

This glossary is intended to provide definitions not only of terms used within the text of this book, but also of some of the terms used in many of the sources listed at the end of each chapter.

Abiotic - Not living.

Acid - Any substance that can release hydrogen ions in a solution.

Actinomycetes - Decay microorganisms that have a fungus-like appearance but, like bacteria, do not contain a well defined nucleus.

Adsorb - See Adsorption.

Adsorption - The adherence of one material to the surface of another via electromagnetic forces, e.g., dust to a television screen.

Adventitious rooting - roots emanating from above ground plant parts.

Aerobic - Needing oxygen to live.

Alkaline - Refers to substances with a pH greater than 7.

Allelopathic - Usually refers to the negative influence a plant has on other plants or microorganisms.

Allelochemicals - Refers to substances produced by one plant that have a negative effect on another.

Amorphous - Without consistency in its structure or form.

Anaerobic - Refers to an environment with little or no oxygen or organisms that require little or no oxygen to live.

Antagonist - Any organism that works against the action of another.

Anthropogenic - Caused by human action.

Apatite - A natural phosphate mineral.

Aragonite - Calcium carbonate (lime) formed by shellfish.

Arthropod - Refers to a group of animals with segmented bodies and exoskeletal structure such as insects, spiders and crustaceans.

Assimilation - Digestion and diffusion of nutrients by an organism for growth and/or sustenance.

ATM - Atmosphere, a measurement of pressure of a gas.

Atmosphere - Refers to the naturally existing gases of any given environment. Also a measurement of pressure (see ATM).

Autoclave - A machine that, with heat and pressure, can react gases with other materials. It is also used to sterilize tools and equipment.

Autotrophs - Organisms that can synthesize organic carbon compounds from atmospheric carbon dioxide, using energy from light or chemical reactions.

Bases - See Base cation.

Base cation - A positively charged ion, historically belonging to the earth metal family (potassium, magnesium, calcium, etc.).

Biomass - The cumulative mass of all living things in a given environment.

Biotic - Pertaining to life or living organisms.

Botany - The study of plants.

Calcite - Calcium carbonate (lime)

Carbon : Nitrogen ratio - A ratio measured by weight of the number of parts carbon to each part nitrogen, e.g., 10:1, 50:1, etc.

Carbohydrates - A group of organic compounds that include sugars, starch and cellulose.

Carnivores - Organisms that consume animals or insects for sustenance.

Cation - An ion of an element or compound with a positive electromagnetic charge.

Cation exchange capacity - The total amount of exchangeable cations that a given soil can adsorb.

Cellulose - The most abundant organic compound on earth, found mostly in the cell walls of plants.

Chelation - The combination of metal (inorganic) and organic ions into a stable compound sometimes referred to as a chelate.

Chlorosis - Loss of normal green color in plants.

Colloids - Very small soil particles with a negative electromagnetic charge capable of attracting, holding and exchanging cations.

Consumer - See heterotrophs.

Cultivar - Refers to a specific plant variety.

Detritus - The detached fragments of any structure, whether biotic or abiotic, that are decomposing or weathering.

Dolomite - Calcium, magnesium carbonate (magnesium lime).

Edaphic - Refers to factors, such as soil structure, atmosphere, fertility, and biological diversity, that influence the growth of plants.

Edaphology - The study of edaphic factors.

Edaphos - Greek word meaning soil.

Entomo - Prefix pertaining to insects.

Enzymes - A group of proteins that hasten biochemical reactions in both living and dead organisms.

Eutrophy - Refers to the excessive nutrient enrichment of ponds or lakes, causing the accelerated growth of plants and microorganism and depletion of oxygen.

Evapotranspiration - Refers to water loss from the soil from both evaporation and transpiration through plants.

Exude - The release of substances from cells or organs of an organisms.

Faunal - Pertaining to microscopic or visible animals.

Fecundity - Refers to the reproductive capabilities of an organism.

Floral - Pertaining to plants or bacteria, fungi, actinomycetes, etc.

Free oxygen - Gaseous oxygen not bound to other elements.

Furrow slice - Plow depth of approximately 6 - 7 inches.

Geoponic - Pertaining to agriculture or the growing of plants on land.

Gustation - Or gustatory refers to an organism's sense of taste.

Hemicellulose - A carbohydrate resembling cellulose but more soluble; found in the cell walls of plants.

Herbivores - Organisms that consume plants for sustenance.

Heterotrophs - Organisms that derive nutrients for growth and sustenance from organic carbon compounds but are incapable of synthesizing carbon compounds from atmospheric carbon dioxide.

Humification - The biological process of converting organic matter into humic substances.

Humology - The study of humus.

Hydrolysis - The reaction of hydrogen (H) or hydroxyl (OH) ions from water with other molecules, usually resulting in simpler molecules that are more easily assimilated by organisms.

Hyphae - A microscopic tube that is a basic component of most fungi in their growth phase.

In situ - Refers to natural or original position. Example: organisms in situ may respond differently to a stimulus than they would in a laboratory.

Ion - Any atom or molecule with either a positive or negative electromagnetic charge.

Kairomone - A chemical substance produced by organisms (e.g., plants or insects) that attracts another species or the opposite gender to it. Example: 1) Fruit produces kairomones that attract certain insects. 2) Many insects produce kairomones called pheromones that attract the opposite sex.

Ligand - A compound, molecule, or atom with the capability of bonding with another compound, molecule, or atom.

Lignin - A biologically resistant fibrous organic compound deposited in the cell walls of cellulose whose purpose is strength and support of stems, branches, roots, etc.

Lodging - When plants become too top heavy to stand upright and instead lie over onto the ground.

Macro - A prefix meaning large.

Meso - A prefix meaning middle.

Metabolism - The biological and chemical changes that occur in living organisms or the changes that occur to organic compounds during assimilation by another organism.

Metabolite - A product of metabolism or a substance involved in metabolism.

Meteorology - The study or science of the earth's atmosphere.

Methodology - A system, or the study of methods.

Micelle - (Micro-cell) A negatively charged (colloidal) soil particle most commonly found in either a mineral form (i.e., clay) or organic form (i.e., humus).

Micro - A prefix meaning small, usually microscopic.

Mineralized - The biological process of transforming organic compounds into non-organic compounds (minerals) e.g., mineralization of protein into ammonium.

Mineralogy - The study or science of minerals.

Mitigate - To lessen.

Mmho or Millimho - A thousandth of a mho, which is a measure of a material's ability to conduct electricity. Usually used in soil tests to determine salt levels.

Molecule - The smallest particle of a compound that can exist independently without changing its original chemical properties.

Monoculture - The cultural practice of growing only one variety of crop in a specific area every season without variance.

Morphology - The study or science of the form or structure of living organisms.

Mucilage - compounds synthesized by plants and microbes that swell in water, taking on a gelatinous consistency, that function to maintain a moist environment and bind soil particles together to form an aggregation.

Myco - A prefix that refers to fungi.

Nitrification - A process performed by soil bacteria that transforms ammonium nitrogen into nitrite and, finally, nitrate nitrogen. Nitrate is the form of nitrogen most often used by plants.

OM - Abbreviation for organic matter.

Oxidation - Usually refers to the addition or combination of oxygen to other elements or compounds.

Oxidize - To add oxygen. See oxidation.

Parent Material - The original rock from which a soil is derived.

Pedology - The study or science of soils.

Pedosphere - The top layer of the earth's crust, where soils exist.

Phenology - The study or science of biological phenomena and their relationship to environmental factors.

Pheromone - A chemical produced by an insect or other animal that attracts another member of the same species, usually of the opposite sex.

Physiology - The study or science of the biological functions and/or activities of living organisms.

Phyto - A prefix referring to plants.

Phytotoxic - A substance that is toxic to plants.

Porosity - Refers to the spaces between soil particles.

Producer - see autotrophs.

Rhizosphere - The area of soil in immediate proximity to roots or root hairs of plants.

Saprophyte - an organism that can absorb nutrient from dead organic matter.

Senescence - The aging process.

SOM - Abbreviation for soil organic matter.

Steward - A person who manages or cares for property of another. In agriculture, the term can refer to someone who cares for his own land but believes that ownership does not entitle one to dispose of the soil's resources for his/her own personal gain.

Substrate - Material used by microorganisms for food.

Symbiotic - A relationship between two organisms, usually obligatory and often of mutual benefit.

Synergy - Where the activities or reactions of two or more organisms or substances are greater than the sum of the agents acting separately.

Taxonomy - The science of classification.

Tectonic - Pertaining to the structure and form of the earth's crust.

Texture analysis - An analysis of soil particles determining the percentages of sand, silt and clay.

Throughfall - Moisture or precipitation that drips from aboveground plants, such as trees, to the ground. Throughfall is thought to contain some substances leached from leaf surfaces.

Topography - Pertaining to the specific surface characteristics of a given landscape.

Trophic levels - Levels of consumers within a food chain in relation to producers of organic nutrients, such as plants. For example, producers - primary consumers - secondary consumers - tertiary consumers - decay organisms.

Valence - A measurement of how many electrons an atom or molecule can share in a chemical combination. A positive valence indicates electrons offered in a chemical bond, whereas a negative valence is the number of electrons that can be accepted.

Volatile - Refers to substances that can easily change, often into a gas.

Index

A

D

M

Q

R

W

Y

Z

Figure and Table Index

HUNTER'S SABBATH: HIPPOCRATIC

the gauzy lichen here
to mask this granite
I know I will not save
invading
as often will be hare's
and cat's
thin trail out
that I may leave
than they incise
in easy passing
nor greater wound
in any less than
today I will not prey
my way may do
but let it do at least

took years
patient earth
not cure
yet today my path
and deer's
described by scat and track
thin trail back
no greater scar
on scarp and peak
unpursued
than weather makes
fevered mood
nor storm
no earthly good
no harm

by
Sydney Lea © <u>Hunting the Whole Way Home</u> (Hanover, NH:
University Press of New England, 1994).

EDAPHOS
Dynamics of a Natural Soil System

Finally, a book that explains the detailed interrelationships the soil has with the earth's environment in terms that anyone can understand. EDAPHOS shows how critically we as humans are linked to our entire ecosystem and how our reverence or apathy for the soil that sustains us affects our future as a civilization.

"An interesting and new approach to an often dull subject... After reading this, one can't help but see soil as part of the whole environment, affected by it and with effects on it."

Professor Leonard Perry, University of Vermont

*"In **EDAPHOS**, Paul answers questions... that growers, gardeners and extension specialists always ask. This book will contribute to our understanding of what sustainable soil management means and how to practice it."*

Karen Idoine, Extension Specialist
University of Massachusetts

"If you have always wanted to understand more about soils, but were discouraged by scientific techno-jargon, then this book is for you."

Professor Wendy Sue Harper, University of Vermont

"..one of the best books on soil science this reviewer has read in years."

B.U.G.S. Quarterly

"We give Paul Sachs high marks for making a potentially boring subject come alive."

Hortideas

"His clarity allows the reader, in a matter of hours, to achieve a general understanding of the soil system that took the author 10 years to achieve."

Ecology Action Newsletter

"Once you read this book, you will never think of the soil in the same way, again!"

Gardener's Home Library

THE EDAPHIC PRESS
P.O. Box 107
Newbury, Vermont 05051

ORDER FORM

Qty	Description	Price	Amount
_____	**Handbook of Successful Ecological Lawn Care**	$18.95	_____
_____	**Edaphos: Dynamics of a Natural Soil System**	$14.95	_____

I understand that I may return the book(s) for a full refund if I'm not satisfied.

Enclosed for book(s) is _____

VT residents, please 5% sales tax _____

Shipping (book rate) $1.50/book _____

TOTAL ENCLOSED _____

Name _____

Business Name _____

Address _____

City _____ State _____

Zip _____ Phone _____